Jewish Economies

Jewish Economies

Development and Migration in America and Beyond

Volume II: Comparative Perspectives on Jewish Migration

Simon Kuznets

Stephanie Lo and E. Glen Weyl, editors

Routledge
Taylor & Francis Group
LONDON AND NEW YORK

First published 2011 by Transaction Publishers

Published 2017 by Routledge
2 Park Square, Milton Park, Abingdon, Oxon OX14 4RN
711 Third Avenue, New York, NY 10017, USA

First issued in paperback 2017

Routledge is an imprint of the Taylor & Francis Group, an informa business

Library of Congress Catalog Number: 2010052449

Library of Congress Cataloging-in-Publication Data

Kuznets, Simon, 1901-1985.
Jewish economies : development and migration in America and beyond / Simon Kuznets ; [editors] E. Glen Weyl & Stephanie Lo.
v. ; cm.
Includes bibliographical references and index.
Contents: v. 1. Economic structure and growth of Euro-American Jewry.
ISBN 978-1-4128-4211-2
1. Jews—Economic conditions. 2. Jews—Europe—Economic conditions. 3. Jews—United States—Economic conditions. I. Weyl, E. Glen (Eric Glen), 1985- II. Lo, Stephanie. III. Title.
DS140.5.K89 2011
330.9730089'924—dc22 2010052449

ISBN 13: 978-1-138-51122-4 (pbk)
ISBN 13: 978-1-4128-4270-9 (hbk)

Contents

Acknowledgments

Help from many people was crucial in making this compilation possible.

We gratefully acknowledge Paul Kuznets and Judith Stein. Their unending support, both through personal interviews and their permission to access and use their father's papers, was pivotal throughout the entire process.

E. Glen Weyl would like to thank Olga Litvak, whose class HIS382 "The Eastern European Jewish Diaspora in Comparative Perspective: Israel, America and the USSR in the Twentieth Century" in the spring of 2007 first stoked this work.

We appreciate the helpful comments of Barry and Carmel Chiswick, Ben Friedman, Mark Guglielmo, Levis Kochin, Vladimir Moskovin, Peter Temin, and seminar participants at Duke University, particularly Malachi Hacohen and Roy Weintraub. We are especially grateful for the thorough discussion of our work provided by Vibha Kapuria-Foreman, and the financial support of the History of Economics Society that made it possible for Weyl to attend the meeting where this discussion was given.

We also benefited from the financial support of the Milton Fund, which, among other things, made possible the excellent research assistance of Yani Petrov and Rui Wang. Critical institutional support for this work came from the creative environment fostered by the Harvard Society of Fellows, without which it is unlikely that we would have pursued this interdisciplinary project.

Permissions

Paul Kuznets and Judith Stein have kindly provided permissions to publish all of the previously undistributed works that appear in this compilation.

We would also like to give full credit to all the publishers who made this work possible. All permissions are nonexclusive.

We thank the National Bureau of Economic Research and, in particular, Claudia Goldin and James Poterba, for allowing us to edit and republish *Immigration and the Foreign Born.* The piece, written by Kuznets in conjunction with Ernest Rubin, was previously published as NBER Occasional Paper 46 in 1954, pp. 1–107.

We are grateful to the editor of the journal *Rivoon L'Calcala* (*Economic Quarterly: The Journal of the Israeli Economic Association*) and the board at the Israeli Economic Association for their permission to translate and publish "Israel's Economic Development," which appeared in their journal in Hebrew in 1973 (vol. 20) on pp. 189–209.

We also appreciate the permissions from the Charles Warren Center at Harvard University, which allowed us to republish "Immigration of Russian Jews to the United States." This work originally appeared in *Perspectives in American History* (vol. IX—1975), edited by D. Fleming and B. Bailyn, pp. 35–124.

We would also like to give credit to Naftali Greenwood, who did a spectacular job providing a professional translation and interpretation of "Israel's Economic Development" from Hebrew to English.

Preface

Stephanie Lo

Simon Smith Kuznets was an economist known for his analytic rigor, having won the 1971 Nobel Prize "for his empirically founded interpretation of economic growth that has led to new and deepened insight into the economic and social structure and process of development." While he remains best known for his development of national income accounts, in fact, Kuznets had interests encompassing a broad range of topics (he has written thirty-one books and over two hundred papers) involving more general work on developmental economics. While some of Kuznets's work is well known to the economics community, much less is known about his studies on the economic history of Jews broadly, which included in-depth work on immigration. In this work, we reveal a lesser known side of Kuznets: the Eastern European Jewish immigrant, who persistently pursued the topic of Jewish history, yet hesitated to make his work more generally known due to his personal interest in the subject and therefore, by his reasoning, his bias. In doing so, we found many unpublished or hard-to-find works by Kuznets—some not previously available in English and most not formerly available to the public—which we hope to make widely available by publishing here. There are many facets of value to these pioneering works on Jewish immigration and economic structure; not only are the data and rigorous analyses valuable on their own, but they also work together to give the readers insight into the personality and intellect of the founder of modern empirical economics.

This compilation, *Jewish Economies: Development and Migration in America and Beyond*, consists of two volumes, entitled "Economic Structure and Growth of Euro-American Jewry" and "Comparative Jewish Migration and Economy."

The first volume starts with an introduction to this work, written by my colleague, E. Glen Weyl, which outlines many of the broader themes that tie the pieces of this work together. Weyl ties the works included in this volume—focusing on Jewish immigration and its economic impact—and thereby Kuznets's personal and cultural background, to his better known work in mainstream economics. This introduction proposes that there was a subtle but significant synergy between Kuznets's own background and his perspective on population, inequality, professions, and economic development, which may have, in turn, shaped his more famous views and hypotheses, including the so-called inverted-U hypothesis about inequality. Many of the works cited in the introduction are included in these volumes, in hopes that our readers will examine, for themselves, the actual evidence for the proposed thematic importance of these works.

The first work in this compilation is a preliminary version of "Economic Structure and Life of the Jews." The final version was published in a compilation entitled *The Jews: Their History, Culture, and Religion*, edited by Louis Finkelstein, in 1961. The work analyzes the economic structure of the Jews as a small minority of relatively recent origin in various countries, demonstrating thematic similarities between the economic structures of Jews in various parts of the world. The preliminary version included here was lengthier and more thorough than the final product, which was likely cut down to fit size requirements by the journal. In fact, two entire tables—Table 3: Association Between Inter-Country Differences in Industrial Structure of Jews and Inter-Country Differences in Other Variables and Table 5: Illustrative Calculations of the Effect of "Recency of Entry Mix" on Movement of Average Income and Income Dispersion, Jews in the U.S.A., 1900–1950—were completely removed between the draft and the final published work. Consequently, the discussion surrounding Table 3, which comprises an entire subsection entitled "Inter-country Differences in Industrial Structure," was removed. Other sections of the draft, in many of which Kuznets highlights *his* particular interpretation of the findings, are noticeably absent in the final version, including a passage in which Kuznets notes that his "calculations are only suggestive; and it is not intended to argue here the desirability or feasibility of continuously tapping this potential." Overall, given that the draft of "Economic Structure and Life of the Jews" differs substantially from the final version, we hope that the publication of this draft in our compilation is valuable to the academic community.

"Economic Structure of U.S. Jewry: Recent Trends" is an English translation of a work previously published in Hebrew. The lecture was delivered at a seminar on Jews in the Diaspora on June 24, 1971. In the speech, Kuznets discusses his statistical analysis of the recent changes of, and ongoing changes to, the economic—and, more deeply, the *occupational*—structure of Jews in the United States. Kuznets begins with a series of observations on the incomes and occupations assumed by Jewish males in the United States, comparing their status in 1970 to that in 1930. He highlights the "major shift among Jews . . . toward the professional and technical occupations" and hypothesizes why the changes may have occurred. He further discusses what he perceives to be the implications of the trends in the occupational structure of the Jews, which include the "radicalization of the Jewish minority" as well as "its possible effect on the attitude of the majority."

Expanding upon his speech at the house of the president of Israel, Kuznets wrote "Economic Growth of U.S. Jewry" in August 1972 to serve as a sequel to "Economic Structure and Life of the Jews" (in Finkelstein's volume). "Economic Growth of U.S. Jewry" is Kuznets's largest and most comprehensive work on the economic history of Jews. The work largely contributes to the data available to scholars interested in Jewish economics in the United States; it includes twenty-two tables, most of which combine data from multiple hard-to-find sources. Kuznets groups his analysis into three broad categories: "numbers and distributions," which gives detailed data on the Jewish population in the United States since 1880 and analyzes the breakdown of the population in terms of sex, language, and foreign born; "education and occupation," which includes data and analysis regarding the average educational level for Jews of different ages, sexes, and generations; and "income levels and structure," which includes analysis on the number of Jews in the labor force and their changing occupational structure over time. The summary section demonstrates both the breadth and the depth of the topics Kuznets explored in this work: each of the twenty-nine summary points is unique—and, in many ways, groundbreaking, particularly given the relative dearth of pieces on the topic—a result of his thorough quantitative and historical analysis throughout the work. The work is unfinished and was, previous to this volume, unpublished. As an accompaniment to this work, we have included a letter from Kuznets to Martin Feldstein on February 26, 1973 (found in Kuznets's archives at Harvard), which details Kuznets's hesitation to publish this work in the Harvard economics departmental paper series. The letter stands as one of the only recorded instances in which Kuznets admitted his personal and cultural motivations for some of his studies and subsequent hesitance to publish those studies.

The second volume is entitled *Comparative Jewish Migration and Economy* and includes the works discussed below.

"Immigration and the Foreign Born" was previously published as a National Bureau of Economic Research Occasional Paper (46: 1954). While this paper is little known even in academic circles, it was actually Kuznets's first work on immigration and was one of the first thorough empirical studies in economics on the subject. The work, coauthored with Ernest Rubin, discusses the impact of the general foreign born (i.e., not just the Jews) in the United States. Kuznets and Rubin claim that the impact of immigration on the economic situation of the United States—more so than in other countries—has been significant, yet "has long been slighted and might richly repay more intensive research." The analytic rigor of Kuznets and his desire to rid his work of personal biases emerge especially in Part Four, the technical appendix, which gives an overview of previous works' treatment of technical problems. Indeed, Kuznets and Rubin acknowledge that "[i]mmigration has had a long history in the United States. For the most part, however, it was seldom treated dispassionately even when an attempt was made only to ascertain the pertinent facts and their reliability."

"Israel's Economic Development" was previously published only in Hebrew in *Rivoon L'Calcala* (*Economic Quarterly: The Journal of the Israeli Economic Association*) in 1973 (20, 189–209). The work discusses the impact of mass immigration upon Israel's increase in productivity, a topic that Kuznets argues is far under-analyzed, leaving a "broad domain of as-yet unanswered questions." He ultimately concludes that Israel's situation was unique due to the ideological and institutional characteristics of the country—most notably, its domestic political stability and national unity, as well as the high educational status of its emigrants—which set the stage for rapid economic growth.

"Immigration of Russian Jews to the United States" was previously published in *Perspectives in American History* (volume IX—1975) by the Charles Warren Center at Harvard University. Unlike the other works in this compilation, this work is well known and has had widespread influence, and has been cited in several books (for instance, *American Judaism: A History* by Jonathan Sarna; *The Encyclopedia of American Jewish History*, by Stephen Norwood and Eunice Pollack; and many others) and papers (e.g., "Jewish Immigrant Wages in America in 1909" by Barry R. Chiswick, *Explorations in Economic*

History). The work was republished in Jeffrey Gurock's 1998 work *American Jewish History*. The work is an epitome of Kuznets's analytic rigor, with numerous tables discussing the details of the labor force, skills, and general structure of the immigrants.

We, as the editors of these two volumes, hope that the works included in this compilation will make clear to the readers the subtle, although complex, personal and cultural understandings that motivated Kuznets and shaped his perspectives on some of his historical and economic studies. Moreover, we hope that these two volumes will make these lesser known and previously unpublished works accessible for the casual reader and the academic alike. While some of Kuznets's work has gained deserved recognition, this volume, we hope, will shed light on some undiscovered gems of work and the fascinating personal and cultural themes underlying them. Moreover, we hope that these works, as unknown precursors to the burgeoning field of the economic history of the Jews, will serve as valuable references for scholars and interested readers alike.

Introduction: Simon Kuznets, Cautious Empiricist of the Eastern European Jewish Diaspora

E. Glen Weyl

The construction of hypotheses is a creative act of inspiration, intuition, invention; its essence is the vision of something new in familiar material. The process must be discussed in psychological, not logical, categories; studied in autobiographies and biographies, not treatises on scientific method; and promoted by maxim and example, not syllogism or theorem.

—Milton Friedman, "The Methodology of Positive Economics"

The announcement, in September 1971, that Simon Smith Kuznets (April 30, 1901–July 9, 1985) was to receive the third Sveriges Riksbank Prize in Economic Sciences in Memory of Alfred Nobel surprised no one[1] in the economics community. Kuznets built the system of national income accounting that allows accurate measurement of national product. Over the course of his more than half a century of service to the profession, Kuznets laid much of the foundation of modern development economics by providing the first comprehensive analysis of international growth data from developing countries. His research also made substantive contributions to the study of economic development, emphasizing the links between inequality and economic growth and highlighting important distinctions, not understood at the time, between today's underdeveloped countries and the state of today's rich countries before industrialization. He also pioneered, jointly with Milton Friedman, the foundational concepts of human capital and lifetime income.

Yet there is another side of Simon Kuznets that is less familiar to his colleagues, which this book highlights. Despite being one of the most distinguished American economists, Kuznets was actually born to a family of well-off Jewish bankers and furriers in Pinsk (formerly in Russia, now in Belarus) and grew up in what is now Ukraine before immigrating via Poland to the United States. Astonishingly, given that his impact on the methodology of economics rivals that of the much-acclaimed economists Kenneth Arrow and Paul Samuelson, there has been hardly any scholarship on Kuznets's life and thought. The few who have studied him see his background as little more than a preamble to his scholarly work.[2] Yet, as I argue below, Kuznets's identity and past, and his attempt to understand them quantitatively through the empirical study of the Eastern European Jewish Diaspora, were central to his understanding of economic development. However, the standard neglect of Kuznets's background, and of him entirely, is not altogether surprising given that Kuznets labored assiduously to maintain a wall of separation between the two facets of his life. The same cautious empirical methodology that has made Kuznets a challenging subject for historians of economics also hid the personal motivation behind the studies to which he applied it. The secular cosmopolitan life he built for his family obscured his Eastern European[3] Jewish ancestry. A universalistic commitment to empirical rigor and appropriate subjects of economic inquiry protected from the economics community his abiding fascination with his past.

My window on Kuznets is therefore his writing about and relation to the history and economics of the Jews. These works are collected for the first time in these volumes. Some of them have been previously published, two of them even in their complete form and in English. Many of the most interesting works were unpublished, published only in Hebrew, or scattered so broadly as to obscure the corpus they represent. Once assembled, even the fairly superficial inspection effected by this introduction demonstrates their close connection to the innovative ideas he brought to early development economics.

In "Economic Structure and the Life of the Jews," Kuznets builds a model of the path of Jewish inequality closely resembling that in his celebrated Presidential Address to the American Economic Association, published in 1955. Beyond the similarity in the formal approach of these two works, his substantive claims about the inverted-U shape of income inequality among Jews parallel his broader "Kuznets curve" hypothesis about economic development and income inequality. Thus, Kuznets's pathbreaking work, perhaps the first to take seriously the relationship between development and inequality, seems inextricable from his coincident work on the economic history of the Jews. In fact, it seems likely that the severe inequality among Jews that Kuznets documents quantitatively in later work[4] and saw throughout his life, along with its connection to the economic history of the Jews, played a key role in motivating his focus on distribution.

The influence of Kuznets's past extends to his emphasis, late in his career, on the role of culture, institutions, and context in economic development. His views, now fairly widely accepted, were initially highly controversial coming against the backdrop of the linear, materialistic, and universalistic theories of development prevalent at the time, such as those of Paul Rosenstein-Rodan, Arthur Lewis, Raul Prebisch, and W. W. Rostow. The turn away from purely measurable economic factors and toward these "softer" considerations begins with, and may well have been driven by, his early study of Jewish economic history, as well as the course of his own multicultural life.

Population, and the promises and threats it posed for development, was one of the last themes Kuznets took up in the late 1960s and 1970s. As a firm, if always balanced, opponent of neo-Malthusian hysteria about population, Kuznets clearly echoes his earlier arguments about the contributions (especially Jewish) immigrants made to the American economy. I would suggest that Kuznets saw in the "population bombers" repeats of the anti-immigrant hysteria that helped halt the wave of Eastern European Jewish immigration that had carried him to America. In his work on "Israel's Economic Development," which appears in an English translation for the first time in the second volume of these works, Kuznets sees that nation's ideological embrace of immigrants as the lifeblood of that nation's exceptionally rapid economic growth.

A final connection between Kuznets's economics and his background is the most speculative, but perhaps the most exciting as well. In the 1940s, Kuznets wrote one of his last major works of pure data assembly on income flows jointly with Milton Friedman, *Income from Independent Professional Practice*. This work made an important step beyond data collection, wading deep into a controversy that almost sunk the book's publication by arguing that medical licensure acted to raise doctor's wages by limiting competition. The book also pioneered the methodology of human capital accounting.

The former is striking given Kuznets's interest in the role of Jewish employment restrictions in spurring emigration and his singular unpublished[5] writing on "The Doctrine of Usury in the Middle Ages." Human capital, on the other hand, clearly plays a prominent role in Kuznets's work beginning with his study of Jewish educational patterns and his concurrent work on income inequality. While his work with Friedman is sufficiently rote and technically empirical that it is difficult to decipher with any certainty either the motivations that led to the study or the conclusions drawn from it, it again seems unlikely that here, its thematic association with the struggles of Eastern European Jews is an accident.

In fact, this opacity of Kuznets's substantive views on economics as well as their motivation are the rule, not the exception, in his work in all fields, as I discuss in the penultimate section of this introduction. Ever the consummate student of his advisor, Wesley Clair Mitchell, Kuznets was the ultimate cautious empiricist, offering caveat upon caveat throughout his career for even the modest hypotheses he dared to venture. This careful positivist attempt to separate facts from conjecture was but one manifestation of a broader set of dualities in his life and work. Never did he reveal in his work the motivation leading him to it and almost never did he show the broader conclusions that might be drawn from it. In fact, whenever motivation was too apparent, as in his work on Jewish economic history, he did his best to conceal his work from his economics colleagues. Despite his status as a first-generation Eastern European immigrant and his passionate identification with the State of Israel, he made every effort to raise his children as any other secular, mainstream, native-born American. Thus, Kuznets poses something of an enigma: motivated and inspired by understanding his past, he assiduously labored for universalism, both methodologically through empiricism and culturally through Americanism.

Yet while Kuznets's story may superficially seem paradoxical, precisely what makes it so interesting, and of at least some broader significance, is how it parallels the broader story of Jews of Eastern European descent in American economics. Jews rose to prominence more in economics than in any other academic discipline during the twentieth century, soaring from total exclusion to dominance of the field. As Derek Penslar[6] argues, while (especially Eastern European) Jews were well integrated into the natural sciences, they had been long excluded from the mainstream of European political and social affairs.

The political events of the late nineteenth and early twentieth centuries (emancipation, immigration, and anti-Semitism) gave American Jews a sociopolitical voice and motivation for the first time. This process paralleled, and often intertwined with, the transformation of economics into a quantitative science. I conclude with the speculation that this unique intersection of technical skill, reinforced by traditional separation from Gentile social affairs, and fresh political motivation, which Kuznets typified, may have ideally suited the Eastern European Jewish Diaspora to transform contemporary economics. Obviously, this is a mere conjecture, drawn largely from a single anecdote, but it potentially offers an important avenue for future research.

The Life of a Scholar

Little is known[7] about the history of the Kuznets family. The name, which means "blacksmith" in Russian, is thought to have been adopted only a few generations before the family's migration to the United States and designed to conceal[8] the family's Jewish background in a culture where few Jews were in fact blacksmiths.[9] Despite their name, Kuznets's father was a banker.[10] Pinsk, where Kuznets spent his childhood and attended primary school, was immortalized in Chaim Weizmann's autobiography as a hotbed of Zionist youth activism.[11] At the age of nine or ten, Kuznets's family moved to Rovno in Ukraine[12] to live with his mother's family, who were well-off furriers.[13] There he was raised according to a combination of cultural practices: Russian (from his mother and aunt) and Yiddish (from his grandparents).[14] While his primary scholastic interests were secular, rather than Talmudic, Kuznets received training in Judaism and Jewish history.[15] After the Jewish expulsion from Ukraine during the Great War, Kuznets moved to Kharkov for his secondary education at the *gymnasium* and university.[16] His education spanned from Kharkov High School No. 2, from October 1916 to May 1917, to the Commercial Institute of Kharkov, from 1918 to July 1921.[17] In Kharkov, Kuznets was exposed to the Bundist school of Jewish, anti-Zionist Marxism,[18] though his interest in and reaction to these influences are far from clear and do not clearly manifest in his later work.

Around the time of his move to Kharkov, his father and elder brother left for the United States through Turkey, while he stayed behind with his mother and younger brother.[19] Because his mother was an invalid,[20] the remaining brothers were hesitant to follow their father. However, Kharkov University shut down with the onset of civil war in Russia following the revolution of October 1917, and Kuznets briefly took up a position as a section head at the bureau of labor statistics in the Ukraine. In 1921, the family was, with many other Jews, deported back to Poland. Simon was briefly arrested for a reason that is not clear from available accounts, persuading the rest of family to join their father in the United States.[21] His mother, who for years had been suffering from symptoms resembling multiple sclerosis, died on the way to the West in Warsaw, and the family eventually left through Dantzig.[22]

Kuznets arrived in New York in 1922, and his life[23] as known to the economics community began. Within two years, he had received his BA and MA, and after two further years of research, he was awarded a PhD in 1926 under the supervision of Wesley Clair Mitchell.[24] Mitchell, the founder of the National Bureau of Economic Research, was undoubtedly the greatest intellectual influence on Kuznets's career. In fact, he was the only economist Kuznets explicitly thanked in his Nobel Prize autobiography, saying that he "owe[d Mitchell] a great intellectual debt."[25] In collaboration with and under the guidance of Mitchell, Kuznets began his early career by investigating empirical regularities in macroeconomic data in a series of books. First, his *Cyclical Fluctuations* investigated cyclical variation in retail commerce.[26] In *Secular Movements in Production and Prices,* Kuznets discovered for the first time the so-called long or Kuznets cycle, a low-frequency (fifteen-to-twenty year), low-amplitude fluctuation in economic activity previously unknown to researchers.[27] Finally, Kuznets completed the trilogy by considering extremely high-frequency seasonal movements in manufacturing output in *Seasonal Variations in Industry and Trade.*[28]

While working on his trilogy, Kuznets met and then married his wife, the Russian Canadian Jewish Edith Handler, in 1929.[29] They lived and had two children, Paul and Judith, in the dominantly Gentile Upper West Side.[30] Reinforcing this spatial divide from his past, Kuznets raised his children in a strictly secular, American manner, never attending synagogue and providing them no education in Russian language or culture. Nonetheless, Kuznets maintained a firm personal interest in Russian affairs, as a strong opponent of the Soviet Union, and was seen by his colleagues as something of an amateur expert on the Soviet economy. He also was an avid consumer of emerging Soviet literature, particularly dissident literature, perhaps building on the education in Russian literature that his mother and aunt instilled in him.[31] Despite this private interest in Russia, his encounters with Soviet economists left him with the impression that they were more political apparatchiks than social scientists, and he engaged in little scholarly dialogue with Russian academics. Furthermore, none of his interest in Russian culture and affairs filtered into his relationship with his wife or children. In addition to the strict line he drew between his past and the family life he was creating, Kuznets divided his personal and professional lives equally stringently, almost never discussing work at home or with friends outside the field. He had many such friends; though they were mostly academics, they were drawn from a variety of fields: psychology, philosophy, sociology, public affairs, religion, and art.[32]

The process of studying data on economic aggregates seems to have persuaded Kuznets that the available information was insufficient to supply the rigor and broad scope economists demanded. Kuznets therefore set out during the 1930s to build a system of comprehensive accounting for productive activity at the national level. His basic insight and approach, familiar to any student who has taken an introductory macroeconomics class, was to measure a nation's productive output by the income it generated. Kuznets set out to comprehensively measure income from all sources within the United States; the framework he developed was eventually applied across the world and forms the basis of modern methods of measuring national product.[33] After rapid success in this ambitious project, Kuznets moved on to measure other, more detailed forms of income. In collaboration with Milton Friedman,[34] he began the work discussed extensively in the *Work with Milton Friedman* section below. During World War II, Kuznets applied his talent for aggregate accounting and statistical analysis to explore the limits of American productive capacity. His analysis helped impose discipline on a political process that demanded far more in service of the war effort than the U.S. economy was capable of turning out.[35]

After the war, Kuznets and his family moved from New York to Philadelphia, where since the early 1930s Kuznets had been commuting to teach at the University of Pennsylvania. When the time came to find a house in Philadelphia, Kuznets reversed course and placed the family in an overwhelmingly Jewish suburb north of the city. The war's end brought other changes. As news of the Holocaust horrors spread throughout the United States, Kuznets, like other American Jews, was deeply shaken. He greeted the founding of the State of Israel with enthusiasm. Almost immediately, Kuznets began to make nearly annual trips to the Holy Land, meeting with and assisting the nation's nascent economic policy elite and eventually becoming a primary force behind the founding of the Maurice Falk Institute for Economic Research in Israel, which remains a primary locus for economic research in the Jewish state.[36]

The end of the Second World War also brought a shift in Kuznets's attention to what he described as "a wider view, using national income estimates and their components to compare the performance of countries in different parts of the world on an international scale."[37] This interest led him to write a series of ten articles under the titles "Quantitative Aspects of the Economic Growth of Nations," published in *Economic Development and Cultural Change* between 1956 and 1967. This set of articles formed the basis for Kuznets's most famous book, *Modern Economic Growth*, published in 1966. Yet, the most cited article of Kuznets's whole career, which emerged from his work on economic growth, was not actually a developed piece of research; rather, it was a hypothesis about the relationship between economic growth and income inequality that he debuted in his address[38] to the American Economic Association as president in 1955.

As his interest shifted from income to development, Kuznets twice changed universities. He left Pennsylvania in 1954 to spend six years in Baltimore at Johns Hopkins before spending the last decade of his career at Harvard University. His last major work focused on the relationship between population, demographics, and economic development. The connections between this work and his immigrant past are perhaps obvious and were first discussed by Kapuria-Foreman and Perlman.

After winning the Nobel Prize in 1971, Kuznets retired from Harvard and his career entered a new phase. He was in constant demand to lecture around the world and under no pressure to produce cutting-edge research; the mathematicization of economic theory and the increasing availability of empirical data eroded the importance of Kuznets's comparative advantages in the field. While he continued to write, he began to explore various areas of economics that had previously been shut out by his drive to address quantitatively the crucial questions of economic development. First, he began, after a long career of sole authorship, to collaborate more closely and more often with his colleagues. Second, he further developed his interest in Jewish history (discussed extensively below), which had lain dormant since his influential "Economic Structure and Life of the Jews" was published in 1960. Finally, he increasingly wrote broader articles and addressed more to methodology, survey, and interpretation than to original empirical analysis.[39]

As he entered the final stage of his life, he also increasingly took advantage of the nearly unlimited opportunities he had to travel. The frequency of his trips to Israel increased, especially with the Falk Institute he helped found flourishing. Despite all this, he remained extraordinarily productive until health intervened: from 1980 to 1982, he published twelve articles. Then, after three years of struggling with Parkinson's disease, Simon Kuznets died on July 8, 1985.

The Development of Development Economics

"Development Economics," the branch of the discipline concerned with poor nations, is a young subfield, even in a comparatively young discipline. As late as the early 1930s, most citizens of the developed world, even economists, did not understand that much of the world's population lived in relative poverty, essentially outside the system of industrial capitalism. Despite pervasive rhetoric about the "barbarism" or "lack of civilization" of colonized regions, Bardhan[40] argues that it was not until the development (by Kuznets) of national income accounting that it became possible to quantify the vast differences in material well-being between the developed and developing worlds.

Following Colin Clark's[41] seminal publication of systematic quantitative evidence of the "economic underdevelopment" in many parts of the world, there were a number of prominent "big theories" of development. Paul Rosenstein-Rodan[42] argued that industrialization is only profitable when undertaken simultaneously by many industries and thus requires a "big push" to succeed. Kurt Mandelbaum[43] attempted, with little success, to apply demand side Keynesian theory in order to explain underdevelopment. Raúl Prebisch[44] pointed to colonial legacy trade patterns that victimized developing nations, while W. Arthur Lewis[45] emphasized the misallocation of labor supply to the rural, rather than industrial, sector. Robert Solow[46] proposed an influential mathematical theory of economic growth in which poor nations were poor because of a lack of capital and technology. Perhaps most infamously, W. W. Rostow[47] argued that developing nations simply needed to position their economies as currently developed nations had been when they developed to begin a "take-off" to sustained economic growth through a series of "linear stages."

All these theories had at least two important broad features in common, which Kuznets called into question. First, all focused overwhelmingly on the aggregate problem of industrialization and growth, rather than on the effects of policies on, or through, their within-country distributions. Second, all viewed currently developing countries as following roughly the same growth trajectory (sharing the same production function, in Solow's terms) today as developed countries had followed in the past. While they disagreed about the causes of development, all believed in a universal recipe that had worked in the past for currently wealthy nations and would work in the future for currently underdeveloped nations. The following section discusses how insights Kuznets drew from his understanding and study of the Eastern European Jewish Diaspora led him to challenge the first of these views, while the section after it discusses the second.

Jewish Inequality and the Kuznets Curve

Economic inequality has proved a severe and persistent feature of the economic life of Jews, especially those of Eastern European descent, for at least the last century and a half. As Kuznets argues within his seminal 1975 article "Immigration of Russian Jews to the United States: Background and Structure," which is reproduced in our second volume, the legal discrimination and urbanity likely combined to create an enormous inequality within the Jewish community between a wealthy commercial and financial elite and the dislocated and discriminated-against masses. In fact, extreme inequality due to professional insecurity among European Jews was bemoaned as early as 1793 by prominent Jewish enlightenment (*maskilim*) intellectual David Friedländer in his classic *Akten-stücke, die Reform jüdischen Kolonien in den Preussischen Staaten betreffend*[48] and has long been seen as the source of the paradox in anti-Semitism that Jews have been viewed both as exploitative economic overlords and detestable paupers.

Kuznets argues that this inequality may have played an important role in the emigration of Eastern European Jews in two ways. First, inequality within the Jewish community may have reinforced prejudices within the non-Jewish population in creating both resentment of Jewish wealth and disdain for Jewish poverty, a theme that Penslar also picks up. Second, the dislocation and low economic position of much of the Jewish population, particularly when contrasted to the wealthy community elite, may have created a strong desire among some for selective migration to countries with broader opportunity, such as the United States. While not discounting the role of Jewish persecution in Eastern Europe in spurring emigration, he argues that much of the differential Jewish migration may be attributable to greater Jewish urbanity and therefore greater exposure to dislocation and inequality associated with early stages of industrialization.

While quantifying the extent of these differential rates of wealth disparity is nearly impossible given the lack of data, Kuznets documents in the 1972 manuscript "Economic Growth of U.S. Jewry," which appears in print for the first time on page 167 of the first volume of this series, that this trend has persisted, if not steepened, after Jewish immigration to the United States. He shows that while Jewish median income is only 10–20 percent higher than that of urban American Gentiles, mean income is almost twice that of the reference group, which suggests far greater Jewish inequality. Dramatic inequalities between impoverished newly arrived immigrants and wealthy established American Jewry, documented by Kuznets in his 1960 "Economic Structure and the Life of the Jews,"[49] were followed, after acculturation, by the wide cleavages of income between and within the professions (almost universally well-educated) Jews chose. Inequality among Jews is made all the more potent by the relative cultural segregation of Jews, which led to close contact among Jews of different classes. These inequalities were not merely an engaging subject for academic study in Kuznets's life, but of pressing personal relevance. From the inequality between wealthy Jewish professional and lower-middle-class academic friends[50] to that surrounding him in his life in New York,[51] inequality among Jews appeared at all stages of his life. One can only speculate that the view down from the wealthy heights of his youth in Pinsk and Kharkov[52] fit the rough patterns described in his academic work.

Thus, it should not be surprising that income inequality became a central theme of Kuznets's understanding of both the economic structure of Jews and the development of economies. The latter theme is perhaps the most widely known of Kuznets's contributions to economics. In his 1954 Presidential Address to the American Economic Association, Kuznets argued that the evolution of income inequality and its relationship to economic growth should be central to the study of economic development. He also laid out a hypothesis about the nature of this relationship, which remains influential to this day, despite having been recently falsified even in the countries Kuznets studied with the advent of richer data.[53] His basic theory was that income inequality should first rise and then fall as a country developed economically. His reasoning ran roughly as follows: an industrializing country may be seen as being divided, à la Lewis,[54] into two broad sectors: one urban and industrial; the other rural, communal, and agricultural. Economic development involves the transfer of population from the second sector into the first. Given the greater inequality of outcomes and uncertainty in urban life, at least the initial stages of this move were sure to exacerbate the divide between rich and poor, even as they spurred the nation's overall economic development. Furthermore, the increasing wealth of the urban sector relative to the rural sector and the accumulation of savings by this capitalist sector exacerbate inequality.

However, countervailing forces emerge as the process of development proceeds. First, the continued thrust of industrialization eventually erases differences of income between urban and rural sectors, as increased mobility and labor market efficiency demand the equalization of wages for comparable work. Second, the increasing availability of education, social welfare, and other government services demanded by urban masses eventually spread economic opportunity widely, holding down early entrepreneurial profits through competition and expanding the range of people to whom the most attractive economic opportunities are available. Finally, the process of development is largely one of capital accumulation, and with such accumulation comes decreasing returns to capital; in fact, in most standard economic models, the share of national income accruing to capital is constant as capital accumulates. Workers, who now have more machines to use, see the returns to human capital rise. Given increasing mass education, human capital is more equitably spread than physical capital. Therefore, wages rise and economic inequality eventually declines.

Much less well known are Kuznets's closely related theories of inequality among Jewish Eastern European migrants. In an early working draft of "Economic Structure," edited and published for the first time in this volume, Kuznets lays out what might be termed the "immigrant Kuznets Curve" hypothesis (pages 51–53 of Volume I of this series). He argues that inequality within an immigrant population should first increase and then fall as that community develops economically within its destination country. His reasoning is that immigrants are likely to rise economically as they become accustomed to the economic conditions and culture of a country. So long as a steady stream of migration continues, inequality will arise between the wealthier migrants who have spent longer in the country and the poorer new arrivals. However, if migration tapers or ceases, inequality will abate as all members of the arrived group equilibrate to their natural income in the new country. Note that this reasoning largely parallels Kuznets's argument for the inverted U in the inequality-development relationship: the initial waves of migration to the city bring inequality between urban and rural areas and as the migration becomes complete, this inequality disappears.

This connection is further reinforced by the modeling exercises Kuznets used to quantitatively analyze these two parallel hypotheses. A core feature[55] of "Economic Growth and Income Inequality" is a toy model Kuznets builds that explores the possibility that the moving of population into a wealthier but more unequal sector might first generate and then reduce income inequality, under different assumptions about the relative income of the sectors. In the early version of "Economic Structure" in the first volume of this series, Kuznets includes a similar exercise (p. 115) where he explores the effects of changing distribution of migrants among cohorts over time on the patterns of intra-Jewish inequality, under different assumptions about the relative wages of the cohorts. The similarities between these are striking. Both consider a discrete number of sectors, assume various relative incomes in the sectors, allow shares of population allocated to the sectors to vary over time, and trace the implications for the path of income inequality (in the latter case, both absolute and relative to the rest of the population). The readers may judge for themselves the stylistic and substantive connections between these from Tables 1 and 2.

The connections between Kuznets's understanding of Jewish and broader inequality are further reinforced at least weakly by the apparent temporal coincidence of "Economic Structure and Life of the Jews" and "Economic Growth and Income Inequality." The former was available in a fairly polished draft in April 1956,[56] and the latter was given at the American Economic Association annual meeting at the end of 1954.[57] Presumably, given that it was not likely his highest work priority, Kuznets had been working on his article on Jewish economics for several years. Thus, it seems plausible that his insight into the relationship between income inequality and development, as well as the right way to model this interaction, actually arose from his work on the history of Jews. At least, his work on

Table 1 **Percentage shares of first and fifth quintiles in the income distribution for total population under varying assumptions concerning per capita income within the sectors, proportions of sectors in total number, and intrasector income distributions**

	Proportion of number in Sector A to total number						
	0.8 (1)	**0.7** (2)	**0.6** (3)	**0.5** (4)	**0.4** (5)	**0.3** (6)	**0.2** (7)
I. Per capita income of Sector A = 50; Sector B = 100							
1. Per capita income of total population	60	65	70	75	80	85	90
Distribution (*E*) for both sectors							
2. Share of first quintile	10.5	9.9	9.6	9.3	9.4	9.8	10.2
3. Share of fifth quintile	34.2	35.8	35.7	34.7	33.2	31.9	30.4
4. Range (3–2)	23.7	25.9	26.1	25.3	23.9	22.1	20.2
Distribution (*U*) for both sectors							
5. Share of first quintile	3.8	3.8	3.7	3.7	3.8	3.8	3.9
6. Share of fifth quintile	40.7	41.9	42.9	42.7	41.5	40.2	38.7
7. Range (6–5)	36.8	38.1	39.1	39.0	37.8	36.4	34.8
Distribution (*E*) for Sector A, (*U*) for Sector B							
8. Share of first quintile	9.3	8.3	7.4	6.7	6.0	5.4	4.9
9. Share of fifth quintile	37.7	41.0	42.9	42.7	41.5	40.2	38.7
10. Range (9–8)	28.3	32.7	35.4	36.0	35.5	34.8	33.8
II. Per capita income of Sector A = 50; Sector B = 200							
11. Per capita income of total population	80	95	110	125	140	155	170
Distribution (*E*) for both sectors							
12. Share of first quintile	7.9	6.8	6.1	5.6	5.4	5.4	5.9
13. Share of fifth quintile	50.0	49.1	45.5	41.6	38.0	35.0	32.2
14. Range (13–12)	42.1	42.3	39.4	36.0	32.6	29.6	26.3
Distribution (*U*) for both sectors							
15. Share of first quintile	3.1	2.9	2.7	2.6	2.6	2.7	3.1
16. Share of fifth quintile	52.7	56.0	54.5	51.2	47.4	44.1	40.9
17. Range (6–5)	49.6	53.1	51.8	48.6	44.8	41.4	37.9

(continued)

Table 1 *(continued)*

	Proportion of number in Sector A to total number						
	0.8 (1)	**0.7** (2)	**0.6** (3)	**0.5** (4)	**0.4** (5)	**0.3** (6)	**0.2** (7)
Distribution (E) for Sector A, (U) for Sector B							
18. Share of first quintile	7.4	6.2	5.4	4.7	4.2	3.9	3.8
19. Share of fifth quintile	51.6	56.0	54.6	51.2	47.4	44.1	40.9
20. Range (9–8)	44.2	49.8	49.2	46.5	43.2	40.2	37.2

Some differences will not check because of rounding.

For methods of calculating the shares of quintiles, see p. 12 and fn. 6 of Simon S. Kuznets, "Economic Growth and Income Inequality," *The American Economic Review* 45, no. 1 (1955): 1–28.

The implications can be brought out most clearly with the help of a numerical illustration (see Table I). In this illustration, we deal with two sectors: agriculture (A) and all others (B). For each sector, we assume percentage distributions of total sector income among sector deciles: one distribution (*E*) is of moderate inequality, with the shares starting at 5.5 per cent for the lowest decile and rising 1 percentage point from decile to decile to reach 14.5 per cent for the top decile; the other distribution (*U*) is much more unequal, the shares starting at 1 per cent for the lowest decile, and rising 2 percentage points from decile to decile to reach 19 per cent for the top decile. We assign per capita incomes to each sector: 50 units to A and 100 units to B in case I (lines 1–10 in the illustration); 50 to A and 200 to B in case II (lines 11–20). Finally, we allow the proportion of the numbers in sector A in the total number to decline from 0.8 to 0.2.

The numerical illustration is only a partial summary of the calculations, showing the shares of the lowest and highest quintiles in the income distribution for the total population under different assumption.[6] The basic assumptions used throughout are that the per capita income of sector B (nonagricultural) is always higher than that of sector A; that the proportion of sector A in the total number declines; and that the inequality of the income distribution within sector A may be as wide as that within sector B but not wider. (p. 12)

(fn. 6) The underlying calculations are quite simple. For each case, we distinguish 20 cells within the total distribution-sets of ten deciles for each sector. For each cell, we compute the percentage shares of both number and income in the number and income of total population, and hence also the relative per capita income of each cell. The cells are then arrayed in increasing order of their relative per capita income and cumulated. In the resulting cumulative distributions of number and countrywide income we establish, by arithmetic interpolation, if interpolation is needed, the percentage shares in total income of the successive quintiles of the country's population.

international income inequality seems to have been instrumental in allowing him to understand the evolution of Jewish economic structure; at most, his thinking about the economics of American Jewry may have led him to the broader connections between development and inequality.

Table 2 Illustrative calculations of the effect of "recency of entry mix" on movement of average income and income dispersion, Jews in the U.S.A., 1900–50

		Assumption I			Assumption II	
	Index of average income (1900 = 100) (1)	Index of absolute dispersion (1900 = 100) (2)	Relative dispersion (absolute average income) (3)	Index of average income (1900 = 100) (4)	Index of absolute dispersion (1900 = 100) (5)	Relative dispersion (absolute average income) (6)
1900	100	100	0.32	1,001	100	0.43
1905	95	97	0.34	94	98	0.45
1910	94	102	0.34	93	100	0.46
1915	102	97	0.31	102	98	0.40
1920	113	86	0.25	117	86	0.31
1925	120	87	0.23	126	87	0.29
1930	130	65	0.16	139	65	0.20
1935	138	33	0.08	150	33	0.09
1940	137	39	0.09	148	39	0.11
1945	140	24	0.05	152	24	0.07
1950	140	24	0.05	152	24	0.07

Assumption I—Ratio of average income of groups by years of residence:
0–5—1; 6–10—1.5; 11–20—2.0; over 20—3.0.
Assumption II—Ratio of average income of groups by years of residence:
0–5—1; 6–10—2.0; 11–20—3.0; over 20—5.0.
This table appears in the early version of "Economic Structure" (p. 99 of that draft), and is also included in the first volume of this series on p. 73.

Development and Culture

Kuznets's second objection to the initial thrust of development theory was his critique of the doctrine that developing countries could or should follow the development paths of presently developed countries. Kuznets was skeptical about how much might be learned about the future of developing countries by studying the past of developed countries. In his book *Modern Economic Growth*,[58] the eponymous 1973 article, and several other articles, he lays out a variety of reasons why the development path of currently underdeveloped countries may differ fundamentally from the past of developed nations.

Some of these differences were what would seem to be fairly obvious and conventional economic and technological distinctions. These are of less interest for my argument, but were not well understood by economists at the time, so I briefly summarize them here. Most currently underdeveloped countries have a lower per capita output than the Western nations, even before their industrialization, and are not great political powers, as were most wealthy nations during their period of development. Furthermore, consumer preferences have, to some extent, leapfrogged over early industrial goods. Service goods are a growing share of modern economies, making global demand faced by developing nations different from that in the nineteenth century.[59] Where currently developed countries existed at or near the technological frontier during much of their process of development, currently underdeveloped nations linger in a sort of limbo. The wide availability of certain technologies has rapidly improved standards of living in developing nations. Vaccinations, television, and other consumer goods have become increasingly available to citizens of poor nations, extending the length and quality of life. At the same time, basic productive technologies, particularly in transport and capital goods, have failed to filter across national borders. This strange combination of consumerism without industrialism puts poor countries in a distinctly different technological state than that facing the West before its industrialization.[60]

More innovative was the emphasis Kuznets put on noneconomic distinctions, such as institutions and culture. These were uncommon topics for study in economics in any form and thus Kuznets's focus on them was itself an important contribution. The first and probably least controversial of these heterodox factors was institutional. Most, though not all, currently developed countries reached that state during periods of growing democratic participation and under governments checked by the demands of individual rights and liberties. They also had developed modern legal systems, largely professional civil services, and other modern governance institutions. To a large extent, these institutions are weak or absent in many, if not most, developing nations. In addition, most developing nations had a far less benign experience with colonization than did the few currently developed nations that were at one time colonies. Their populations are largely the colonized, rather than the colonizers. As an exception that proved the rule on the plight of most developing countries, Kuznets in his work on Israel emphasizes the institutions that developed to deal with the state of constant war and the status of colonizer rather than colonized.

Compounding these problems for most developing countries is the fact that colonialism, as well as the presence of a developed global market outside the country, means that many sources of significant wealth, far beyond the usual productive capacity of the country, are available to select internationalized elites. This exacerbates problems of income and wealth inequality that may have been less severe in Europe during its development. Consequently, if institutions play an important role in economic development, as it seems likely they do, then it would be surprising if the development paths of currently developing countries were similar to the past of currently developed nations.[61]

More controversially, Kuznets highlights the cultural contrasts between currently backward nations and the past of wealthy nations. Unlike other divergences, he has little data to formalize these distinctions. Religious differences, absence of Western cultural heritage, and "colonial hangover" all make the cultures of developing nations systematically different from those of developed nations at their time of industrialization. Kuznets concedes that little is known about the relationship between such cultural factors and economic growth and therefore that the implications of such differences may or may not be important. But he emphasizes that it is worth keeping in mind the role such cultural elements may play in supporting an entrepreneurial society by facilitating risk sharing and informal trade, efficiently allocating resources to new endeavors, and fostering a focus on the educational and intellectual culture important to developing human capital.[62]

While certainly not opposed to the use of economic history to learn about the economic future, Kuznets was strongly skeptical of simplistic, de-contextualized extrapolation from a hazy Western economic past.[63] In moving economic theory beyond such "linear" and purely economic theories of growth, Kuznets helped give birth to modern development economics, which has focused on understanding the economics of currently developing countries on their own terms. At the same time, Kuznets was not, like some of his more radical colleagues such as Albert Hirschman,[64] opposed to economic theorizing or committed to the notion that development policy should be based on purely "case-based" or "pragmatic" considerations.[65] Rather, Kuznets argued for a vision of development economics that worked to develop generalizing theories, but theories that took into account and understood the most dramatic and important distinctions while abstracting from less important differences. Thus, beyond the narrower point of difference between past and future development, Kuznets's emphasis on culture and institutions was revolutionary within development economics and has had a large and lasting impact on the field.

Many of these distinctions between currently developing nations and the past of developed nations parallel the distinctions he draws between Jewish and Gentile economic structures in his work on the economic history of the Jews. Most prominent among these parallels is structural. In his analysis of Jewish and Gentile economic structure, Kuznets primarily stresses the broadest and most theoretically justified distinctions between the economics of a small minority within a country and that of the majority, eschewing Jewish-specific explanations.[66] This parallels Kuznets's later belief in the utility of theories addressing the broad sweep of developing countries, rather than considering development on a case-by-case basis, while at the same time emphasizing the distinction between the current state of developing nations and the past of developed nations.[67] The basic approach, in both cases, is one of carefully complicating theory one level at a time and of avoiding a rush either to overgeneralization or to a purely case-based, infinitely flexible antitheoretical analysis. This parallel is further reinforced by the differing "development paths" that he envisions small (immigrant) minorities following relative to the majorities within the same country. Small minorities, unwedded to majority customs, are likely to participate most heavily in the fastest growing technological sectors of the economy, paralleling the possible technological and product-space "leapfrogging" that Kuznets suggests may be possible for developing nations.[68]

Yet, perhaps the greatest relationship between Kuznets's thinking about the history of Jews and development economics comes in his emphasis of cultural and social factors. Of all the foci Kuznets suggested, these are perhaps the most controversial within the economics community, which tends to view such claims as vague at best and culturally deterministic (even crypto-racist) at worst. Despite this widespread hostility within the economic community, Kuznets was deeply committed to the importance of culture, as is perhaps most dramatically demonstrated by the title of the journal he helped found and make prominent, *Economic Development and Cultural Change*. Kuznets's interest in culture and society as driving forces in economic development likely had roots in the continual dialogue he maintained in his personal life with academics of widely varying fields, particularly sociologists and anthropologists,[69] but was also tightly connected to his understanding of the distinctive cultural and social structure of the Jewish community that underlay its economic success and more general economic structure.

In fact, the first time, as far as I know,[70] that Kuznets discusses the relationship between culture and economics is in "Economic Structure." After the publication of that article, it explodes into a primary theme in his research interests. While the founding of *Economic Development and Cultural Change* predates his completion of a draft of "Economic Structure" by four years, it seems plausible that Kuznets's interest in the cultural factors underpinning economic development was reinforced, if not spurred, by his study of Jewish history.

A major theme of "Economic Structure" is the notion that economic patterns of the Jewish community might be explained by the desire within the community to maintain cultural cohesion and that Jews might be willing to sacrifice a substantial economic advantage in order to work in sectors of the economy where other Jews work. Kuznets also emphasizes that Jewish urbanity may be seen as an outgrowth of the greater anonymity afforded by cities, allowing for increased cultural cohesion without excessive fear of a backlash from the majority population. Furthermore, in the context of Israel/Palestine, although he implies this may be a feature of Jewish economic structure more broadly, he emphasizes the importance of "social capital" that allowed informal social insurance and efficient allocation of financial resources for investment within the Jewish community.

Kuznets's interest in the connection between Jewish cultural and social conditions to Jewish economic structure further highlighted the speech he gave, later in his career, at the home of the president of Israel, which appears in the first volume of this compilation on pages

149–164. In particular, Kuznets stresses the cultural inheritance that appears to spur Jews toward the aggressive pursuit of education, leading to their eventual prominence in the highly trained professional and academic sectors of the American economy (volume 1, pages 113–114). Interestingly, he also stresses the tendency of Jewish intellectuals to be more radically left wing than intellectuals at large. He argues that, given that more Jews are intellectuals in the first place, this fact has important implications for the political, and eventually economic, composition of the Jewish workforce. In particular, he feared that the increasing trend of radical intellectuals "dropping out" of school, the workforce, and mainstream society in general might lead Jews to follow this misguided trend particularly zealously. In understanding the economic position of Jews in the United States after immigration from Eastern Europe, Kuznets emphasizes the fact that Jews had much stronger family ties and were much more likely to bring their entire family along when they immigrated than were other immigrants to the United States.[71] He also makes fairly vague references to the selectivity of Jewish history for intelligence and a culture focused on education, an argument controversial anywhere, but particularly among economists.

Finally, Kuznets emphasizes the potential economic inefficiencies and inhibitions of development that ethnic division in developing countries might create.[72] Considerations of the importance of such ethnic conflict dates to years before those writings, however, when he first took up this theme in his discussion of the economic structure of the Jewish minority, in fact, of any ethnic minority.[73] Beyond his writing on Jewish history, Mark Perlman[74] also emphasizes more direct connections between Kuznets's, and other Jewish economists', past of separateness and youth in Russia and a hesitance to see the past of developed countries as an appropriate model for current developing countries.

Jewish Immigration and the Population Debate

The 1960s were a time of ferment for neo-Malthusian worries about exploding world population, culminating in Paul Ehrlich's famously alarmist and hugely influential *The Population Bomb*. In the economics community, too, population problems became a focus, including the topic of Joseph Spengler's 1965 Presidential Address to the American Economics Association. The dominant view of academics outside economics followed broadly Ehrlichian lines: population growth threatened a Malthusian implosion of living standards. Economics was somewhat more optimistic, but still concerned; Solow's neo-classical growth model indicated that increased population growth would reduce the level, but not the growth rate, of per capita incomes.

Kuznets influentially[75] took a different perspective, beginning with his article "Population Change and Aggregate Output."[76] Kuznets argues that population growth could actually be an important source of per capita income growth, as population growth offered increased opportunities for specialization and, more importantly, greater numbers of people meant greater numbers of rare geniuses who advanced technological progress, accelerating economic development. Inspired by and drawing upon Kuznets's work, Edmund Phelps[77] summarized this argument eloquently:

> One can hardly imagine how poor we would be today if it were not for the rapid population growth of the past to which we owe the enormous number of advanced technologies we enjoy today . . . If I could redo the history of the world, halving population from the beginning of time on some random basis, I would not do it for fear of losing Mozart in the process.

Phelps's argument is perhaps nowhere more palpable and present than in the Jewish community: how much richer would today's world be if the Jewish intellectuals murdered in the Holocaust had survived? Kuznets was also particularly skeptical about the more limited and widely accepted claim that developing countries could not afford their rapid rates of population growth. In a 1967 piece for the *Proceedings of the American Philosophical Society*, "Population and Economic Growth," Kuznets sought to bring a more balanced perspective to the broader academic community's understanding of the costs and benefits of population growth.[78] Kuznets argues that current technology, if simply applied to developing countries, would be more than sufficient to supply food for not only all current inhabitants but also all projected future inhabitants for at least forty years without any increase in arable land.[79] The capacity of population growth to be supported by the adoption of new technology is clearly echoed in Kuznets's comments on the high rates of population growth within the Jewish community. These have hardly retarded Jewish economic advance, given the expansion of Jewish human capital through education to support these greater numbers.[80] However, in his typical style, Kuznets was exceedingly cautious in advancing these arguments beyond the bounds of what is clear from data. For example, he writes on page 184 of "Population and Economic Growth," "intellectual caution and modesty should compel one to stop right here—with this confession that economic analysis alone is inadequate in dealing with such a fundamental aspect of economic growth as its relationship to population increase." Thankfully, Kuznets did not stop right there, instead expressing the cautious insights he had gained from a lifetime of studying population and development.

Kuznets's emphasis on the role of immigration in economic development also manifests itself in his work on "Israel's Economic Development." Section 3 of that article (119–134) is devoted to arguing that half or more of the excessive growth of Israel compared to other developing nations is due to the combination of immigration and the young nation's astonishing ability to raise the torrent of immigrants consistently to the level of income of those who immigrated earlier. This success, and the astonishingly rapid economic growth he documents and argues it fostered, contrasts favorably even when compared to the impressive track record of Jews in the United States and likely represents one more force that drew the migrant-friendly Kuznets's affections toward the blossoming new state.

From a careful review of his bibliography,[81] it appears that Kuznets's inclination in favor of immigration in his academic work begins within his pioneering research, jointly with Ernest Rubin, on the subject.[82] On page 1 they write, "The growth of a national economy may be stimulated by the increase of its population, which strongly affects consumer demand and the size of the labor force . . . In the United States population growth has traditionally been regarded as a source of strength and a sign of material progress." Yet, as they discuss, views on population policy reversed sharply in the 1920s: the titanic wave of immigration to the United States that carried the Eastern European Jewish Diaspora to the United States ended with the Immigration Act and National Origins Quota of 1924. Opposition to such policies was one of the few political issues about which generally apolitical Kuznets was passionate, believing that immigration was the foundation of American success.[83] This is unsurprising, given that Kuznets barely made it into the country before the restrictions were imposed.

While such restrictions were almost certainly motivated more deeply by racist and eugenicist popular sentiment in the country, they were often justified publically, and gained crucial support from (even Jewish) organized labor, by arguments about the excessive overcrowding and wage depression caused by immigration.[84] Kuznets and Rubin argue, again on page 1, that while these "interests (may have been) acting in supposed accordance with their economic advantage," they were likely misled due to a lack of "carefully considered . . . scientific research in the national interest," research they hope to provide. Kuznets in *Demographic and Economic Change in Developed Countries* (Massachusetts: National Bureau of Economic Research, 1960, 324–51) goes on to emphasize, in a strikingly theoretical article by his standards, the importance of allowing free migration and communication of intellectuals in order to achieve maximal rates of technical progress. What he saw as mistaken Malthusian views of immigration clearly struck Kuznets close to home.

Work with Milton Friedman

Superficially, Milton Friedman and Simon Kuznets do not seem like the most natural collaborators. Arch-free-marketeer and adherent of the Keynesian mainstream, father of modern neo-Marshallianism and persistent skeptic of simple models, bold public intellectual and ever-cautious empiricist: Friedman and Kuznets had very different professional inclinations. Nonetheless, their lives overlapped significantly for many years. They shared a common mentor and advisor, Wesley Clair Mitchell, who taught them both empirical economics; moreover, Friedman became Kuznets's assistant during the war years. Eventually, the pair published the bulk of Friedman's dissertation, first as an article in 1939[85] and then as a book in 1945,[86] both as *Income from Independent Professional Practice.*

This work typified the Mitchell-Kuznets school of empirical work: it was several hundred pages devoted overwhelmingly to the dispassionate tabulation of patterns of income earned by professionals in various careers. The book sowed the seeds of two ideas that, largely through Friedman's advocacy of them, were to be the central concerns of labor economics for the following half century: first, occupational licensure as a means of reducing competition, and second, modeling educational choices as investment in "human capital."

The breakthrough idea of Friedman and Kuznets regarding occupational licensure was typified by a quote they include from Harold Rypins on page 12 of their book, who noted, "In all the professions there has developed in the last few years an aristocratic, or at least restrictive movement which, in a sense, is reminiscent of the medieval guilds." Morris Kleiner[87] cites Kuznets and Friedman's work as having major influence on views among economists; particularly influential was the idea, much espoused by Friedman, that occupational licensure may and often does act as a anticompetitive barrier to entry.[88] Prominent citations of this argument by Theodore Schultz[89] and Gary Becker[90] confirm this view. In fact, this view was so controversial at the time of the publication of the volume that it caused a five-year delay in the publication of the work due to the objections of a National Bureau of Economic Research board member affiliated with the American Medical Association. While I am not aware of any work on the history of this contentious proposition, I think most casual readers, including myself, would initially assume this argument was likely of Friedman, the libertarian, not Kuznets, the moderate leftist's, invention.

While I have no clear proof that this view is mistaken, several elements of Kuznets work suggest that it may be. First, it should be recalled that at this time, Friedman's ardent free-market views were just developing.[91] Second, the medieval guild system was hardly an interest of Friedman's and therefore the Rypins quote is unlikely to have caught his eye among the myriad of other references from which the pair chose. On the other hand, Kuznets, eventually in 1960 and more extensively in 1975,[92] wrote on the guild system and its destructive impact on Jewish life in Eastern Europe. While it is unclear when in his career this interest began, an unpublished, handwritten manuscript that I discovered in the Kuznets archive, "The Doctrine of Usury in the Middle Ages," indicates that Kuznets had an abiding interest in medieval professional and economic regulation. I include a version of these notes, transcribed by my coeditor Stephanie Lo, on my website http://www.glenweyl.com.

While the manuscript is classic Kuznets in concealing its motivation and (perhaps partly due to the Bureau's censorship) ultimate conclusions, it stands out from the rest of the corpus of Kuznets's work in several ways. First, it is one of the only writings of his I have encountered with absolutely no quantitative dimension. Second, it is purely a work of intellectual history, tracing the evolution of the doctrine of usury through the Middle Ages. This is, as far as I know, the only intellectual history work Kuznets ever did. Finally, the work is exceptional among treatments of usury in that it makes no mention whatsoever of the Jews that ended up filling the money lending roles proscribed to Christians. This omission seems particularly odd given that it seems apparent that the connection to Jewish economic regulation must have played an important role in the motivation for the manuscript. Of course, it is hard to know whether this was the beginning of an academic paper (as the fact that the paper shows signs of having been edited throughout), a set of personal notes (as the fact that he never after referred to or built upon as it suggests), or somewhere in between. Furthermore, while the positioning of the manuscript in the archive indicates that it was from his early career, I have not been able to associate a date to the paper with any certainty (i.e., before or after his work with Friedman). Regardless, it seems clear that Kuznets, not Friedman, was the primary student of the economic and professional system of the old world. In fact, a thorough review of a bibliography of Friedman compiled by Niels Thygesen[93] indicates that Friedman's only explicit research on history through 1977 was his celebrated work with Anna Schwartz on money in the United States.

The second idea for which the book is famous sprung from the authors' effort to understand the first. Friedman and Kuznets tried,[94] and failed,[95] to explain the income differentials between professional and nonprofessional careers as a return on capital investments necessary to enter the professions. Their failure led them to conclude that occupational licensure and other barriers made professionals a "noncompeting group" (p. 93). Their method of accounting for the fair market return of such "human" capital investments, which improved on earlier work by J. R. Walsh,[96] became the foundation of an enormous literature on the returns to education.

In fact, the pioneers of the theory of human capital, Yoram Ben-Porath,[97] and to a lesser extent Jacob Mincer,[98] Theodore Schultz,[99] and Gary Becker,[100] attribute the genesis of their ideas to Friedman and Kuznets's book; for instance, Ben-Porath establishes in his opening paragraph the importance of "[t]he development by Friedman and Kuznets[101] of the theory . . . of . . . human capital." Friedman carried the idea of human capital developed in his work with Kuznets forward to his classic theory of permanent income,[102] the fundamental ideas of which he attributed to his work with Kuznets in his Nobel autobiography.[103] Friedman's interest in education and its implications for income continued throughout his career, albeit somewhat obliquely through his interest in lifetime, as opposed to temporary, income,[104] another idea[105] he attributed to his work with Kuznets, and reform of the educational system.[106] Likely through his influence, including his role as Becker's advisor, human capital became a dominant theme of the Chicago school, occupying much of the attention of scholars such as Becker, Schultz, and Ben-Porath. Thus, there is little doubt that, despite its relative obscurity, *Income from Independent Professional Practice* set off a quiet revolution in labor economics.

Yet, from where did its emphasis on human capital originate? The most I can do is speculate as I found no information concerning the process of writing the work. However, the connections to Jewish economic history, and Kuznets's understanding of it, could hardly be more apparent. Perhaps the primary focus of virtually all of Kuznets's work on the economic history of the Jews[107] was upon their outstanding educational attainment and the role this played in accounting for their outstanding differential economic advance beyond the position of the general immigrant and native population. It is widely known that education and (religious) study were central values of Judaism at least since the advent of Christianity, and Kuznets documented quantitatively the universal popular perception that this translated into far higher Jewish educational attainment in the United States than among other immigrant or native groups. For example, Kuznets[108] found that Jews of Eastern European descent completed college at twice the rate of the general American population.

Any direct connection between Jewish educational attainment and the human capital theory of Kuznets's work with Friedman is at best speculative. Nonetheless, it seems a plausible potential source of motivation for that important research. Furthermore, it is not just its connection to Jewish economic history that is hard to draw out of *Income*. In typical Kuznets style, the book is written in a highly technical and concrete style that entirely masks both the motivation for its writing as well as the broad generalizations based on the research that Friedman and others obviously took away from it. For example, the most influential passage of the book, the basis of subsequent interest in licensure as a barrier to entry (p. 93) reads,

> The inference from this analysis is that professional workers constitute a "non-competing" group . . . Our data suggest that this group is sufficiently small to lead to underinvestment . . . that in the absence of . . . limitations on entry, incomes in the professions would exceed incomes in other pursuits by less than they do now. The limitations of the data and the speculative character of our analysis make this conclusion tentative.

This bears comparison with Friedman's later writing, in *Capitalism and Freedom* on occupational licensure on pages 141–42:

> Licensure therefore frequently establishes essentially the medieval guild kind of regulation in which the state assigns power to the members of the profession . . . the problem of licensing of occupations is something more than a trivial illustration of the problem of state intervention, that it is already in this country a serious infringement on the freedom of individuals to pursue activities of their own choice, and that it threatens to become a much more serious one with the continual pressure upon legislatures to extend it.

The reserve, modesty, and scientific demeanor with which Kuznets expressed his claims mean that any hopes of understanding the sources of his ideas must be somewhat indirect. The most we may hope for in understanding the motivation behind this work is a series of circumstantial, mutually reinforcing connections between Kuznets's understanding of Jewish history and various areas of his mainstream economics.

The Cautious Empiricist of the Eastern European Jewish Diaspora

While it certainly carries its frustrations for the historian, Kuznets's reticence about the personal causes and consequences of his work is key to understanding him and his contribution. When Bertil Ohlin presented Simon Kuznets, his committee's selection as the 1971 Nobel laureate in Economics, he said, "Kuznets, of course, makes use of models which demonstrate the connections between strategic elements in the economic system, but he shows a very limited sympathy for abstract and generalizing models which provide few opportunities of empirical testing. He chooses and defines concepts which (sic) correspond as closely as possible to what can be observed and statistically measured." Fogel[109] discusses extensively Kuznets's careful, humble, empirical approach to economics.

His hesitance to extrapolate from data or propose hypotheses not directly based in observation is apparent throughout his research. I consider a couple of examples. The conclusion of his famous AEA Presidential Address in which he proposed the inverted U hypothesis begins, "In concluding this paper, I am acutely conscious of the meagerness of reliable information presented. This paper is perhaps 5 per cent empirical information, 95 per cent speculation, some of it possibly tainted by wishful thinking." The apology for this, one of the most empirically based presidential addresses for many years, continues for almost half a page. His extreme caution applied even to the most mundane extrapolations from data. On page 21 of

"Economic Growth of U. S. Jewry," he ends a paragraph of apologies for the assumptions he was forced to make in order to generate the first estimates of a time series of American Jewish population with "We shall have to rest content with these rough approximations." To the jaded reader who is accustomed to daily encounters with the most complex contortions of structural econometrics, it is astonishing[110] to see such fervent caution about steps of data collection that would probably not even be reported in most contemporary papers.

Kuznets's painstaking effort to separate conjecture from fact reflects a related, but broader, set of dualities that pervaded his life and work: between his work on Jewish history and its motivation in his past, between that work and his professional life as an economist, and between his loyalty to his heritage and the strict American life he built for his family. To gain a richer perspective on Kuznets as a thinker and as a person, it is useful to consider each of these, briefly, in turn.

It could hardly be more apparent that Kuznets's past and identifications led him to do his research on Jewish economic history. In fact, in a 1973 letter to Martin Feldstein, which we have published on page 273 of the first volume of this series, Kuznets writes, "I did this paper (and other in the series) because of my interests and associations as a Jew (I frankly doubt that were it not for these interests and associations, I would have, as a general economist, devoted much thought or effort to this topic)." However, absolutely no clues to such motivations, or even any mention of his past, appears in any of Kuznets's scholarly work on the history of the Jews. His first article on the Jews[111] begins in typically universalistic fashion, "The economic structure and life of any group, within a given historical epoch, is largely a matter of its natural and social environment." In the most informal and personal of his writing on the history of the Jews, a speech he gave at the home of the President Zalman Shazar of Israel,[112] Kuznets touches on a wide range of topics very close to his life, yet never explicitly betrays the slightest personal interest or emotion. When he discusses the forcing of Jews in Eastern Europe, like his parents, toward a limited range of professions,[113] when he analyzes the cultural inheritance of Jews and the role it plays in their success,[114] when he discusses the difficulties immigrants faced with language,[115] when he analyzes the constraints on occupational choice imposed by anti-Semitism,[116] and even when he notes the overwhelming preponderance of Jews among Ivy League faculty,[117] he never mentions his own or his family's experience nor lapses into any sort of discernable emotion.

Even with motives so carefully absent, Kuznets worried that his research on the economic history of the Jews was too personal to constitute real professional work. He therefore sought to separate it entirely from his mainstream work in economics. In fact, of the half dozen colleagues and students of Kuznets's I interviewed for this project, not a single one ever remembers discussing with him about any for his work on the history of the Jews, despite all of their being of Eastern European Jewish descent themselves! When Martin Feldstein asked in 1973 to include his unpublished "Economic Growth of U. S. Jewry" in a Harvard Departmental working paper series, Kuznets[118] replied, after noting as above his personal motivation in writing the paper, "I would deem it inappropriate to (publish the paper in the series) . . . [O]bjective as the tools employed may be, the very choice of topic reveals a concern with, and interest in, a highly specialized aspects (sic). I would feel differently if this were a paper on trends in the structure of several ethnic minorities in the United States."[119]

Kuznets ensured his past was, in fact, two steps removed from his profession. It was not only his interest in Jewish history that Kuznets clearly separated from his professional life and relationships, but also the entirety of his personal views and opinions. Rosovsky,[120] an advisee of Kuznets and one of his close friends and colleagues, reports that all throughout the 1960s, perhaps the most political moment of U.S. history, he remembers Kuznets as being perhaps the only member of the Harvard department who expressed no political views he could recall. In fact, none of the dozens of colleagues and family members of Kuznets's I interviewed had a recollection of *any* strong political views (other than on immigration as described above) held by Kuznets and almost all described him as apolitical. While Rosovsky also attests that Kuznets was also one of the few Jews at Harvard who made no attempt to conceal his background, he made no attempt to discuss any aspect of his personal background or views professionally. The separation between his past and his present extended beyond work, back another level, into a separation between his private past and the future he built for his family.

Unlike the fabled and stereotypical first-generation Eastern European Jewish immigrant, but typically for Jewish fathers of his generation, Simon Kuznets taught his children almost nothing of the "old world" he had left behind. He never spoke with them in Yiddish nor in Russian, never forced or even encouraged them to attend synagogue or remember their Jewish heritage, and never cooked them Russian food nor played them Russian or Yiddish music.[121] While he maintained a personal interest in contemporary Russian literature and affairs, as many accounts attest, he never imposed these interests on his family. Kuznets took Judah Leib Gordon's *maskilim* mantra "Be a Jew in and a man in the street" to an extreme: he was a fervent (cultural) Jew in his heart but a man to all the world.

Thus, I hope, the full portrait of Kuznets I wish to paint has come into view. He was a consummate inductive empiricist whose interpretation of the facts that confronted him was shaped by the categories of his past and his struggle to understand it. He was a passionately dispassionate analyst of the history of an interesting ethnic minority, which happened to be his own people. He was an apolitical fervent supporter of the State of Israel from the day of its birth,[122] making regular trips to the Falk Institute there and becoming a fixture of the Israeli economics community.[123] The unifying theme of his life and work was a series of dualities and apparent contradictions, a straightforward enigma: the cautious empiricist of the Eastern European Jewish Diaspora.

Eastern European Jews and Modern Economics

What interests me in Kuznets's story is not its idiosyncrasy or quirkiness, but rather how it takes to a logical extreme a broader story of the Jews of Eastern European descent who played such a crucial role in transforming economics in the twentieth century. That the Eastern European Jewish Diaspora was at the center of creating Economics, as we understand it today, can hardly be doubted. However, some simple statistics may be instructive.

According to data collected by jinfo.org[124] and systematized for this article by Yanislav Petrov,[125] since 1969, when the Economics prize was first given, 50 percent of economics Nobel laureates have been Jews. This compares with 29 percent in Physics and 27 percent in Chemistry over the same time frame. Similarly, since the awards began at similar times in the late 1940s and early 1950s, 63 percent of the recipients of the John Bates Clark medal have been Jews, compared to 27 percent of the comparable Fields medal in mathematics (Table 3).

These statistics are particularly striking given their contrast with history. During the nineteenth century, economics had few, if any, Jews and was in fact dominated by Christian activists; almost 40 percent of those who founded the American Economic Association in 1885 were either ordained ministers or lay religious activists.[126] Also,

Table 3 Jewish accomplishments in economics and other scientific fields

	Percentage Of Jewish Recipients (%)
Nobel Prizes	
Economics (1969–2009)	42.2
Chemistry (1969–2009)	28.4
Physics (1969–2009)	27.6
John Bates Clark Medal (Economics) (1947–2009)	62.5
Fields Medal (Mathematics) (1936–2006)	27.1

Sources: "The Jewish Contribution To World Civilization," Http://Www.Jinfo.Org/; "All Laureates In Economic Sciences," Http://Nobelprize.Org/Nobel_prizes/Economics/Laureates/; "John Bates Clark Medal," Http://Www.Vanderbilt.Edu/Aea/Clark_medal.Htm; And "International Mathematical UniOn: Fields Medal," Http://Www.Mathunion.Org/General/Prizes/Fields/Details/ (All Accessed 10 February 2010).

anti-Semitism was common in the profession, as discussed in Melvin Reder[127] and immortalized in the famous story, recounted by Richard Swedberg,[128] of Paul Samuelson's decision to found an economics department at the Massachusetts Institute of Technology after being rejected for an assistant professorship at Harvard despite having written one of the best dissertations of the century.

The cold statistics are very much visible in the everyday life of the profession. My hair has always had the characteristically tight Jewish curls, but despite growing up in heavily Jewish communities my whole life, I had never met so many fellow Jewish curlyheads as I did when I came to Harvard's economics department. And the trend is even more pronounced if one focuses even more narrowly than the leaders and prizewinners in the field on the few figures who were truly revolutionary in building the framework of modern economics.

Simon Kuznets built the accounting methodologies underlying most of modern empirical economics. Paul Samuelson, father of the dominant algebraic-computational school of modern economic theory, was the son of Polish Jewish immigrants living in Indiana.[129] Kenneth Arrow, father of the other main geometric-mathematical strain of economic theory, was born to a New York Jewish family in the early 1920s. Two of the three founders of the Neo-Marshallian second Chicago School, Milton Friedman and Gary Becker, were, respectively, the son of very recent Jewish immigrants from Hungary[130] and the son of an Eastern European Jewish immigrant mother.[131] Jacob Marschak, founder of modern structural econometrics, who died before he could be awarded the Nobel Prize, was a Jewish immigrant[132] from Kiev. Many of the other heroes of any account of the forging of the modern quantitative, empirical-mathematical Neo-Classical economics, such as that given by Roy Weintraub,[133] are of Eastern European Jewish extraction. Of course there are many exceptions: John Hicks in theory, George Stigler in the Chicago School, Trygve Haavelmo and Tjalling Koopmans in econometrics. Nonetheless, it is astonishing that a group representing less than three in every hundred people in the United States and less than two in every *thousand* worldwide was the overwhelming force in the development of modern economics, far beyond even the outsized role they played in physics, mathematics, and other fields.

Why? The most straightforward and essentialist answer, one that borders dangerously on standard anti-Semitic images of Shylock the moneylender, is that there is some inherent connection (perhaps through occupational restrictions in the old country and their legacy) between the Jewish cultural inheritance and the questions in which economists take interest. Equally speculative, but more plausible to me, is a story suggested by Kuznets's own life: there was something that placed the generation of Jews that arrived in the United States between 1880 and 1920, and their children and grandchildren, in an ideal position to lead a revolution in economics. I conclude by exploring a possible causal mechanism for this conjecture. Any attempt to actually provide evidence for it, to test it against alternative hypothesis, or even to formulate such alternatives, is left squarely to future research.

Perhaps the most striking feature of the revolutions wrought by the great economists of Eastern European Jewish extraction was their fundamentally methodological nature. Kuznets, Samuelson, Arrow, Friedman, Becker, and Marschak certainly added important substantive insights to the field. But what they are overwhelmingly remembered for was the methodological lenses (empirical, mathematical, statistical, and "price theoretic") they made central to the discipline. None of these had any discernible connection to anything Jewish; in fact, by stripping away historicist and institutionalist traditions, they represented a forceful universalizing push within the discipline. As Friedman's quote with which I began this paper suggests, the sources of this revolution must be sought elsewhere than in their formal writings as these sources themselves impelled them to hide their tracks.[134] To paraphrase Chaim Weizmann's (who also hailed from Pinsk, 1949) famous dictum, the great Eastern European Jewish Diaspora economists of the twentieth century were just like any other economists, only more so.

On the "demand side," the universalizing thrust of "scientific"[135] economics offered a natural defense against anti-Semitic hostility to Jewish influence in the more culturally implicated humanities and social sciences. This made economics a unique outlet for Jewish political and social thinkers. Furthermore, Eastern European Jews' past prepared them with the skills for which modern economics called, but had not prepared them for the problems it would pose, leaving them with fresh eyes. Derek Penslar's[136] impressive recent book, *Shylock's Children: Economics and Jewish Identity in Modern Europe*, traces the history of modern Jewish economic thinking in Western Europe and the lack thereof in Eastern. Penslar argues that Jewish learning through the early *Haskalah* focused overwhelmingly on the natural sciences, neglecting social sciences given the lack of Jewish influence over or interest in the policies of Gentile host societies.[137] While Jewish politico-economic thinking developed over the course of the early nineteenth century, it was confined almost entirely to (a radical fringe of) German Ashkenazi and especially Western European Sephardic Jewry.[138] The aspiration of Eastern European Jewish students remained firmly religious or, if secular, natural scientific. Cut off from political influence, concern, and learning by repression, Eastern European Jews came to the United States with extraordinary training in and devotion to the study of natural scientific method but with an equal political naïveté.

Yet the rapid succession of emancipation, immigration to democratic America, the rise of political anti-Semitism in Germany, and economic catastrophe worldwide quickly forced them to come to terms with social affairs. Rapidly upwardly mobile, powerfully organized through unions given their professional concentration in America, and finally offered a voice through American free speech and universal franchise, Jews rapidly emerged as a political force in the United States. A select, but disproportionate, few of these immigrants and immigrants' children had extraordinary, rigorous scientific and mathematical training. Free from the cultural burden of a long-standing political tradition, application of these tools to those social problems via a science of economics[139] they helped build must have seemed the most natural and accessible means of confronting academically the new range of challenges they were invited to address. While it was socially sophisticated Western European Jews like Albert Einstein, Wolfgang Pauli,[140] and Niels Bohr who helped make modern physics, it was the unwashed but upwardly mobile easterners that made modern economics.

More than any of those pioneers, Simon Kuznets typified that spirit. I have argued that what he brought to economics was, to a large extent, *not* a series of substantive political, economic, or social commitments. Rather, he arrived from Kharkov with rigorous training in statistical and empirical methods and an earnest desire to understand the forces that had shaped and were shaping his life. His beloved cultural inheritance was an ability to see the economy and his own past with a *tabula* close to *rasa*: a rigorous empirical lens unburdened by preconceived theory. That, I think, is something of the resolution to the enigma of his life and work. He was committed to, inspired by, and grateful for his past *precisely for the rigorous, scientific, and universalistic perspective it lent him.*

And it is precisely this commitment that interested me in his story. Born to two atheists, culturally assimilated Jewish parents, I always resented the social expectations accompanying my Judaism, seeking always a secular universalist vision of my identity. Yet, I have come to realize the inevitability, and intellectual attraction, of my Jewish heritage as I found so many of my fellow travelers in that struggle for universalism to be themselves born to atheist, culturally assimilated Jewish parents.

Of course, the story I have just told is explicitly and disproportionately shaped by my experience and by Kuznets's story, through which I have come to understand it. It is at best a provocative reflection and at worst self-indulgent speculation. Yet, I hold out some hope that it can be more the former than the latter. I believe that the story of the rebirth of economics as a mathematical science in the twentieth century cannot be, as it has in the past been, easily separated from the story of the Eastern European Jewish immigrants' struggle to understand political, social, and economic affairs. Perhaps someday the pogroms, the great wave of Jewish immigration at the turn of the twentieth century, the rise of German anti-Semitism, and the birth of the State of Israel will be seen as rivaling the Great Depression in having shaped modern economic thought. Only through future scholarship on this important neglected subject will we be able to tell.

Notes

1. A possible exception was Wassily Leontief, who upon hearing that a Russian economist was to be announced to have won the Nobel Prize, prepared to make a statement.
2. See, for example, Robert W. Fogel, "Some Notes on the Scientific Methods of Simon Kuznets," *Working paper series (National Bureau of Economic Research) no. 2461* (1987); Robert W. Fogel, "Simon S. Kuznets: April 30, 1901–July 9, 1985," *Working paper series (National Bureau of Economic Research) no. 7787* (2000); Kapuria-Foreman and Perlman, "An Economic Historian's Economist: Remembering Simon Kuznets," *Economic Journal* (November 1995): 1524–47; Moses Abramovitz, "Simon Kuznets, 1901–85," *Journal of Economic History* 46, no. 1 (1986): 241–46.
3. To avoid Russian chauvinism, I use the term "Eastern European" to broadly refer to the entirety of the Russian imperialist-Jewish pale. However, it should be noted that Kuznets, in his work, along with many others at the time, did not respect such contemporary distinctions and typically refers to what I call Eastern European Jewry as simply Russian Jewry.
4. Simon S. Kuznets, "Economic Growth of U.S. Jewry," *Papers of Simon Smith Kuznets, 1923–1985 (inclusive), 1950–1980 (bulk), Correspondence and other papers relating to Jewish studies, ca.1959–1977, Box 1, in folder \em Economic Structure of U.S. Jewry. Call Number: HUGFP88.25*, 1972.
5. I believe I am the first to discover this writing in the course of my research for this paper. I owe a tremendous debt to Stephanie Lo, coeditor of this volume, for transcribing it in a legible form that made it possible for me to review it in detail. So other scholars may have the same benefit, this article is available at http://www.glenweyl.com, given that it is not directly relevant to this volume.
6. Derek J. Penslar, *Shylock's Children: Econonomics and Jewish Identity in Modern Europe* (Berkeley and Los Angeles: University of California Press, 2001), 56–57.
7. In several places, which I flag, secondary sources disagree on the sequence, and sometimes substances, of events. I have done my best to reconcile the sources, privileging those whose authors are more confident of their facts or closer to the actual events, such as family members.
8. In fact, Simon was the only member of the family who maintained his name upon arriving in the United States; the rest of the family adopted the anglicized "Smith" (Encyclopedia Britannica, *Kuznets, Simon*, 2007).
9. Paul Kuznets, Personal Interview, May 3, 2007.
10. Judith Stein, Personal Communication, February 10, 2010.
11. Chaim Weizmann, *Trial and Error: The Autobiography of Chaim Weizmann* (New York: Harper, 1949), 16–28.
12. Ruth Kuznets Pearson Hauptman, Personal Communication, February 6, 2010.
13. Judith Stein, Personal Communication, February 10, 2010.
14. Ruth Kuznets Pearson Hauptman, Personal Communication, February 6, 2010.
15. Vibha Kapuria-Foreman and Mark Perlman ("An Economic Historian's Economist: Remembering Simon Kuznets," *The Economic Journal* 105,

no. 433 (1995): 1524–47) and Fogel ("Simon S. Kuznets: April 30, 1901–July 9, 1985") disagree about whether Kuznets attended primary school in Kharkov or Pinsk. I privilege the Kapuria-Foreman and Perlman (1995) account as the authors cite a personal interview. Indeed, Judith Stein (Personal Correspondence with Vladimir M. Moskovkin, 2009) points to a memoir that Kuznets's niece wrote to deduce that the family moved from Pinsk to Kharkov when Kuznets was fourteen years old.

16. Fogel, "Simon S. Kuznets: April 30, 1901–July 9, 1985," 1.
17. Judith Stein, Personal Correspondence with Vladimir M. Moskovkin, 2009.
18. Kapuria-Foreman and Perlman, "An Economic Historian's Economist: Remembering Simon Kuznets."
19. How and through where his brother and father left for the United States are not exactly clear, but this was the best I was able to piece together from various secondary accounts. See Encyclopedia Britannica, *Kuznets, Simon* and Kapuria-Foreman and Perlman, "An Economic Historian's Economist: Remembering Simon Kuznets."
20. Paul Kuznets, Personal Interview, May 3, 2007.
21. Ruth Kuznets Pearson Hauptman, Personal Communication, February 6, 2010.
22. Paul Kuznets, Personal Interview, May 3, 2007; Ruth Kuznets Pearson Hauptman, Personal Communication, February 6, 2010.
23. I do not provide a comprehensive biography of Kuznets's career, as its relevance to the contents of these volumes is limited. Instead, I aim here to provide an outline with emphasis on the aspects of his life most relevant to the connection between his thinking and his Eastern European Jewish heritage. For a more complete intellectual biography, see Kapuria-Foreman and Perlman, "An Economic Historian's Economist: Remembering Simon Kuznets."
24. Fogel, "Simon S. Kuznets: April 30, 1901–July 9, 1985."
25. Simon S. Kuznets, *Autobiography*, 1971. Accessed from http://nobelprize.org/nobel_prizes/economics/laureates/1971/kuznets-autobio.html, May 2011.
26. Simon S. Kuznets, *Cyclical Fluctuations* (New York: National Bureau of Economic Research, 1926).
27. Simon S. Kuznets, *Secular Movements in Production and Prices: Their Nature and Their Bearing Upon Cyclical Fluctuations* (Boston: Houghton Miflin, 1930).
28. Simon S. Kuznets, *Seasonal Variations in Industry and Trade* (New York: National Bureau of Economic Research, 1933).
29. Ibid., 1.
30. Judith Stein, Personal Communication, February 10, 2010.
31. Ruth Kuznets Pearson Hauptman, Personal Communication, February 6, 2010.
32. Paul Kuznets, Personal Interview, May 3, 2007.
33. Kapuria-Foreman and Perlman, "An Economic Historian's Economist: Remembering Simon Kuznets," 1529–33.
34. Milton Friedman and Simon S. Kuznets, *Income from Independent Professional Practice* (New York: National Bureau of Economic Research, 1945).

35. Kapuria-Foreman and Perlman, "An Economic Historian's Economist: Remembering Simon Kuznets," 1534–35.
36. Paul Kuznets, Personal Interview, May 3, 2007.
37. Kuznets in statements transcribed by Fogel, "Some Notes on the Scientific Methods of Simon Kuznets," 34.
38. Simon S. Kuznets, "Economic Growth and Income Inequality," *The American Economic Review* 45, no. 1 (1955): 1–28.
39. Edith Kuznets, Robert W. Fogel, Marilyn Coopersmith, and Kathleen McCauley, "Bibliography of Simon Kuznets," *Economic Development, the Family and Income Distribution* (1989): 439–60.
40. Pranab Bardhan, "Economics of Development and the Development of Economics," *Journal of Economic Perspectives* 7, no. 2 (1993): 129–42, 130.
41. Colin Clark, *The Conditions of Economic Progress* (London: MacMillan, 1939).
42. Paul N. Rosenstein-Rodan, "Problems of Industrialisation of Eastern and Southeastern Europe," *Economic Journal* 53, nos. 210–211 (1943): 202–11.
43. Kurt Mandelbaum, *Industrialisation of Backward Areas* (Oxford: Oxford University Press, 1945).
44. Economic Commission for Latin America, United Nations, and Raúl Prebisch, *The Economic Development of Latin America and Its Principal Problems* (New York: United Nations Department of Economic Affairs, 1950).
45. W. Arthur Lewis, "Economic Development with Unlimited Supply of Labour," *The Manchester School* 22, no. 2 (1954): 139–91.
46. Robert M. Solow, "A Contribution to the Theory of Economic Growth," *Quarterly Journal of Economics* 70, no. 1 (1956): 65–94.
47. Walt W. Rostow, *The Stages of Economic Growth: A Non-communist Manifesto* (Cambridge, UK: Cambridge University Press, 1960).
48. Penslar, *Shylock's Children: Econonomics and Jewish Identity in Modern Europe.*
49. Simon S. Kuznets, "Economic Structure and Life of the Jews." In *The Jews: Their History, Culture and Religion*, edited by Louis Finkelstein, 3rd ed., vol. 2. (New York: Harper and Bros. Publishers, 1960, 1597–1666) 1621–23.
50. This was described to me by his son Paul Kuznets in 2007 in a personal interview.
51. Fogel, "Simon S. Kuznets: April 30, 1901–July 9, 1985."
52. Paul Kuznets, Personal Interview, May 3, 2007.
53. Tony Atkinson, Thomas Piketty, and Emmanuel Saez, *Top Incomes in the Long Run of History* (Cambridge, Mass.: National Bureau of Economic Research, 2009).
54. Lewis, "Economic Development with Unlimited Supply of Labour."
55. Kuznets, "Economic Growth and Income Inequality," 13.
56. It was sent to David Landes as a draft, which I have a copy of, on that date. Simon S. Kuznets, "Economic Structure and Life of the Jews," Baltimore, MD: S. Kuznets. 1956.
57. Kuznets, "Economic Growth and Income Inequality."

58. Simon S. Kuznets, *Modern Economic Growth: Rate, Structure, and Spread* (New Haven: Yale University Press, 1966).
59. Kuznets, *Modern Economic Growth: Rate, Structure, and Spread,* 435–36.
60. Simon S. Kuznets, *Nobel Prize Speech,* 1971.
61. Kuznets, *Modern Economic Growth: Rate, Structure, and Spread.*
62. Kuznets, *Modern Economic Growth: Rate, Structure, and Spread,* 458–60.
63. Ibid., 433–35.
64. See, for example, Albert O. Hirschman, *The Strategy of Economic Development* (New Haven: Yale University Press, 1959).
65. Kapuria-Foreman and Perlman, "An Economic Historian's Economist: Remembering Simon Kuznets."
66. Kuznets, "Economic Structure and Life of the Jews," 1600–4.
67. Simon S. Kuznets. "Notes on the Takeoff." In *The Economics of Takeoff into Self-Sustained Growth,* edited by W. W. Rostow. Proceeding of a Conference held by the International Economic Association. (Macmillan: London, 1963).
68. Ibid., 1601.
69. Paul Kuznets, Personal Interview, May 3, 2007.
70. The most comprehensive bibliography of his work was compiled by Robert W. Fogel, Marilyn Coopersmith, and Kathleen McCauley and edited and supplemented by Edith Kuznets to be published in a book of posthumous essays in 1989. I will refer to this simply as Kuznets et al. (1989).
71. Simon S. Kuznets, "Immigration of Russian Jews to the United States: Background and Structure," *Perspectives in American History* 9 (1975), 35–124, 97–100.
72. Kuznets, *Modern Economic Growth: Rate, Structure, and Spread,* 454–56.
73. Kuznets, "Economic Structure and Life of the Jews," 1602–3.
74. Mark Perlman. "Jews and Contributions to Economics: A Bicentennial Review." In *The Character of Economic Thought, Economic Characters and Economic Institutions,* (Ann Arbor, MI: University of Michigan Press, 1996) 307–18.
75. Perhaps the most popularly known pro-population economist Julian Simon (*A Life Against the Grain: The Autobiography of an Unconventional Economist* (New Brunswick, NJ: Transaction Publishers, 2003)) attributed many of his ideas to Kuznets and even asked Kuznets to write the introduction to his 1977 *The Economics of Population Growth.* Kuznets, in characteristically non-confrontational fashion, demurred. I thank Pierre Desrochers for pointing me to this story.
76. Simon S. Kuznets, "Population Change and Aggregate Output," in *Demographic and Economic Changes in Developed Countries* (1960), 326–30.
77. Edmund S. Phelps, "Population Increase," *The Canadian Journal of Economics* 1, no. 3 (1968): 497–518, 510–13.
78. Simon Kuznets, "Population and Economic Growth," *Proceedings of the American Philosophical Society* 111, no. 3 (1967): 170–93.
79. Ibid., 185.

80. Kuznets, "Immigration of Russian Jews to the United States: Background and Structure."
81. Kuznets et al. (1989).
82. Simon Kuznets and Ernest Rubin,"Immigration and the Foreign Born," *National Bureau of Economic Research Occasional Papers*, paper no. 46, 1954.
83. Judith Stein, Personal Communication, February 10, 2010.
84. Claudia Goldin, "The Political Economy of Immigration Restriction in the United States, 1890 to 1921," in *The Regulated Economy: A Historical Approach to Political Economy* (1994).
85. Milton Friedman and Simon Kuznets, "Income from Independent Professional Practice," in *National Bureau of Economic Research Bulletin*, no. 72–73, 1939.
86. Friedman and Kuznets, *Income from Independent Professional Practice.*
87. Morris M. Kleiner, "Occupational Licensing," *The Journal of Economic Perspectives* 14, no. 4 (2000): 189–202, 190.
88. Milton Friedman and Rose D. Friedman, *Capitalism and Freedom* (Chicago: University of Chicago Press Chicago, 1962), 137–60; Milton Friedman, *Autobiography*, 1976.
89. Theodore W. Schultz, "Investment in Human Capital," *American Economic Review* 51, no. 1 (1961): 1–17, 14.
90. Gary S. Becker, "Investment in Human Capital: A Theoretical Analysis," *Journal of Political Economy* 70, no. S5 (1962): 9–49, 10.
91. Lanny Ebenstein, *Milton Friedman: A Biography* (New York: Palgrave Macmillan, 2007), 31–52.
92. Kuznets, "Immigration of Russian Jews to the United States: Background and Structure," 56–57.
93. Niels Thygesen,"The Scientific Contribution of Milton Friedman," *Scandinavian Journal of Economics* 79, no. 1 (1977), 56–98.
94. Friedman and Kuznets, *Income from Independent Professional Practice*, 83–84.
95. Ibid., 84–86.
96. J. R. Walsh, "Capital Concept Applied to Man," *Quarterly Journal of Economics* 49, no. 2 (1935): 255–85.
97. Yoram Ben-Porath, "The Production of Human Capital and the Life Cycle of Earnings," *Journal of Political Economy* 75, no. 4 (1967): 352–65, 352. Admittedly, Ben-Porath was not as central of a figure to this developing literature as the others, but he does offer the clearest articulation of the role played by Friedman and Kuznets. A more important figure was Barry R. Chiswick (Gary S. Becker and Barry R. Chiswick, "Education and the Distribution of Earnings," *American Economic Review* 56 (1966): 358–69.), especially given that he has become something of an heir to Kuznets in his interests in immigration and the economic history of Jews.
98. Jacob Mincer, "Investment in Human Capital and Personal Income Distribution," *Journal of Political Economy* 66, no. 4 (1958): 281–302, 284.
99. Schultz, "Investment in Human Capital," 14.
100. Becker, "Investment in Human Capital: A Theoretical Analysis," 10.
101. Friedman and Kuznets, *Income from Independent Professional Practice.*

102. Milton Friedman and National Bureau of Economic Research, *A Theory of the Consumption Function* (Princeton: Princeton University Press, 1957).
103. Milton Friedman, *Autobiography*, 1976.
104. Friedman and National Bureau of Economic Research, *A Theory of the Consumption Function*.
105. Stein (2009) suggests Kuznets may also have been the genesis of the emphasis of the Chicago school on home production, having emphasized in his work during the war that national income accounts should consider women's work in the home, a fight he lost. Given that I can find no references to this in any written work by Kuznets or Friedman it remains a speculation and given that it is not directly connected to my thesis I will not explore it further.
106. Milton Friedman, "The Role of Government in Education." In *Economics and the Public Interest*, edited by Robert A. Solo, (New Brunswick, NJ: Rutgers University Press, 1955) 123–44.
107. Kuznets, "Economic Structure and Life of the Jews"; Kuznets, "Economic Growth of U.S. Jewry"; Simon S. Kuznets, *Economic Structure of U.S. Jewry: Recent Trends* (Jerusalem: Institute of Contemporary Jewry, Hebrew University of Jerusalem, 1972); and Kuznets, "Immigration of Russian Jews to the United States: Background and Structure."
108. Kuznets, "Economic Growth of U.S. Jewry."
109. Fogel, "Some Notes on the Scientific Methods of Simon Kuznets."
110. In fact, Kuznets's extreme care is likely a good part of the reason why, despite his enormous contribution to economics, Kuznets has few contemporary followers. In an age where fights over empirical methodology are between an "atheoretical" camp using instrumental variables and regression discontinuity analysis and a "structural" camp advocating complex models of entire industries, it is hard to imagine where a skeptic of even multiple linear regression, as Fogel ("Some Notes on the Scientific Methods of Simon Kuznets," 16–17) describes Kuznets as being, could fit in.
111. Kuznets, "Economic Structure and Life of the Jews."
112. Kuznets, "Economic Growth of U.S. Jewry."
113. Ibid., 11–12.
114. Ibid., 12–14.
115. Ibid., 14–16.
116. Ibid., 18. Rosovsky reports that anti-Semitism played a role in Kuznets's residential choice in Philadelphia.
117. Ibid., 26–27.
118. Simon S. Kuznets, "Personal letter to Martin Feldstein," *Papers of Simon Smith Kuznets, 1923–1985 (inclusive), 1950–1980 (bulk), Correspondence and other papers relating to Jewish studies, ca.1959–1977, Box 1, in folder Correspondence, Tables and Worksheets on Jewish Economics. Call Number: HUGFP88.25*, 1973.
119. See page 273 of the first volume of this series.
120. Henry Rosovsky, Personal Interview, January 28, 2010.
121. Paul Kuznets, Personal Interview, May 3, 2007; Judith Stein, Personal Communication, February 10, 2010.

122. Paul Kuznets, Personal Interview, May 3, 2007.
123. Rosovsky recalls that every time one came to visit Cambridge, they would make a mandatory pilgrimage to the Kuznets residence on Francis Avenue, just a block and a half from my current apartment.
124. *Jews in Economics*, JInfo.org, 2009.
125. Yanislav Petrov, "Data on Jewish Accomplishments in Economics and Other Scientific Fields," 2010, http://www.people.fas.harvard.edu/~weyl/JewsinScience.xls.
126. Fogel, "Simon S. Kuznets: April 30, 1901–July 9, 1985," 3–4.
127. Melvin W. Reder, "The Anti-Semitism of Some Eminent Economists," *History of Political Economy* 32, no. 4 (2000): 833–56.
128. Richard Swedberg, *Schumpeter: A Biography* (Princeton: Princeton University Press, 1991), 139.
129. Michael M. Weinstein, "Paul A. Samuelson, Economist, Dies at 94," *New York Times*, December 13, 2009.
130. David J. Theroux, *Milton Friedman (1912–2006)*, 2006.
131. Gary S. Becker, *Autobiography*, 1992.
132. According to a correspondence between Jacob Viner and Joseph Schumpeter reviewed by Amartya Sen, Marschak was nearly barred from becoming one of the first fellows of the Econometric Society because Schumpeter believed he was "both a Jew and a socialist."
133. E. Roy Weintraub, *How Economics Became a Mathematical Science* (Durham, NC: Duke University Press, 2002).
134. In fact, Kevin Hoover pointed out to me that Friedman's quote parallels a distinction Hans Reichenbach (*Experience and Prediction: An Analysis of the Foundations and Structure of Knowledge* (Chicago: University of Chicago Press, 1938)) dwelled on between psychology and epistemology, between the historical and logical origins of an idea. Ronald Giere (*Science without Laws* (Chicago: University of Chicago Press, 1999), 228) argues that this distinction was important to Reichenbach, and perhaps by extension to Friedman, precisely because of its connection to the anti-Semitic attempt to discredit many modern scientific ideas as "Jewish" science. This highlights the "demand side" cause of the universalizing, methodological thrust of the Eastern European Jewish contribution to modern economics that I discuss below.
135. David Hollinger (*Science, Jews and Secular Culture* (Princeton: Princeton University Press, 1996)) makes a similar argument regarding the sciences and public intellectual culture more broadly. Steven Beller (*Vienna and the Jews: 1867–1938* (Cambridge, UK: Cambridge University Press, 1989)) suggests such demand side factors were the driving forces in establishing the dominantly Jewish professions in Vienna prior to German annexation, while also emphasizing, along the lines of my argument, the importance of heterogeneous and often surprising Jewish reactions to Jewishness.
136. Penslar, *Shylock's Children: Econonomics and Jewish Identity in Modern Europe.*
137. Ibid., 56.
138. Ibid., 81–84.
139. Of course there is no reason why economics should have assumed such a dominant role compared to other quantitative social sciences. Thus, a

natural implication of my hypothesis is that Eastern European Jews should have had a similarly transformative quantifying impact on other potentially quantitative social sciences, such as political science and sociology. Paul Lazarsfeld is a leading example that would seem to confirm this conjecture, as founder of modern quantitative sociology, but neither quantitative evidence of the form made possible by the awards nor a strong personal knowledge of the field make it possible for me to test this hypothesis. It therefore remains as an interesting direction for future research.

140. Pauli's father converted to Catholicism before his birth, but came from a prominent Jewish family.

1

Immigration and the Foreign Born

Simon Kuznets (with Ernest Rubin)

Part I

Summary

Discussions of basic economic problems and policies have always been concerned with population. Labor is a primary resource of production: with any given store of natural wealth, equipment, and technological skill, the limits of production are set by the size of the labor force.

The growth of a national economy may be stimulated by the increase in its population, which strongly affects consumer demand and the size of the labor force. Economic conditions in turn may influence the growth of population. In the United States, population growth has traditionally been regarded as a source of strength and a sign of material progress.

In few other nations, perhaps in none of major industrial rank, has immigration played so large a role in augmenting population as in the United States. Although from the beginning the native birthrate, to be sure, has been a greater source of increase than foreign arrivals, yet none can doubt the importance of recruitment from abroad. That it must have had significant economic as well as social effects in a commonplace.

Before and during World War I, there was extensive controversy concerning the consequences of immigration, some of it scholarly and well informed, much of it pervaded by the prejudices of the time. During that war, immigration was sharply curtailed, and in the early 1920s, legal restrictions greatly reduced the volume of arrivals. This reversal of a historic policy was in part the consequence of pressures by interests acting in supposed accordance with their economic advantage, but few would maintain that the decision was a carefully considered conclusion resting on adequate scientific research in the national interest. Since the early 1920s, the change has been accepted as a fait accompli with little curiosity concerning its effects.

Now, a generation later, at a time when little public excitement over the question exists and when it has become possible with additional information and newer techniques of investigation, to arrange the data so that they bear on major problem areas, it may be pertinent to look back over the whole course of immigration. The present chapter constitutes only a small beginning of this task. It asks rather than answers questions that might be of importance for economic policy. The questions themselves arise from statistical results that should be accepted with the reservations explained in part II. Yet the possibility of misrepresentation is small enough so that the conclusions should be reported.

The Basic Trends

What was the magnitude of the long-term flow of immigration? In order to obtain an impression of the trends, the variations associated with business cycles and the longer swings were eliminated from the picture, for the time being. Early figures are less complete and reliable; few statistics of any sort are available before 1820. It is clear, however, that there was a tremendous jump in the net difference between immigrant arrivals and departures beginning in the late 1830s and extending to the time of the Civil War. After the Civil War, the net inward flow increased somewhat more moderately until World War I, when it began to suffer a sharp decline.

If the net difference between annual arrivals and departures is stated as a percentage of the total existing population, it reached its peak at 7–8 percent in the years between 1838 and the Civil War and then tended downward until it approximated 2 percent of the total population after 1918. These estimates are probably on the conservative side.

Another long-term tendency of importance is a rising trend of the ratio of departures of immigrants to arrivals. This change began in the early years, but can be measured only since the 1870s. For the period 1878–97, the ratio of departures to arrivals was about 17 percent; in the period 1908–14, when also there was no war and no restrictive legislation, it exceeded 30 percent. After 1918, it was even higher. For a short period during the depression of the 1930s, departures even exceeded arrivals.

Immigrant Contribution to Population Increase

The change in the number of the foreign born measures the influence of immigration on population, since it accounts both for net arrivals and for the deaths of resident immigrants. Between 1850 and 1860, the foreign-born population increased by 1.89 million, while the total population was increased by 8.25 million. Immigration therefore was responsible for 22.9 percent of population growth in that decade. Never again was the percentage quite so high, though it reached 17.1 percent in 1860–70, 20.1 percent in 1880–90, and 19.9 percent in 1900–10. Lower figures were registered for decades marked by serious depression—10.8 percent in 1870–80 and 8.4 percent in 1890–1900. The percentage of increase in the foreign born to total increase dropped to 2.9 in 1910–20, the World War I decade.

The revolutionary change in immigration policy following World War I must be largely responsible for the low figure of 1.7 percent in 1920–30. This change, augmented by the impact of depression, reduced the figure to -29.3 percent in 1930–40. In that troubled decade, the number of the foreign born *declined* to 2.61 million, while the total population grew to 8.89 million. New net immigration failed by a wide margin to make up for deaths of immigrants already here.

Incoming immigrants, many of whom in the nineteenth and early twentieth centuries, were young unmarried men or men who came without their families, added to the labor force even more relatively than they did to the population as a whole. Reliable figures of the gainfully occupied by nativity are not available prior to 1870, but in the decade that followed, checkered though it was by unemployment and crisis, the increase in the foreign-born population accounted for 16.2 percent of the total growth in the labor force. The figure jumped to 30.1 percent in 1880–90, declined to 10.1 percent in 1890–1900, and rose again to 24.9 percent in 1900–10.

Then came the drastic decrease to -1.2 percent in 1910–20, followed by -5.3 percent in 1920–30, and -40.7 percent in 1930–40. In these years, not only did net immigration drop, but also a larger proportion of the immigrants were dependents of men already here.

It is impossible to estimate how much the population would have grown if immigration had not been so high in the earlier years or if it had remained large in the later ones. Were the immigrants in any degree a substitute for native births that might have occurred had the incomers not arrived? Too many influences on the birthrate may exist to encourage even a guess.

In any event, immigration contributed about one-seventh of the total growth in population between 1870 and 1910, and about one-fifth of the growth in the labor force in the same period. In more recent decades, it has contributed less than nothing. The change in itself is dramatic and can scarcely have been without consequences. These figures disregard the secondary contribution of immigration to population, through the founding of new families and an increase in the second and later generations.

The Long Swings

If the effect of short business cycles is eliminated from the figures, longer swings in immigration remain, each swing covering a period of about twenty years. For example, the average of annual arrivals during the business cycle 1871–77 was 319,000; from this figure, the average rose to 534,000 during the cycle of 1882–88, then a decline began to 318,000 in 1895–97. Three of these twenty-year swings may be observed between the 1870s and the early 1940s. Apparently, they also occurred in former years. Similar and still wider swings are found in *net* immigration.

Did the long immigration swings arise from swings in business activity and levels of living in the United States? As a rough test of the possibility, comparison was made between changes in net immigration and changes in gross national product per worker. (By far, the largest component of national product is consumer goods.) Since the national product has a persistent upward trend, the series representing it was stated in percentages by which the year-to-year change differed from the trend; the curve therefore shows a drop when the actual rise for any year is less than the long-term rate of increase. The gross national product curve reveals long swings of about the same duration as those in net immigration.

Before 1914, the twenty-year swings in immigration tend to *follow* those in gross national product per worker. It would be hazardous to conclude without further analysis that the swings in immigration were caused by similar changes in the improvement of levels of living in the United States, but the fragmentary evidence here presented may serve to reinforce the pertinence of the question.

Did the long swings in immigration have an effect on the economic activity of the nation? To make a beginning at investigation of this question, net immigration was compared with the course of housing construction, since increasing arrival of immigrant families might augment the demand for housing, while a slackening in immigration might bring a similar reduction in housing demand. Swings in housing construction (in constant dollar volume) of about twenty years' duration roughly coincide with the swings in net immigration. In this case, the changes in immigration flow *precede* the changes in housing construction, as would be expected if the number of immigrants produced an effect on real-estate markets. Here again no conclusion can safely be drawn; the correspondence merely suggests a much broader problem for research.

Migration and Business Cycles

Correspondence between migration and the business cycle has been carefully studied in the past. Reexamination of the figures up to World War II reveals the general conformity noted previously by others. With some exceptions, the number of arrivals increases in prosperity and falls in depressions, while the number of departures follows the opposite course. This conclusion must be modified by the steadily rising trend in departures.

It was suggested by Harry Jerome in his report for the National Bureau of Economic Research in 1926, *Migration and Business Cycles,* that if immigrant workers were less available to supplement the labor force in booms, the consequent rise in labor costs might damp down the boom and hence moderate the ensuing depression. It was perhaps irrelevant that the restriction of immigration that had occurred shortly before the book was written exerted no visible damping effect on the boom then in progress and that the ensuing depression was as far from moderate as can easily be imagined.

The present study suggests some fragmentary reasons for supporting the opposite conclusion—that cyclical changes in inward and outward migration might serve to moderate the cycle or at least its effect on unemployment of the native labor force. There is some evidence to show that most of the departures were from the pool of the recently arrived. A large proportion of the arrivals and departures were of men, and of members of the labor force. Under conditions of a free in- and outflow, one might therefore regard foreign labor supply as a sort of stabilizing reservoir. Here is a possibility that merits further investigation.

Immigration and Variations in Population Growth

Restriction of immigration had at least one result that may have decreased the stability of the economy. Increase in the population of the United States proceeded at a steadier rate—that is, fluctuations in growth were less sharp—during the long period when immigration was larger than after it was drastically reduced. Steadiness of population growth, at whatever rate, would seem to favor stability in aggregate consumer demand and in business expectations. In addition, it might make it easier to avoid the disturbance to production or employment that could arise from variations in growth of the labor supply.

This effect on regularity of population growth is apparently accounted for by the fact that additions to the population consisting of second-generation Americans tend to cancel out alterations in the birthrate for native-born American parents. Swings in immigration and in the rate of increase in native born of *native* parentage are roughly synchronous; apparently, they respond to the same forces within the economy. But swings in the rate of increase in native born of *foreign* parentage lag a decade behind immigration, presumably reflecting the lag in the founding of families and childbearing. Because of this difference in phase, the net additions to population from the two sources together are steadied—as long as immigration remains an important factor.

Before the 1920s, the proportional increase in total native-born population was comparatively free from swings. It was only in the 1930s that the sharp drop of births within the country, in combination with the virtual absence of immigration during the decade, produced a sudden and drastic fall in the rate of increase in the nation's population. This fall was soon felt in elementary and later in secondary schools. It is now affecting higher education and the labor supply. A correspondingly drastic increase is in prospect as a consequence of the rise in birthrates during the 1940s.

Proportion of Foreign Born in the Labor Force

A wide divergence of opinion has prevailed in the United States concerning the effect on the nation's culture and institutions of the fact that a large proportion of the population was of foreign birth, and that of these, many were recent arrivals. A pertinent fact, however, was seldom if ever observed—a given volume of immigration contributed a progressively smaller increase to the foreign-born population as time went on. With a larger resident body of foreign born, more new arrivals were needed to offset the deaths of the resident population. And with a larger proportion of departures to arrivals, more gross arrivals were needed to preserve the same net additions. In 1870–80, less than three arrivals resulted in one additional foreign-born resident; in 1900–10, the ratio was more than three to one; and by 1920–30, it had jumped to eight to one. In addition, the proportion of the foreign born who were recent arrivals steadily declined, even before immigration was restricted.

In 1890 and 1910, perhaps as much as 50 percent of the foreign born who were gainfully occupied had been in the country only ten years or less. If so, they constituted more than 10 percent of the total labor force of the nation. What were the consequences of this fact to the relations between management and labor, to union organization and policy, to distribution of income, to the social and political environment? And what changes in these respects may be attributed to the fact that by 1940 the number of recent arrivals had become insignificant?

Other questions, less frequently discussed in this connection, also deserve examination. Does the drastic decline of demand for unskilled labor, directly consequent upon the introduction of mechanized processes for heavy work in construction, industry, transportation, and agriculture—a change that became prominent in the 1920s—have any relationship of cause or effect to the decline of immigration? What are the interrelationships among a rapidly advancing technology, an open or a closed frontier to labor migration, and the labor market? What are the implications of these matters for economic growth, or for cyclical or longer undulations in economic activity? The area of investigation touched by this chapter has long been slighted and might richly repay more intensive research.

Part II

The Comparison and Some General Implications of Its Results

Introduction

The flow of people from abroad added millions of workers, consumers, and family heads to the population of this country. This movement directly affected the size and structure of the country's population and had far-reaching influences through the chain reaction of internal migration and economic mobility that it stimulated. According to many historians, the development of the United States has been dominated by the character and movement of the frontier *within* the country. One may argue that it has also been affected by the relation of the country to the rest of the world—for a long time the frontier outpost and, more recently, the giant economic leader of the older civilization of Europe, the ancestral home of most of its population.

Since migration across our borders is so strategic in the economic development of this country, it is a shock to find that the basic quantitative records of this movement are subject to numerous errors. The records have not been made consistent with others relating to the foreign born, and, perhaps as a consequence, the long-term aspects of migration in relation to economic growth have not been analyzed adequately. We have annual data on arrivals of alien passengers back to 1820, and immigrants and nonimmigrants have been distinguished since 1869. But even these series are incomplete, if only because for most of the period they do not include immigration by land. We have data on emigration, but only back to 1908. We have census of population enumerations of foreign-born residents since 1850, but they are affected by varying treatment of nonimmigrant aliens and are generally believed to understate the true number of foreign born. We have, again from the census of population, data on the foreign-born labor force since 1870, but they are subject to biases similar to, and perhaps larger than, those in the data on all foreign born.

Under these circumstances, careful examination of the scope and character of the series and a systematic check on their consistency with one another are indispensable before analysis can be undertaken. In this review of the basic series, a systematic comparison of data on migration with those on the foreign born is one of the first steps. The analytical relationship between the two series is obvious, and some attempts to cross-check them for selected census decades have been made.[1] Yet despite a clear realization of the potential value of the task,[2] it has not been undertaken on a systematic basis for a period long enough to permit study of economic trends.

It is to this task that our efforts have been devoted, and part III describes in detail the data and devices employed and the results of the comparison. In part II, an attempt is made to present to the general reader, less interested in details of estimation, the nature of the statistical experiment conducted and, particularly, some of the findings relating to the long-term movements in migration and the foreign born, and their bearing upon other long-term trends in the American economy.

The Comparison

During any interval between two population censuses, the number of foreign-born residents at the initial date is increased by immigration and diminished by deaths and emigration. Hence, incoming aliens must be added to and deaths and departing aliens subtracted from the foreign born at the beginning of the census period. The resulting estimated number of foreign born at the end of the period can then be compared with the number yielded by the census enumeration of that date. If the three sets of statistics—foreign born, migration, and mortality—are all true, or at least subject to errors of similar size and sign, the *estimated* number of foreign born at each census date should equal the *enumerated.*

The successive steps in the comparison are set forth in Table 1.1. Lines 1–12 describe the sequence as it has been followed in the detailed calculations, which are explained in full in part III. Lines 14–20 recapitulate the procedure in terms of total additions and subtractions. The figures were taken from the work sheets for the 1900–10 decade, one for which the computations are most detailed.

Table 1.1 conceals a great mass of detail. Mortality rates could not well be applied to either the resident foreign-born or the migration population *en gros,* without distinction of age and sex. The calculations were made for numerous age-groups, for each sex separately. In fact, for the one decade lines 1–12 were repeated some thirty times for the fifteen-odd age-groups by which males and females were classified.

These computations could have been made for each year in the decade since the data on arrivals and the estimates of departures are available and the death or survival rates can be interpolated annually. But because of the approximate character of these rates and the assumptions involved in estimating volume, sex, and age of departures, the laborious procedure was limited to only two periods within each decade, usually quinquennia.[3] This meant that the cumulative total of arrivals and departures over a five-year period had to be treated as if it were for a single year of that period, the middle one.

That an attempt to follow even such a condensed procedure for the several age-groups of each sex in the foreign-born and migrant

Table 1.1 Illustrative calculation of survival and migration for a single census period, 1900–10 (in thousands)

1. Foreign-born whites, census, June 1, 1900	10,214
2. Survivors of line 1, July 1, 1903	9,536
3. Arrivals, all aliens, June 1, 1900–July 1, 1905	4,158
4. Departures, all aliens, June 1, 1900–July 1, 1905	1,739
5. Net balance (line 3 – line 4)	2,420
6. Line 2 + line 5	11,956
7. Survivors of line 6, July 1, 1907	11,108
8. Arrivals, all aliens, July 1, 1905–Apr. 15, 1910	5,422
9. Departures, all aliens, July 1, 1905–Apr. 15, 1910	2,557
10. Net balance (line 8 – line 9)	2,865
11. Line 7 + line 10	13,973
12. Survivors of line 11, Apr. 15, 1910; equal to *estimated* foreign-born whites on that date	13,330
13. Foreign-born whites, census enumeration, Apr. 15, 1910	13,346
Recapitulation for the census period	
14. Foreign-born whites, at beginning of decade (line 1)	10,214
15. Total inflow (line 3 + line 8)	9,580
16. Gross total (line 14 + line 15)	19,794
17. Deaths ((line 1 – line 2) + (line 6 – line 7) + (line 11 – line 12))	2,169
18. Departures (line 4 + line 9)	4,296
19. Total draft (line 17 + line 18)	6,465
20. Foreign-born whites, at the end of decade (line 16 – line 19)	13,330

Because of rounding, detail will not necessarily add to total. *Source*: Table B.5.

populations back to 1870 would run into numerous difficulties with inadequate, inconsistent, and recalcitrant data need not be emphasized, and since these difficulties are discussed in part III, there is no need to deal with them in detail here. The major ones, however, are briefly listed. First, the census data are limited to foreign-born whites—no consistent and long series, with detailed age and sex classes, is available for total foreign born, including nonwhites. This limitation is, however, of minor importance since the number of nonwhite foreign born in 1930, the census year in which total foreign born was at its peak, was only about 0.2 million out of 14.2 (see part III, section Race). Second, the data on arrivals (as well as departures) include nonwhites but for most of the period do not cover movement across land borders. Third, the data on departures of aliens are available only since 1908 and must be estimated prior to that date on the basis of departures of all passengers (including American citizens), and the sex and age classifications are particularly difficult to make for the earlier decades. Fourth, specific death rates for foreign-born whites are available back to 1900 only and had to be extrapolated for earlier periods largely on the basis of trends in the death rates for Great Britain.

Despite these difficulties and the other numerous gaps and inconsistencies that necessitated extensive statistical patching, the comparison of the estimated and enumerated series does not show enormous and bizarre disparities. Column 2 of Table 1.2 gives the estimate that flows directly from the systematic calculations indicated in Table 1.1, and column 4 shows the disparity between the census enumeration and the estimate before any allowance for the identifiable sources of discrepancy. For some of the latter (the movement to and from Canada, arrivals and departures of nonwhite aliens, alien seamen, etc.), a rough approximation can be made. The revised estimate in column 3 and the revised difference in column 5 take account of these identifiable sources of discrepancy, the effect of which can be estimated only roughly and not even consistently through all the decades.

The summary comparison in Table 1.2 (available for each age and sex class) suggests the following conclusions (see also Chart 1.1). First, the census enumeration falls short of the unadjusted migration–survival estimate by percentages ranging from 1 to 4 and exceeds the estimate significantly at only one point, in 1900. The shortage of the census enumeration, after allowance has been made in the estimate for known sources of discrepancy, is reduced in most cases, and the census enumeration yields a slightly larger number of foreign born than the estimate in three of the seven comparisons (for the totals).

Second, the proportional (and of course, absolute) discrepancies between the census enumeration and the migration–survival estimate are larger for foreign-born males than for females. But even for the former, the largest unrevised shortage is 7 percent, in 1890. Most differences, for males and females taken separately, are less than 4 percent, and the majority of these are less than 3 percent.

The comparisons in Table 1.2 confirm the belief that census enumerations tend to understate the number of foreign born. One explanation is that they reflect the assimilation process and the inclination of some foreign-born groups to claim native birth. But the tendency

Table 1.2 Comparison of census enumerations and migration–survival estimates of foreign-born white population, 1880–1940 (absolute figures in thousands)

Date	Census enumeration (1)	Estimate (2)	Revised estimate (3)	Difference (1 – 2) (4)	Revised difference (1 – 3) (5)	Percentage difference is of column 2 (6)	Percentage revised difference is of column 3 (7)
Total							
June 1, 1880	6,560	6,638	6,538	–78	+22	–1.2	+0.3
June 1, 1890	9,122	9,489	9,507	–367	–385	–3.9	–4.0
June 1, 1900	10,214	9,705	10,190	+509	+24	+5.2	+0.2
Apr. 15, 1910	13,346	13,330	13,318	+15	+27	+0.1	+0.2
Jan. 1, 1920	13,713	14,198	14,076	–485	–363	–3.4	–2.6
Apr. 1, 1930	13,983	14,241	14,236	–257	–253	–1.8	–1.8
Apr. 1, 1940	11,419	11,541	11,630	–121	–211	–1.1	–1.8
Males							
June 1, 1880	3,522	3,640	3,555	–118	–33	–3.2	–0.9
June 1, 1890	4,952	5,306	5,295	–354	–343	–6.7	–6.5
June 1, 1900	5,515	5,144	5,419	+371	+96	+7.2	+1.8

Apr. 15, 1910	7,524	7,504	7,490	+20	+34	+0.3	+0.4
Jan. 1, 1920	7,528	7,819	7,786	−291	−258	−3.7	−3.3
Apr. 1, 1930	7,502	7,622	7,644	−120	−141	−1.6	−1.8
Apr. 1, 1940	6,011	6,007	6,096	+4	−85	+0.1	−1.4
Females							
June 1, 1880	3,038	2,998	2,983	+40	+55	+1.3	+1.8
June 1, 1890	4,170	4,183	4,212	−13	−42	−0.3	−1.0
June 1, 1900	4,699	4,561	4,771	+138	−72	+3.0	−1.5
Apr. 15, 1910	5,822	5,826	5,828	−4	−6	−0.1	−0.1
Jan. 1, 1920	6,184	6,379	6,290	−194	−105	−3.0	−1.7
Apr. 1, 1930	6,481	6,618	6,592	−137	−111	−2.1	−1.7
Apr. 1, 1940	5,408	5,534	5,535	−126	−126	−2.3	−2.3

Because of rounding, detail will not necessarily add to total. *Source:* Table 1.10.

is far from a marked one. For the present purpose, the most relevant aspect of the comparison is the limited magnitude of the discrepancy. This is all the more significant since the series on migration and deaths, the former completely and the latter partly independent of the census data on foreign born, account for such a large part of the totals. Total additions (arrivals) and deductions (departures and deaths) during the 1900–10 decade amounted to about 16.0 million (Table 1.1, lines 15 and 19). The census figure of foreign born in 1900 was about 10.2 million (Table 1.1, line 14) in all decades, at least through 1910, and the migration–survival flows were appreciably larger, relatively, than either the initial or terminal census enumeration of foreign born. In light of this large proportion of the migration–survival flow, the relatively small discrepancy between the estimate and the census enumeration becomes significant.

Several qualifications must, however, be noted. First, the comparison is from decade to decade and accepts the census enumeration of foreign born at the beginning of each decade. If the census totals are consistently short of the migration–survival estimates, should we not cumulate these shortages to derive the true discrepancy in 1940, for example? While the answer to this question is "yes," the cumulative discrepancy between census enumerations and migration–survival estimates cannot be derived by *adding* the successive differences in column 4 or 5 of Table 1.2. It is much smaller than either of these totals since the totals would have to be reduced by deaths of the foreign-born population (suggested by the estimate and missing in the census enumeration). Thus, even if we argue that seventy-eight thousand foreign born were not included in the census enumeration of 1880, few of them would have survived by 1940 to swell the shortage in that year. Yet the survival calculations underlying the estimates given in columns 2 and 3 were not applied to the group missing at each terminal census date. In other words, if we tried to guess at the cumulative shortage in the census enumeration of foreign born in 1940, and used column 4 for the purpose, we would assume that the differences in 1880–1910 were so reduced by mortality by 1940 as to have little effect and would allow for only part of the discrepancy in 1920 and 1930.

Roughly speaking, the cumulative discrepancy in 1940 in either column 4 or 5 would fall far short of half a million, which is less than 5 percent, for total foreign born.

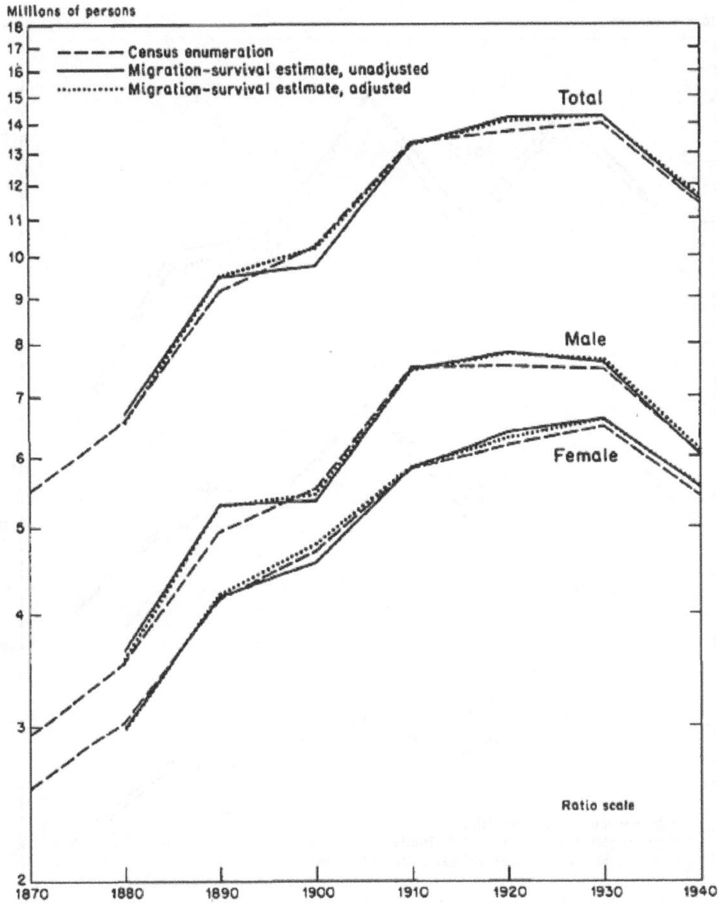

Chart 1.1 Panel A Census enumerations and migration–survival estimates of foreign-born white population, census dates, 1870–1940

Another qualification is suggested by comparing the decadal *changes* in the number of foreign born, that is, first differences in column 1, between columns 1 and 2, and between columns 1 and 3. Since these changes can be small in any decade, the *percentage* differences between them can be quite large. But percentage discrepancies of changes are probably not significant, and since the size of the discrepancy varies from census date to census date, there will be substantial differences between changes in *estimated* and *enumerated* foreign born. The

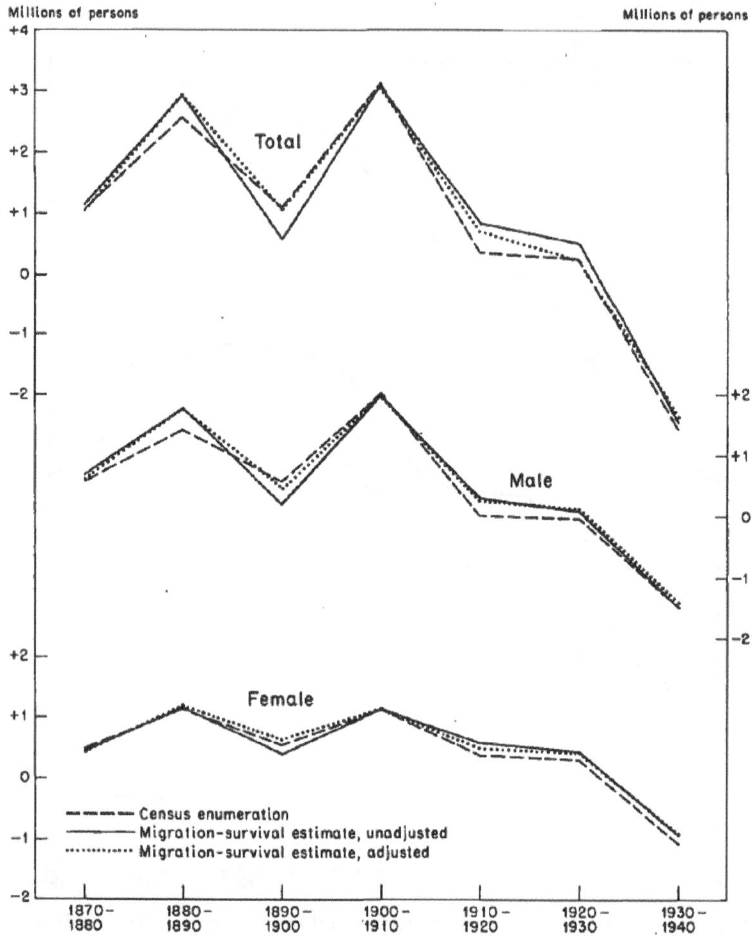

Chart 1.1 Panel B Changes between census enumeration at beginning of census period and census enumeration and migration-survival estimates at end of census period, 1870–1940

important point is that these series of changes move in unison: when there is a large increase or decrease in the enumerated foreign born, there is also a large increase or decrease from the enumerated to the estimated foreign born, and when there is a small change in one series, there is also a small change in the others (Chart 1.1, panel B). The only systematic, and interesting, difference is that the *estimated* series appear to be more sensitive than the census *enumeration* series—the fluctuations in the decade changes in the former are of wider amplitude than those in the decade changes in the latter.

But the chief qualification on the consistency of the two series is revealed by studying the discrepancies by different age-groups (see Table 1.11). The outstanding conclusion is that for the youngest age-group, under fifteen years of age, the census enumerations substantially *exceed* the migration–survival estimates. This discrepancy holds for males in six of the periods and for females in all seven, and particularly in the early census years, 1880–1900. By contrast, the census enumerations are short of the migration–survival estimates for the middle age-groups, between twenty-five and sixty-five years of age, and there is a tendency toward excess for the advanced age-group, sixty-five and over.

The discrepancies in the middle age-groups, from twenty-five to sixty-five years of age, are important since the foreign-born sector of the labor force is recruited largely from them and in greater proportion from the males than from the females. The shortage of the census enumerations is marked in 1880 and 1890. Consequently, at least for these dates the foreign-born component of the labor force may be understated by more than 7 percent. This discrepancy, and the effect of its variations on changes in the foreign-born labor force from census date to census date, must be taken into account in any analysis of the contribution of migration and the foreign born to the growth of the labor force in this country, and via the latter to the longer term trends in the growth of the economy at large.

Despite these qualifications, the census enumerations and the migration–survival estimates of foreign born are on the whole consistent. However, there may be downward biases in both; even the migration–survival estimates may understate the true number of foreign born because of possible shortages in the migration figures themselves. Such shortages, if they exist, will not be revealed by comparison with the census enumerations if the latter are undercounts. Admittedly, the analysis and comparisons cannot reveal errors in both series when the errors are in the same direction. But for practical purposes, the important question is the probable magnitude of such errors—over and above those that can be identified and have been used to revise the differences in Table 1.2. It is the assumption, supported by some evidence on emigration from Europe in comparison with the reported immigration here, that the errors cannot be so large as to vitiate the long-term trends and the towering long swings revealed by the record of immigration and net changes in foreign born as the two series stand.

Arrivals and Departures

Arrivals of all alien passengers (available from the official data) and departures of alien passengers (official since 1908 and estimated back to 1870) are plotted in Chart 1.2, together with the difference between the two, an approximation to net immigration. It might have been preferable to confine both arrivals and departures to immigrants and emigrants, excluding the entrance and departure of alien visitors and the departure of resident aliens intending a temporary visit abroad. But it is not possible to do so for the full period nor is it desirable here, since the census data on foreign born prior to 1930 include aliens in the country temporarily. Besides, while data are available since 1908, the distinction between an immigrant and a nonimmigrant had no legal meaning prior to the 1920s and that between an emigrant and a nonemigrant may even now not be too reliable since it depends upon a declared intention that need not necessarily be fulfilled.[4] However, we do make use of the distinction between immigrants and other alien passengers in the data since 1908 and present alternative calculations in the tables that follow.

The major impression of Chart 1.2 is that arrivals, departures, and, naturally, the net differences are subject to marked fluctuations, both over short periods closely associated with business cycles in this country and in towering swings ranging in duration from eleven to twenty-five years. The longer record of arrivals, available back to the 1820s, indicates that both the cycles and the long swings were prominent even before the Civil War. The data on immigrants since 1908 suggest a similar picture, except that the absolute volumes and the ratio of departures to arrivals are significantly smaller. It follows that the secular, long-term trends in the flows of people into and out of the country are obscured not only by sensitive responses of these flows to business cycles, but also by longer and in some respects even more prominent swings.

The comments that follow on the underlying trends, the long swings, and the responses of the flows to business cycles are intended merely as a sketch of the major findings, but more importantly, they suggest some major problems for further research. They can scarcely do justice to the record and to the full variety of facts and questions that it suggests.

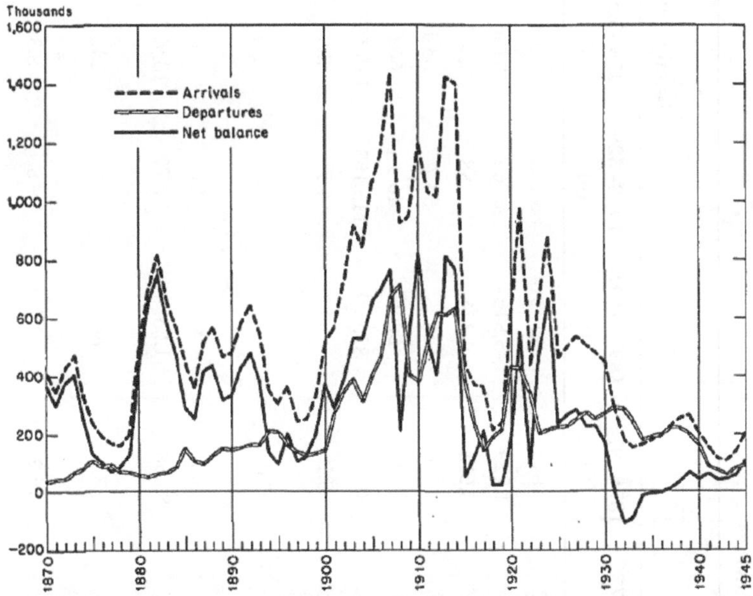

Chart 1.2 Arrivals, departures, and net balance of alien passengers, fiscal years ending June 30, 1870–1945

The Underlying Trends

Since there are long swings of wide amplitude in the flows of immigrants and of all alien passengers, the underlying trends can best be discerned if we date these swings and take averages for the periods marked off by them—either from peak to peak or from trough to trough. Each average represents a level in which the fluctuations that constitute a swing have been canceled out, and the movement of these averages should reveal the characteristics of the underlying secular trend.[5]

Table 1.3, which was calculated along these lines, carries us back to the 1820s, before the period covered by the new estimates. The detailed estimates could not be extended for years before 1870 since relevant data on departures and mortality of foreign born are almost completely lacking. We have made rough assumptions concerning ratios of departures to arrivals for such long swings as can be established before the 1870s, but these assumptions, based on the ratios and their movements since the Civil War, can hardly be in such error

Table 1.3 Average volume per decade of arrivals, departures, and net balances, trough-to-trough and peak-to-peak long swings, all alien passengers, 1823–1932, and immigrants, 1910–32 (absolute figures in thousands)

A. Trough-to-trough swings							
	All alien passengers						Immigrants
	1823–38[a] (1)	1838–67[b] (2)	1862–77[c] (3)	1878–97[c] (4)	1897–1918[c] (5)	1918–32[c] (6)	1918–32[c] (7)
1. Arrivals	358	1,969	2,892	4,840	8,172	5,153	3,463
2. Departures	36	197	434	1,229	3,846	2,765	1,156
3. Net balance	322	1,772	2,458	3,611	4,326	2,388	2,307
4. Departures as percentage of arrivals	(10.0)	(10.0)	(15.0)	25.4	47.1	53.7	33.4
5. Net balance as percentage of arrivals	(90.0)	(90.0)	(85.0)	74.6	52.9	46.3	66.6
6. Total population	13,258	23,522	39,839	60,063	87,979	115,153	115,153
7. Arrivals as percentage of population	2.7	8.4	7.3	8.1	9.3	4.5	3.0
8. Departures as percentage of population	0.3	0.9	1.1	2.0	4.4	2.4	1.0
9. Net balance as percentage of population	2.4	7.5	6.2	6.0	4.9	2.1	2.0
10. Foreign-born population		2,245	5,567	8,658	12,374	13,972	13,972
11. Arrivals as percentage of foreign-born population		87.7	51.9	55.9	66.0	36.9	24.8
12. Departures as percentage of foreign-born population		8.8	7.7	14.2	31.1	19.8	8.3
13. Net balance as percentage of foreign-born population		78.9	44.2	41.7	35.0	17.1	16.5

B. Peak-to-peak swings						
	All alien passengers					Immigrants
	1834–54[b] (1)	1854–72[b] (2)	1873–84[c] (3)	1884–1910[c] (4)	1910–24[c] (5)	1910–24[c] (6)
1. Arrivals	1,736	2,427	4,037	6,313	7,310	5,891
2. Departures	174	303	756	2,536	3,756	2,010
3. Net balance	1,562	2,124	3,281	3,777	3,554	3,881
4. Departures as percentage of arrivals	(10.0)	(12.5)	18.7	40.2	51.4	34.1
5. Net balance as percentage of arrivals	(90.0)	(87.5)	81.3	59.8	48.6	65.9
6. Total population	19,827	34,066	48,982	72,717	102,747	102,747
7. Arrivals as percentage of population	8.8	7.1	8.2	8.7	7.1	5.7
8. Departures as percentage of population	0.9	0.9	1.5	3.5	3.6	1.9
9. Net balance as percentage of population	7.9	6.2	6.7	5.2	3.5	3.8
10. Foreign-born population	2,000	4.136	6,814	10,294	14,065	14,065
11. Arrivals as percentage of foreign-born population	86.8	58.7	59.2	61.3	52.0	41.9
12. Departures as percentage of foreign-born population	8.7	7.3	11.1	24.6	26.7	14.3
13. Net balance as percentage of foreign-born population	78.1	51.4	48.2	36.7	25.3	27.6

(continued)

Table 1.3 *(continued)*

[a]Years ending September 30.

[b]Years ending December 31.

[c]Years ending June 30.

Because of rounding, detail will not necessarily add to total.

Notes: Figures in parentheses are approximate. See notes below for the specific items.

The turning points were established by observation of the gross and net arrivals; the peak year 1884, derived from a nine-year moving average, is the only one that does not coincide with the turning points in the annual series.

Panel A

Line 1

Column 1: Average of annual data given in Imre Ferenczi, *International Migrations,* vol. I (New York: National Bureau of Economic Research, 1929), Table 1, 377. (For 1832–38, the figures reported for calendar years were adjusted to years ending September 30 by straight-line interpolation.)

Column 2: Ibid. for 1843–50, the figures reported for years ending September 30 were adjusted to calendar years by straight-line interpolation.

Column 3: Ibid. for 1862–68. The figures reported for calendar years were adjusted to years ending June 30 by straight-line interpolation. For the year ending June 30, 1869, the estimate is the sum of the number of immigrants reported in ibid., Table II, 384, and the number of nonimmigrant aliens admitted; the latter is an average of the number for 1868 (derived from ibid., Tables I and IV) and for 1870 (derived from Table B.1 and ibid., Table II). For 1870–77, the figures are derived from Table B.1. Columns 4–7: From Table B.1.

Line 2

Columns 1–3: Product of lines 1 and 4.

Columns 4–7: From Table B.1.

Line 4

Columns 1–3: Rough extrapolation of columns 4–7.

Line 6

Average of estimates for calendar years. For 1823–69 from *Historical Statistics of the United States, 1789–1945,* Bureau of the Census, Series B, 31; for 1870–1919, unpublished estimates derived as the sum of foreign-born population (Table B.6) and native-born population (derived by logarithmic straight-line interpolation between census dates); for 1919–32 from ibid.

Line 10

Column 2: Census figures for 1850, from ibid., Series B 193. Includes white and free colored population only.

Column 3: Census figure for 1870. See note to column 2.

Columns 4–7: From Table B.6.

Panel B

Line 1

Column 1: For source, see notes to panel A, line 1, column 1. For 1844–50, the figures reported for years ending September 30 were adjusted to calendar years.

Column 2: For source for 1854–67, see notes to panel A, line 1, column 1. The estimates for 1868 and 1869 are derived similar to that for 1869 in panel A (see notes to panel A, line 1, column 3). For 1870–72, the figures are from Table B.1.

Columns 3–6: From Table B.1.

Line 2

Columns 1 and 2: Product of lines 1 and 4.

Columns 3–6: From Table B.1.

Line 4

Columns 1 and 2: Rough extrapolation of columns 3–6.

Line 6

See notes to panel A, line 6.

Line 10

Column 1: Rough estimate.

Column 2: Census figure for 1860, from *Historical Statistics of the United States, 1789–1945,* Series B, 193.

Columns 3–6: From Table B.6.

as to vitiate the marked trends that the record indicates. It therefore seemed justifiable to extend the view to cover the longer period and get a better perspective of the secular trends.

It might be expected that the volumes of both arrivals and departures would tend to grow—given the growth of this country and of its attractive and absorptive capacity, and given a correlative increase in the total of foreign born, resident and transient, the pool from which departures take place. Of particular interest here is the rate of this growth in comparison with the country's total population and its foreign-born component.

If we try to abstract from visitors and read the major conclusions in terms of immigrants and emigrants alone, the following results may be discerned.

First, the really sizable influx began during the twenty to twenty-five years preceding the Civil War, that is, between the mid-1830s and 1860. The percentage of transients among the arrivals of that period must have been quite small, probably not over 5 percent. The percentage of departures, while roughly estimated, is, if anything, on the high side. Hence, net immigration is probably understated. For these reasons, the levels of net balance shown for the long swings of 1838–61 (trough to trough) and 1834–54 (peak to peak) are, if translated into those of net *immigration,* fairly close to the true level and perhaps slightly short of the latter.

Second, both arrivals and departures have moved upward since that time. But when these movements are adjusted for the nonimmigrant component, and related either to total or foreign-born population in the country, the *relative* magnitude of both total arrivals and net immigration declines from the level established during 1835–60, and the latter thus represents the highest secular level. While the ratio of total arrivals to total population is higher in 1897–1918 than in 1838–61, an allowance of about 15 percent of arrivals for nonimmigrants in the later period (suggested by the figures for 1908–14, when total arrivals were 7.9 million and immigrants 6.7 million) would reduce the percentages in those years to levels below those in the early period.[6] This conclusion is conspicuously shown by the ratio of net arrivals, roughly equivalent to net immigration because of the cancellation of transient arrivals and departures, to total population. And it is even more striking when we compare arrivals and net immigration with the resident foreign population: the percentage of the former to the latter is at its secular peak in the two to two-and-a-half decades preceding the Civil War and falls far short of this level during all the long swings that follow.

Third, the proportion of departures to arrivals has been rising. Complete data are not available before the 1870s, and those given in Table 1.3 should be adjusted for the inclusion of nonimmigrants. During 1908–14 (years free from war and restrictive immigration), the ratio of departures to arrivals for immigrants alone was 30.8 percent and for all aliens 48.8 percent. On the basis of these figures and the entries in Table 1.3, line 4, it is clear that the ratio of departing to arriving immigrants must have risen appreciably from the 1870s onward, let alone the period prior to the Civil War. We know that the proportion of nonimmigrant arrivals was small in the 1870s and 1880s. If we assume that it was not much higher than 10 percent, and that all the nonimmigrants departed, the ratio of immigrant departures to arrivals can be calculated. Thus, for 1878–97, gross immigration was 4.36 million per decade, and departures, 0.74 million per decade. The ratio is about 17 percent, compared with a similar ratio of well over 30 percent for the immigrant–emigrant flow in the long swing of 1897–1918 or the even higher ratio for 1918–32. This increase in the turnover of the immigrant flow is important in its bearing upon the constitution of the foreign-born population and particularly in its effect upon the adaptation of the flow to the changing conditions in this country.

The Long Swings

Just as we established the underlying trends by average values for each observed long swing, so we can study the latter by distinguishing the observed short-term cycles and calculating averages for them. These averages would presumably be free from fluctuations that characterize short-term cycles, and their movements would reveal the long swings. Since our major interest is in *net* arrivals, we set the dates of the shorter cycles in that series and on the basis of these dates computed averages—for complete cycles, from trough to trough and from peak to peak—for arrivals, departures, and net inflow of alien passengers.[7] For the more recent periods, we made similar calculations for immigrants and emigrants (Table 1.4 and Chart 1.3).

There was a swing in arrivals from a low average of 319,000 per year for the cycle of 1871–77 to a peak of 534,000 in the cycle of 1882–88 and back to a trough of 318,000 in the cycle of 1895–97. The fluctuation in *net* arrivals was even wider: from a first trough of 241,000 to a peak of 433,000 and then to a trough of 153,000. The amplitude in the other long swings is appreciably wider.

Three conclusions may be drawn with respect to the long swings in the inflow of aliens or immigrants. First, arrivals of alien passengers and of immigrants were subject to long swings of wide magnitude, three such swings being observable during the period from the early 1870s through the early 1940s. If we center the average of each cycle at its midpoint, as was done in Chart 1.3, the dates of the turning points in the long swings in arrivals are not too different from those for the annual data used in Table 1.3.[8]

Second, there is no negative correlation between arrivals and departures, although one would expect that conditions favoring a long *upswing* in arrivals would also favor a long *downswing* in departures, and vice versa. During the first long swing, departures do rise to a date almost coincident with the *trough* in arrivals, but there is no downswing in departures during the upward phase, that is, from the early 1870s to the middle or late 1880s. In the second swing, departures move parallel rather than opposite to arrivals, though with some lag. After World War I, departures describe two swings, one with a peak in the early 1920s and the other with a peak in the late 1920s.

A partial explanation may lie in the fact that as transportation and other conditions affecting migration were improved, the flow into and out of the country became easier and departures tended to be swelled by large arrivals. The growth of arrivals greatly augments the pool from which departures are likely to occur. In other words, attractive conditions may induce a large volume of immigration, but a sizable number of the immigrants may shortly find conditions not to their liking and may be willing or forced to leave.[9] From 1895 through 1915 particularly, the easy flow into the country was accompanied by a large increase in departures. After World War I, changes in the law began to affect departures if only because they affected arrivals—but not necessarily at the same time.

Third, net arrivals reveal swings with characteristics of their own, since net arrivals (or immigration) are the difference between the inflow and the outflow, and the outflow is characterized by different amplitudes and somewhat different timing from the inflow. These swings are of far wider amplitude, particularly on a relative basis, than those in gross arrivals and departures. What is of even more interest, during the first two swings, peak net arrivals tend to precede peak gross arrivals. Thus, the peak level in net arrivals is reached in

Table 1.4 Average volume per year of arrivals, departures, and net balance during cycles established in net balance, all alien passengers, 1871–1942, and immigrants, 1908–43 (in thousands)

Trough-to-trough cycles				Peak-to-peak cycles			
Period	Arrivals	Departures	Net balance	Period	Arrivals	Departures	Net balance
(1)	(2)	(3)	(4)	(5)	(6)	(7)	(8)
All alien passengers							
1. 1871–77	318.7	78.0	240.7	1873–82	345.3	76.8	268.5
2. 1877–86	473.0	79.6	393.4	1882–88	534.4	101.2	433.2
3. 1886–89	497.4	118.2	379.2	1888–92	531.7	149.3	382.4
4. 1889–95	495.7	169.4	326.2	1892–96	424.0	185.2	238.8
5. 1895–97	317.8	165.2	152.5	1896–1900	317.5	138.0	179.5
6. 1897–1901	377.0	153.2	223.8	1900–3	671.3	295.3	376.0
7. 1901–4	784.6	342.4	442.3	1903–7	1,061.7	427.2	634.4
8. 1904–8	1,136.9	513.0	623.8	1907–10	1,062.4	547.1	515.3
9. 1912–15	1,035.9	419.0	544.9	1910–13	1,120.0	543.2	576.8
10. 1912–15	1,185.3	581.8	603.5	1913–17	774.8	409.5	365.2
11. 1915–18	350.9	225.3	125.5	1917–21	435.2	280.9	154.3
12. 1918–22	539.7	334.9	204.8	1921–24	678.2	289.1	389.0
13. 1922–25	666.0	234.3	431.8	1924–27	554.4	229.5	324.9
14. 1925–32	436.8	261.2	175.6	1927–39	287.9	238.0	49.9
15. 1932–40	203.8	209.9	–6.1	1939–41	209.4	155.6	53.8
16. 1940–42	155.9	104.4	51.5				

Source: Table B.1.

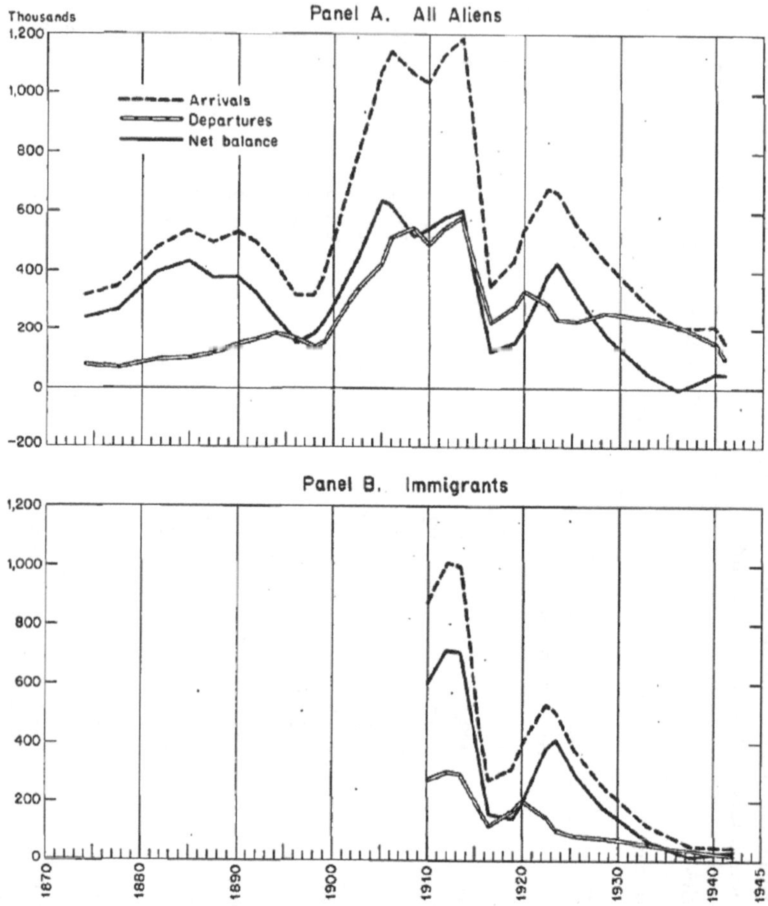

Chart 1.3 Average volume per year of arrivals, departures, and net balance during cycles (trough to trough and peak to peak) established in net balance, all alien passengers, 1871–1942, and immigrants, 1908–48

1882–88, not in 1888–92, in 1903–7 not in 1912–15. Also the first clearly marked trough in net arrivals is in 1895–97 and precedes that in gross in 1896–1900.

While the differences in timing are minor, they are unmistakable. Furthermore, they are not unexpected. Departures are more resistant than arrivals to pressures of worsened conditions in this country. Because of this difference in responsiveness, net arrivals are bound to show a wider relative amplitude than gross arrivals, and perhaps some lead at the peaks. Beginning with World War I, this "normal" relationship of gross and net flows is completely disturbed, and the timing sequence not only disappears but also reverses: here the peak in net inflows (in 1922–25) follows that in gross (in 1921–24).[10]

The causes and consequences of these long swings in migration constitute a wide and as yet inadequately explored subject, and it would be impracticable and presumptuous to attempt to deal with it here. But the intriguing and far-reaching character of the problem may be suggested by the graphic comparison shown in Chart 1.4. The top line is net arrivals, based on averages for successive short-term cycles, and identical with the solid line given in Chart 1.3. The second to top line, based on an approximation to annual gross national product per worker in 1929 prices, represents the general level of economic production per worker. In view of the strong upward trend in this series, the data are annual values—not averages for successive short cycles—expressed as relatives of trend values read from a second-degree potential equation fitted to the logs. Of the two lines at the bottom, one represents the annual volume of expenditures for private nonfarm housekeeping units in 1929 prices, and the second, the index of the number of urban housekeeping dwelling units started.[11] These series have not been modified in any way since the long cycles are readily apparent.

All three series, net arrivals, gross national product per worker, and residential construction, show long swings of approximately the same duration. One should note in passing that the series are completely independent statistically since they are based on entirely different bodies of primary data.[12] Nor is there anything about the technique used in deriving them that would introduce similar long swings.

Of even more interest is the timing, although comparison is difficult because of the different ways in which the series were treated and because of the problems involved in assigning specific dates to the turns in the long swings. But it would seem that, before wars and legislation affected net immigration, the long swings in net immigration tended to *follow* those in gross national product per worker and to *precede* those in the constant dollar volume of residential construction. Thus the first peak in product per worker indicated is in the late 1870s, that in net immigration in the middle 1880s, and that in residential construction in the late 1880s. The next trough in product per worker is in the middle 1890s (1894), in net immigration somewhat later (cycle 1895–97), and in residential construction around 1900. The following peak in product per worker is about 1907, in net immigration either

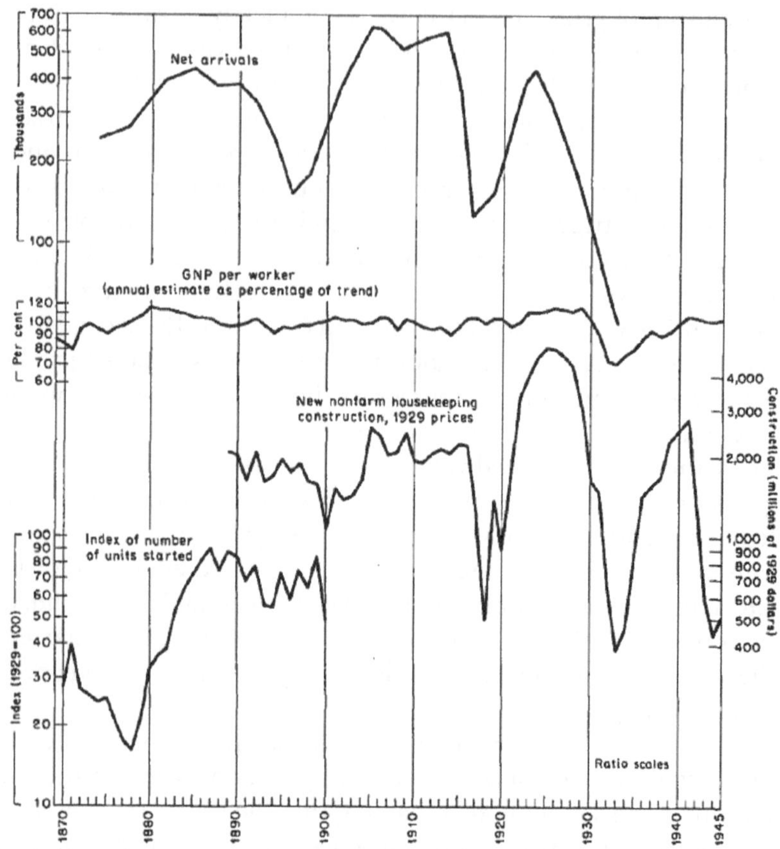

Chart 1.4 Net arrivals, gross national product per worker, and residential construction, total value in 1929 prices and index of number of units started, 1869–1945 (1929 = 100)

about that time or somewhat later, and in residential construction, when smoothed by a nine-year moving average, at about 1910 but with a plateau formation until 1914. Finally, the trough in product per worker is in 1914 and those in net immigration and residential construction sometime during World War I. In the 1920s and 1930s, while general agreement in the long swings exists, the sequence is upset, with net immigration preceding not only construction but also national product per worker.

At the present stage of analysis, and in the present connection, this chart and comparison must remain an intriguing picture and guess.

But there are reasons for expecting similar long swings in the three aspects of economic and social activity with the timing suggested for the years prior to World War I. The dominant proportion of national product, even of gross product, is flow of goods to consumers, and the swings in the product, on a per worker basis, suggest variations in the rate of increase in consumer real income per worker.

To the extent that immigration depends upon the superior economic opportunities that this country offers, we should expect long swings in product per worker to be reflected, with some lag, in a greater influx of people and more net immigration.[13] These additions to the country's population presumably need housing, and since they are sufficiently numerous and mostly in the age-groups associated with the founding of new families, they should have a marked effect on new residential construction, again possibly with some lag.

Yet plausible as these relations seem, they require more exploration. Can we assume that variations in the *rate of increase* of product per worker, given the generally higher level of income in this country, necessarily affect the flow of immigrants? To what extent can we claim that such variations in the rate of growth of product per worker influenced people abroad, and what was the mechanism of this influence? Was it the assistance of foreign born already here that induced relations or friends to come, or was it some effective grapevine of letters and reports? Was there any connection between the rapidity of growth in this country and a similar course in countries of would-be emigration, so that dislocation of industrialization widened the source of emigration in agreement with the timing of the fluctuations in the rate of growth here? Furthermore, can we assume that the newly arrived immigrants, with their relatively low purchasing power, had a truly major effect on residential construction? Were the swings in residential construction perhaps associated with those in the number of native born of native parentage—touched upon below? Alternatively, were the residential construction swings delayed beyond those in product per worker because, particularly in pre-World War I days, the economy did not have the capacity to accelerate the rates of growth of both consumer goods and some capital equipment *and* also of residential construction, so that construction swings had to wait until the limited capacity permitted an upswing? This argument might explain why the swings in residential construction lagged behind those in national product before World War I and coincided with them in post-World War I days.

These questions should not be interpreted to mean that the association suggested by Chart 1.4 is necessarily illusory. They are rather intended to indicate both that the mechanism of these long swings is complex and that their further exploration promises to shed light on the past behavior of this country's economy—and perhaps also of other economies. The only hypothesis urged here is that immigration, arrivals, and departures may have played a significant part in this mechanism.

Response to Business Cycles

Even though only annual data are available through most of the period, cyclical fluctuations in arrivals, departures, and net inflow can be studied in some detail. This is hardly the place to do so, particularly since this aspect of the migratory flows appears to have been studied most, notably by Harry Jerome in his *Migration and Business Cycles* (National Bureau of Economic Research, 1926). Instead, we limit ourselves to a brief comment based largely on measures of the consistency with which arrivals, departures, and net balance responded to cycles in general business conditions.

We use the reference chronology of business cycles in this country, established by the National Bureau of Economic Research, to calculate measures of conformity (Table 1.5). In general, a plus sign indicates that the series moves with business cycles: rises during reference expansions, declines during reference contractions, and shows a decline in the rate of change from expansion to the following contraction, and a rise in the rate of change from contraction to the following expansion. Perfect positive conformity, that is, the expected behavior observed in each reference cycle phase in the period, yields indexes of +100, and perfect negative conformity, that is, declines during expansions, rises during contractions, and so on, yields indexes of −100. Indexes close to 0 signify inconsistent response to business cycles.

The indexes in Table 1.5 were computed separately for the cycles preceding World War I, for those following it, and for the full period—to reveal the effects of war and legislation on short-term responsiveness of arrivals and departures. If we accept indexes of about thirty or larger as significant, particularly for periods including a fair number of reference cycles, the major conclusions can easily be summarized.[14]

First, arrivals change fairly consistently with business cycles (see lines 1–3). This is particularly true for periods preceding World War I

Table 1.5 Indexes of conformity to business cycles, arrivals, departures, and net balance, 1871–1939

	Expansion (1)	Contraction (2)	Full cycle: Trough to trough (3)	Full cycle: Peak to peak (4)	Full cycle: Combined (5)
A. All alien passengers					
Arrivals					
1. 1871–1915 (11 ref. cycles)	+82	+45	+64	+64[a]	+64
2. 1915–39 (6 ref. cycles)	0	0	+33	+60[b]	+45
3. 1871–1939 (17 ref. cycles)	+53	+29	+53	+62[c]	+58
Departures					
4. 1871–1915 (11 ref. cycles)	+27	−45	−27	−45[a]	−36
5. 1915–39 (6 ref. cycles)	−33	0	−33	−60[b]	−45
6. 1871–1939 (17 ref. cycles)	+6	−29	−29	−50[c]	−39
Net balance					
7. 1871–1915 (11 ref. cycles)	+64	+64	+82	+64[a]	+73
8. 1915–39 (6 ref. cycles)	+33	0	0	+60[b]	+27
9. 1871–1939 (17 ref. cycles)	+53	+41	+53	+62[c]	+58
B. Immigrants and emigrants, 1915–39					
10. Arrivals	0	0	0	+60[b]	+27
11. Departures	−67	−17	−67	−20[b]	−46
12. Net balance	0	0	+33	+60[b]	+45

[a]Eleven reference cycles, 1873–1918.

[b]Five reference cycles, 1918–37.

[c]Sixteen reference cycles, 1873–1937.

Source: Table B.1.

although even after the war and subsequent legislation, which obviously disturbed this positive association, the differential response still remains (see lines 2 and 10, columns 4 and 5). In view of the repeatedly claimed effect of the "pull" on the short-term changes of immigration flows, this was to be expected.

Second, departures move invertedly to business cycles, that is, tend to contract during expansions and expand during contractions. While this also should have been expected, it is the exceptions that are interesting. An entry of +27, rather than minus, for line 4, column 1, that is, during reference expansions prior to World War I, reflects the rising long-term trend in departures, already commented upon above—a trend that more than cancels the short-term downward movements during reference expansions. Another point of interest is that the inverted conformity of departures to business cycles is at least as consistent during the period beginning with World War I as prior to it. Perhaps departures are more sensitive to economic conditions than the more rigidly controlled (by law) arrivals.

As already suggested (see note 9), there is some evidence to indicate that most of the departures were from the pool of the newly or recently arrived. The magnitude of the movement during business cycles is not measured in Table 1.5, nor do we need to measure it here: Chart 1.2 demonstrates clearly that the fluctuations were quite substantial. We also know from the age and sex structure of these flows that a considerable proportion of the arrivals and departures were members of the labor force and largely men. We thus get a glimpse of the mechanism of adjustment of the labor force to changing economic conditions which, however problematical in some of its social concomitants, was not necessarily without some economic advantages. This is a highly disputable thesis to which justice cannot be done here. We merely wish to suggest that the opposite conclusion, viz, that the easy influx and outflow of labor aggravated the magnitude of business cycles in this country, is far from firmly established. There is something to be said for the ability of an economy to increase additions to its labor force during prosperous times and to reduce them, if not necessarily convert them into declines, during periods of contraction.

Intradecade Flows

In the preceding section we considered migration flows alone. But changes in the foreign-born resident population, and hence its contribution to changes in labor force or total population, are determined not only by the net balance of arrivals and departures but also by deaths. Estimates of deaths were made along the lines indicated in section The Comparison (see particularly Table 1.1), and we can use them to build up the total flow for each census decade.

However, stocks at the beginning and the end of census intervals and flows (migration and death) during the intervals are in some instances for periods shorter or longer than a decade, depending upon the date on which the census was taken. To facilitate comparison of flows among decades, we adjusted the estimates to cover ten-year periods. Furthermore, our calculations permit us to break the 1910–20 decade at 1915, separating the prewar and prerestrictive legislation decades from those that follow. Comparison of the decade estimates for 1910–20 and 1915–25 thus reveals the effect of war and legislation on the flows. Finally, in the last two decades, the flows are limited to immigrants and emigrants—excluding the transients, who were proportionately much more numerous than that in the earlier decades.

The general impressions concerning the relative magnitudes of arrivals and departures conveyed by Table 1.6 (panel A, columns 2 and 4, and first four columns of panel B) only confirm what has already been indicated—the upward trend in the ratio of departures to arrivals or to the total pool on which outflow could draw—the sum of foreign born and arrivals. This trend continues through the first half of the second decade in this century, but then ceases primarily because of the restrictive effects of war and legislation. We also find that the ratio of *net* arrivals to initial foreign-born population is higher in the 1880s than later, but we know from the analysis in Table 1.3 that the secular peak in the ratio in fact precedes the Civil War.

The new data in Table 1.6 relate to deaths, calculated for both the initial census population of foreign born and the net balance of arrivals over departures. Offhand, one would expect that the ratio of deaths to the total for which it is calculated, that is, the sum of initial foreign born and net arrivals, would decline because of the reduction in mortality rates over the period. But the calculations yield ratios that fluctuate with some tendency to rise toward the end (panel B, fifth column). Further thought suggests that death rate trends are a product of several factors, of which the general decline in death rates is only one. To begin with, the foreign-born population ages during the decade, and if there were no new immigrants, this aging process might result in a rapid *rise* in the death rate. Second, the relative contribution of the net balance of arrivals over departures during the

Table 1.6 Migration and deaths by decades, total alien migration, 1870–1920, and immigrants and emigrants, 1920–40

A. Absolute totals (in thousands)							
Period	Foreign-born, initial census total[a] (1)	Arrivals (2)	Gross total (1 + 2) (3)	Departures (4)	Deaths (5)	Total draft (4 + 5) (6)	Calculated residual, end of decade (3 – 6) (7)
1870–80	5,494	3,000	8,493	730	1,124	1,855	6,638
1880–90	6,560	5,536	12,095	1,043	1,564	2,607	9,488
1890–1900	9,122	4,124	13,246	1,591	1,948	3,540	9,706
1900–10[b]	10,214	9,702	19,916	4,350	2,196	6,546	13,370
1910–15[b]	13,345	11,613	24,959	5,859	2,590	8,449	16,510
1915–20[b]	14,681	3,166	17,847	2,190	2,250	4,440	13,407
1920–30[b]	13,713	4,158	17,871	1,148	2,495	3,643	14,228
1930–40	13,983	571	14,554	467	2,547	3,014	11,540

	B. Ratios (percent)					
Period	**Arrivals ÷ initials (2 ÷ 1)**	**Arrivals – departures ÷ initials [(2 – 4) ÷ 1]**	**Departures ÷ arrivals (4 ÷ 2)**	**Departures ÷ gross total (4 ÷ 3)**	**Deaths ÷ (initial + net) [5 ÷ (3 – 4)]**	**Total draft ÷ gross total (6 ÷ 3)**
1870–80	54.6	41.3	24.3	8.6	14.5	21.8
1880–90	84.4	68.5	18.8	8.6	14.2	21.6
1890–1900	45.2	27.8	38.6	12.0	16.7	26.7
1900–10	95.0	52.4	44.8	21.8	14.1	32.9
1910–15	87.0	43.1	50.5	23.5	13.6	33.9
1915–20	21.6	6.6	69.2	12.3	14.4	24.9
1920–30	30.3	21.9	27.6	6.4	14.9	20.4
1930–40	4.1	0.7	81.8	3.2	18.1	20.7

[a]Census dates are June 1, 1870, 1880, 1890, and 1900; April 15, 1910; January 1, 1920; April 1, 1930 and 1940. The 1915 figure is for January 1 (derived from Table B.6).

[b]For periods of less or more than ten years, the flows are adjusted to a decade basis. Hence the estimates in column 7 are for dates different from those of the census; they are at dates exactly ten years from the date of the entry in column 1. The adjustment factors are 9.875 for 1900–10, 4.708 for 1910–15, 5 for 1915–20, and 10.25 for 1920–30.

Because of rounding, detail will not necessarily add to total.

Source: For column 1 and data underlying columns 2, 4, and 5, Tables B.4 and B.5.

successive decades is a variable one, with respect both to totals and to the proportions of sexes and ages—which are subject to markedly different mortality rates. Finally, the downward movement of age- and sex-specific mortality rates is not necessarily constant from decade to decade. A full analysis of the various factors involved is beyond our competence here. But in this complex of factors, the aging of the foreign-born population is perhaps dominant and is largely responsible for whatever upward drift there is in the ratios in the fifth column of panel B. The large increases in this ratio in 1890–1900 and 1930–40 are due to the relatively low net immigration, which could not sufficiently counteract the effects of the higher age of the initial foreign-born population.[15]

Before World War I, the sum of deaths and departures grew more than proportionately to the total pool from which they were drawn (sixth column of panel B). Consequently, it took an increasing number of arrivals to yield a unit addition to the foreign born in the country. Thus, from 1870 to 1880, the total of foreign born increased to 1,145,000 and gross arrivals amounted to 3,000,000 so that less than three arrivals resulted in one additional foreign-born resident. In 1900–10, the ratio was 9,702,000 arrivals to an increase of 3,156,000, or more than three arrivals per person added to foreign born, and in 1920–30, it was 4,158 to 515, or about 8 to 1—despite the fact that for this decade we counted immigrants alone, not all alien passengers. In general, the ratio will increase rapidly as net migration recedes in importance and deaths mount with the aging of the resident foreign-born population. It is therefore not surprising to find the ratio climbing from 3 to 1 in 1900–10 to 8 to 1 in 1920–30. What is more significant is the rise from 2.6 to 1 in the early decades to 3.1 to 1 in 1900–10.

The trends in the mechanism of intradecade flow revealed in Table 1.6 also affected the structure of the foreign-born population with respect to length of residence in the United States. We may assume, as already indicated, that departures are overwhelming from recent arrivals. This assumption is supported by a comparison of the composition of arrivals by the country of origin with that of departures by the prospective countries of residence. For 1908–14, the major groups of arrivals by country of origin were Austria-Hungary, 22 percent; Italy, 21 percent; Russia and Finland, 20 percent, whereas the major countries of "old" immigration accounted for much lower percentages—the United Kingdom for about 9 and Germany for about 3. For the same period, the major groups of departures, by countries of future residence were Austria-Hungary, about 26 percent; Italy, about 32 percent; Russia and Finland, about 10 percent, whereas the major countries of "old" immigration showed much smaller percentages—the United Kingdom, about 3 percent and Germany, about 2 percent. In 1910, to show the contrast, of the *resident* foreign-born population, Austria-Hungary accounted for only 10 percent; Italy, for about 10 percent; Russia and Finland, for about 10 percent, whereas the United Kingdom accounted for 19 percent and Germany for 17 percent.[16] We shall, therefore, commit no grievous error by assuming that *all* departures during a decade are from arrivals in the same decade. On this assumption and roughly apportioning total deaths between the initial foreign-born population and the net balance of arrivals over departures, we calculated the number of the initial foreign-born population in each decade that survived and were in the country at the end of the decade (Table 1.7). This calculation yields maximum estimates of such survivors and, therefore, minimum estimates of the proportion of foreign born at the end of the decade who were in the country only a decade or less.[17] But the differences between the minimum and true estimates are not so large as to invalidate the results of the calculation.

To repeat, the percentages in Table 1.7 of the foreign-born population that have been in the country ten years or less are underestimates.[18] But even at that, they are quite large at some dates.

Thus in both 1890 and 1910, they were about 40 percent of all foreign born. Since at both dates the proportion of foreign-born population to the total was close to 15 percent, 6 percent of total population, largely adult, were in the country ten years or less—a sizable proportion, particularly if concentrated in a few areas.

The share of the labor force was probably even greater. The newly arrived foreign born were, in general, in age and sex classes that participated more heavily in the labor market than the older resident foreign born. Therefore, those in the country less than ten years might have constituted close to half of the foreign-born labor force in 1890 and 1910. At the same dates, all foreign born gainfully engaged were well above 20 percent of the total labor force in the United States. This means that in 1890 and 1910, over 10 percent of the total labor force of this country were adults who had been in the country for ten years or less.

Whatever may be said about the social advantages and disadvantages of this process by which large segments of the labor force were

Table 1.7 **Estimated minimum proportion or foreign-born population who were in the country ten years or less, 1880–1940 (absolute figures in thousands)**

Period	Foreign-born, initial census total (1)	Rough estimate of deaths (2)	Survivors (1–2) (3)	Estimated foreign born, end of decade (4)	% in country over 10 years (3 ÷ 4) (5)	% in country 10 years or less (100.0 – column 5) (6)
1870–80	5,494	998	4,496	6,638	67.7	32.3
1880–90	6,560	1,334	5,225	9,488	55.1	44.9
1890–1900	9,122	1,843	7,279	9,706	75.0	25.0
1900–10	10,214	1,783	8,431	13,370	63.1	36.9
1910–20	13,346	2,106	11,240	13,407	83.8	16.2
1920–30	13,713	2,212	11,502	14,228	80.8	19.2
1930–40	13,983	2,547	11,436	11,540	99.1	0.9

Because of rounding, detail will not necessarily add to total.

Column 1: Table 1.6, panel A, column 1.

Column 2: Derived from Tables B.4 and B.5. For 1870–1900, mortality of residents at the beginning of the period is estimated directly for males and females. For 1900–40, deaths, male and female, were distributed between foreign born in the country at the beginning of the period and net arrivals during the period on the assumption of the same death rate for both, and further adjusted to strict ten-year periods (see Table 1.6, note b). Column 4: Table 1.6, panel A, column 7.

recent arrivals, it obviously created a situation that had consequences in a variety of fields—relation between labor and capital, union organization, distribution of income, adaptability to environment, and the like. The sharp break occurred with World War I, and the transition was virtually completed with the 1930–40 decade of the Great Depression. By 1940, the proportion of recently arrived residents to either the total foreign-born population or the foreign-born labor force, and hence to total population or labor force, had dwindled to insignificance.

Contribution to Increase in Population and Labor Force

Having considered the magnitudes of the flows and their effect on the foreign-born population, we may conclude with a brief glance at their contribution to the increases in total population and in the labor force. Analysis of labor force estimates is beset with particular difficulties since the concepts and accuracy of enumeration shift from one census date to the next. No attempt has been made to improve the basic figures: the major conclusions would scarcely be affected, and the statistical adjustment of the census totals for gainfully engaged or labor force, subdivided by nativity status, would be extremely difficult.

Rather than study the customary proportionate shares of the foreign-born component in the total at successive census dates, we compare the *changes* in both. The question then is "How much of the increase in total population and labor force through the successive decades can be assigned to the increase in foreign born?" The increases in both total and foreign born are net: they are results of gross additions, by natural birth and immigration, and of drafts, by death and emigration. Furthermore, the calculation of the contribution of the foreign born is purely arithmetical; no attempt is made to guess what would have happened had there been no immigration and foreign born. The latter is practically impossible since immigration was such an important factor both in the internal growth of the country's economy and in its relations with the rest of the world; to visualize the course of events without it is beyond the imagination of an analyst. The experience of countries in the Western Hemisphere that, despite abundant natural resources, did not benefit from international migrations, may offer a clue. But since it would serve no useful purpose, we have not pursued the question here.

In the simpler and more tangible terms, the question is answered in Table 1.8. For both population and labor force, we derive changes from one census date to the next in the totals and in the foreign-born component (columns 1 and 2), and then take the ratio of change in foreign born to change in total. Since the changes in foreign born are much more variable than those in the total, the decade ratios of the former to the latter are also variable. We have, therefore, added the changes for two successive decade intervals and recalculated the ratios in column 6.

Obviously, a foreign-born person can become a resident of this country only by immigration; hence a net increase in foreign born that swells the country's increase in total population is the net residual effect on population of migration streams. Viewed in this light, Table 1.8 shows that in the 1850–60 decade, for example, close to one-quarter of the total increase in population was contributed by net immigration (in excess of deaths of already resident foreign born). If one may infer from the data for the later decades for which changes in both total population and the labor force are available, this would mean that in the early decades perhaps as much as a third of total additions to the labor force was contributed by net immigration. If we take a cumulative total from, say, 1870 to 1910, of the fifty-two million net increase in total population, about 7.9 million, or more than a seventh, was contributed by the increase in foreign born, and of the twenty-five million net increase in labor force, about five million, or a fifth, was contributed by the increase in foreign born. Thus, in purely arithmetical terms, let alone more far-reaching analytical implications, the share of the migration processes in the long-term increase in population and labor force is sufficiently large to merit thoroughgoing analysis.

Table 1.8 also confirms the impression conveyed by Table 1.3 that the largest proportional contributions of the migration streams to the growth of the economy occurred just before the Civil War. Thus, the peak share in panel A, column 3, is for the decade 1850–60, and it is quite likely that if both population and labor force were available by nativity classes for earlier periods, the secular peak ratio might have emerged in both the interval from 1840 to 1860.

Table 1.8 reveals the variations in the decade changes in both total and foreign-born components of population and labor force. Some of these changes are due to the use of census dates that do not mark off exactly equal time intervals, and we have made the necessary adjustments in Table 1.9. But even so, the additions to population and labor force do not form an even progression. The fluctuations in them

Table 1.8 Proportion of changes in foreign born to changes in total population and labor force, census intervals, 1860–1940 (absolute figures in millions)

	Change from preceding census year			Change from the second preceding census year		
Census year	Total (1)	Foreign born (2)	(2) as % of (1) (3)	Total (4)	Foreign born (5)	(5) as % of (4) (6)
A. Total population						
1860	8.25	1.89	22.9			
1870	8.37	1.43	17.1	16.63	3.32	20.0
1880	10.34	1.11	10.8	18.71	2.54	13.6
1890	12.79	2.57	20.1	23.13	3.68	15.9
1900	13.05	1.09	8.4	25.84	3.66	14.2
1910	15.98	3.17	19.9	29.02	4.27	14.7
1920	13.74	0.41	2.9	29.72	3.58	12.0
1930	17.06	0.28	1.7	30.80	0.69	2.2
1940	8.89	−2.61	−29.3	25.96	−2.33	-9.0
B. Gainfully occupied or labor force						
1880	4.88	0.79	16.2			
1890	5.35	1.61	30.1	10.23	2.40	23.5
1900	6.33	0.64	10.1	11.68	2.25	19.3
1910	8.30	2.07	24.9	14.63	2.71	18.5
1920	5.06	−0.06	−1.2	13.36	2.01	15.0
1930	6.40	−0.34	−5.3	11.46	−0.40	-3.5
1940	3.96	−1.61	−40.7	10.36	−1.95	−18.8

Source: Panel A, columns 1 and 4 from *Historical Statistics of the United States, 1789–1945,* Bureau of the Census, Series B, 2; columns 2 and 5 from ibid., Series B, 193. Panel B, columns 1, 2, 4, and 5 from Simon Kuznets and Raymond Goldsmith, *Income and Wealth of the United States, Trends and Structure, Income and Wealth,* Series II (Cambridge, England: International Association for Research in Income and Wealth, 1952), Table 44, 197.

reflect the long swings that affect not only migration but many other processes in the economy as well. In view of their importance, not only in the analysis of long swings in residential construction but also of these long alternations in the rate of secular growth of the economy at large, the few details in Table 1.9 may be of interest.

Here, after adjusting the absolute change to a strict per decade basis we calculated, wherever the changes in the successive decades were positive, link relatives (lines marked b) to see whether the rate of growth was steady. This simple analysis was carried through for several components of total population by nativity, and the results are illuminating. The additions to the native-born white population of native parentage show fluctuations from decade to decade similar in timing to, if narrower in amplitude than, those in the additions to foreign-born population (compare lines 1b and 4b). Swings in the foreign-born population clearly reflect long swings in gross and net immigration. Obviously, whatever conditions favored upswings in the rate of immigration also favored upswings in the rate of net additions to native-born population of native parentage, that is, essentially births to native-born parents. By contrast, fluctuations in addition to native-born population of foreign parentage differ in timing from those in addition to native born of native parentage or to foreign born—at least until the last decade (compare line 2b with lines 1b and 4b). There may be a significant lag of about one decade in the effect of additions to foreign born on additions to native born of foreign parentage. Hence upswings and downswings in addition to foreign born will be reflected in similar movements about a decade later in addition to native born of foreign parentage.

The effect on fluctuations in addition to *total* native-born whites, whether of foreign or native parentage, is curious (lines 3a and 3b). Since the swings in addition to native-born whites of foreign parentage lag one decade behind the swings in addition to foreign born, they also lag one decade behind the swings in addition to native-born whites of native parentage. The swings in addition to the two components of native-born whites, therefore, tend to cancel out, and, as a result, up to the 1930s, the series of additions to *total* native-born whites fluctuates least in its rate of growth from decade to decade (compare line 3b with the other b lines for population). Even additions to the entire population, which includes, besides the components in lines 1–4, the native-born nonwhites, show wider fluctuations in the rate of growth than additions to the narrower group of total native-born whites.

The mechanism by which long swings in addition to population were damped because of the lag between the swings in arrivals of foreign born and their effect on native born of foreign parentage is important to any analysis of the consequences to long cycles of residential construction, to the process of urbanization and territorial

Table 1.9 Absolute changes in population and labor force by nativity components on a strict decade basis, 1870–1940 (absolute figures in thousands)

Item	1870–80	1880–90	1890–1900	1900–10[a]	1910–20[a]	1920–30[a]	1930–40
Total population							
1a. Native-born whites, native parentage	5,404	6,661	7,271	9,138	9,722	12,420	13,464
1b. Link relative		123	109	126	106	128	108
2a. Native-born whites, foreign parentage	2,417	2,474	3,345	2,803	3,383	2,404	–2,484
2b. Link relative		102	135	84	121	71	–
3a. Total native-born whites (1a + 2a)	7,821	9,135	10,616	11,941	13,105	14,824	10,980
3b. Link relative		117	116	112	110	113	74
4a. Foreign born	929	2,570	1,091	3,215	417	276	–2,609
4b. Link relative		231	42	295	13	66	–
5a. Total population	10,338	12,792	13,047	16,179	14,152	16,648	8,894
5b. Link relative		124	102	124	87	118	53
Gainfully occupied or labor force							
6a. Native born (8a –7a)	4,090	3,740	5,690	6,309	5,274	6,576	5,570
6b. Link relative		91	152	111	84	125	85
7a. Foreign born	790	1,610	640	2,096	–62	–332	–1,610
7b. Link relative		204	40	328	–	–	–
8a. Total	4,880	5,350	6,330	8,405	5,212	6,244	3,960
8b. Link relative		110	118	133	62	120	63

[a]For factors used to adjust to a strict decade basis, see Table 1.6, note b.

Lines 1 and 2: Underlying data from *Statistical Abstract, 1931,* Table 7, 4, and *Statistical Abstract, 1946,* Table 33, 34. The 1870 figures are adjusted for undercount. Native-born whites of mixed parentage are apportioned half to native and half to foreign-born parentage.

Lines 4 and 7: Table 1.8, column 2. Population in 1870 is adjusted for undercount.

Lines 5 and 8: Table 1.8, column 1.

distribution, and the like. One point in this connection is that the damping effect ceased after 1920–30, so that in 1930–40 everything converged and additions to total population were reduced sharply. The bearing of the sharp decline in the rate of population growth upon the severity of the depression, at least in residential construction, is obvious.

The fluctuations in addition to the labor force raise some questions to which we have no easy answer. The changes in the foreign-born component are a direct and immediate reflection of changes in total foreign born, since new entries are largely of working age and promptly become members of the labor force. Consequently, the movements of entries in lines 7b and 4b are very similar, with one significant difference. The foreign born in the labor force show an absolute decline in advance of the total foreign-born population. This is due to changes in the character of immigration in the 1910s and particularly the 1920s and later: partly because of war but largely because of legislative changes, immigration became more a matter of bringing in relatives and dependents, and the ratio of males and of persons fit for or expecting to join the labor force dropped appreciably.

The puzzle lies in the fluctuations of additions to the native-born labor force. Offhand, one would expect these fluctuations to reflect those in addition to the native-born population (line 5b), with a two-decade lag: the former are largely affected by births, whose maturity and entrance into the labor force should not occur until after a lapse of about two decades. True, line 3b refers to whites only and line 6b to all races, and there are quirks in the definition and coverage of gainfully occupied and labor force from census date to census date that do not affect total population by nativity. But even so it is curious that the additions to the native-born labor force fall off in 1900–10 compared with 1890–1900, whereas additions to native-born whites are greater in 1880–90 than in 1870–80—an excess that would be even larger if the 1870 census figure of native-born whites was corrected for undercount. Likewise, the proportional additions to the native-born labor force rise from 1910–20 to 1920–30, whereas those to the total native-born population decline from 1890–1900 to 1900–10.

Whatever the explanation of the fluctuations in addition to the native-born component of the labor force, they serve to cancel some of the fluctuations in the additions to the foreign-born component—again at least until the last decade or two. While the cancellation of fluctuations here assumes a different locus than that in the case of total population, it again smoothes out fluctuations, in this case in addition to the total labor force (compare line 8b with lines 6b and 7b). Here also both components converge to produce a particularly sharp decline in additions in 1930–40 compared with those in 1920–30.

Part III
Statistical Methods and Problems

General Outline of Method

Three factors produce changes in the size of a given foreign-born population over a specified time interval: immigration, emigration, and mortality. The estimating equation may be given as

$$P_n = P_0 - \sum_0^n (M_{P_0}) + \sum_0^n (i-e) - \sum_0^n (M_{i-e}),$$

where

P_n = population after interval of n years

P_0 = original population

$\sum_0^n (M_{P_0})$ = mortality occurring in original population in n years

$\sum_0^n (i-e)$ = net difference over n years between immigration (i) and emigration (e)

$\sum_0^n (M_{i-e})$ = mortality occurring in net migration total for n years.

For maximum accuracy, it would be desirable to use the smallest possible subdivision of the n-year interval: apply annual death rates, on an age-specific basis, to the foreign-born population, and use a sequence of annual migration estimates. But mortality data are not available on an annual basis. Furthermore, in computing the mortality of net migration, we had to apply rates that pertain to the foreign-born whites already in the country. Theoretically at least, a different set of mortality rates is needed for this immigrant group, but it is not available.

The method of annual estimation, even if annual mortality rates were available, would require an inordinate amount of labor and time. It is doubtful whether the results would be substantially more accurate and worthwhile than those obtained by a simplified procedure that preserves the fundamental aspects of the basic method. To reduce extensive computations, a system of centering was adopted. It was assumed, for the decades 1900–30, that the following procedure for centering net immigration during the decade would not do violence to the facts: (a) calculate survivors of the foreign-born population at the beginning of a decade for three years, using rates reflecting mortality for this period; (b) redistribute the surviving population into the usual census age-groups and add net immigration occurring in the first quinquennium of the decade in question; (c) calculate survivors of the population obtained by the addition in (b) for a four-year interval using rates that approximate mortality for this particular interval; (d) redistribute the surviving population obtained in (c) into the regular census age-groups and add the net immigration occurring in the second quinquennium of the decade; (e) calculate survivors of the population obtained in (d) for the last three-year interval, using rates reflecting mortality for this period; and (f) redistribute the surviving population obtained in (e) into census age-groups (see Table B.3 for sequence of operations for males, 1920–30).

For 1930–40, the total volume of recorded migration was very small and almost balanced out completely for the decade. Consequently for this decade, we assumed that net immigration could be centered at the midpoint, reducing the number of operations required.

For the decades 1870–1900, the survival ratios used for the foreign-born whites are based on extrapolation of English life tables over this period. In view of the approximate nature of these ratios, a simplification of the procedure similar to that for the 1930–40 decade was adopted. Five- and ten-year survival ratios were prepared for each decade. The entire foreign-born white population at the beginning of the census period was survived for ten years, for example, from 1870 to 1880 using the appropriate ten-year survival ratios. Net migration during the 1870–80 decade was centered at the midpoint, 1875, and survived for five years, that is, to 1880. Both survived groups were then combined to give the estimated foreign-born white population of 1880. Since net migration was somewhat heavier in the first quinquennium than that in the second for each decade between 1870 and 1900, this method tends to underestimate slightly foreign-born mortality. However, we felt that further refinement of centering was not warranted.

Census Data on Foreign-Born Population

Race

For the entire period, only the foreign-born whites in continental United States are considered. This is at variance with the migration statistics that include all foreign born (whites and nonwhites) and certain possessions outside continental United States. In the 1930 census, Mexicans were returned as nonwhite although in all the other censuses from 1870 to 1940 they were regarded as white. For the purpose of this analysis, the revised 1930 census returns, showing Mexicans as whites, were used.

Foreign-born nonwhites and foreign born in territorial possessions were excluded from analysis because consistent treatment was impossible and particularly because adequate mortality data were not available. But the omission is small relative to all foreign-born whites or to the total migration streams. The census figure of foreign born in 1930, when it was at its highest, was 14.2 million (see *Historical Statistics of the United States, 1789–1945,* Bureau of the Census, Series B 193, p. 30), and the total of whites (including Mexicans) was 14.0 million: nor did any significant part of the stream of foreign migrants flow to the territorial possessions.

Treatment of Transients

Prior to the census of 1930, the written instructions to enumerators did not indicate any explicit limitation on the count of the foreign born in the United States.[19] In 1930, the following instruction was observed:[20] "502. *Foreigners temporarily in the United States*—Foreigners visiting in the United States for a purely temporary period are not to be enumerated unless they are employed here. If they are working they are to be enumerated no matter how short their intended stay." The census of 1930 does not indicate how many foreign born, here temporarily, were employed. A modification of this instruction for the enumeration of the foreign born was adopted for the 1940 census.[21] Essentially, the count of foreign born in 1930 and 1940 referred to the resident foreign-born population, that is, naturalized citizens[22] and immigrants. It is also likely that some aliens, temporarily or illegally in the United States in 1930 and 1940, were also enumerated while some foreign-born residents were missed in the census operation. Aliens who had temporarily left the country prior to January 1, 1920, were not enumerated in the 1920 census because "... nothing definite can be known as to whether such aliens intend to return"; a similar instruction applied to the 1930 census.[23]

It is fairly clear that enumerations in the censuses of 1930 and 1940 represent primarily the foreign-born resident in this country while in previous censuses they include nonresident foreign born. This discontinuity is directly related to the development of the immigration laws. Prior to 1921, when the first immigration quota act was passed, the difference between foreign born permanently in the United States and those here for temporary residence had no real basis in law: except for special minor classes, aliens were admitted to the United States with no restriction on their *intended* length of stay. The admission of an alien for temporary or permanent residence became a matter of law as a result of the quota system. Aliens admitted temporarily, that is, as nonimmigrants, subsequent to the Quota Immigration Act of 1924, who overstayed the period for which they were admitted, were subject to deportation.[24] Thus, the nonenumeration of foreign born in the United States who were in fact nonimmigrants and were required to leave after a temporary stay in this country was a justifiable procedure in the 1930 and 1940 censuses.

This varying definition of foreign born in the successive censuses compelled certain decisions in our statistical analysis concerning the treatment of migration flows. For all decades prior to 1920–30, we used arrivals of all alien passengers, whether immigrants or nonimmigrants, and departures of all aliens, whether emigrants or nonemigrants. This procedure would have been followed for most decades in any case, since migration data distinguish immigrants and emigrants from other aliens only from 1908 onward. But regardless of lack of data, this distinction was unrealistic and inconsistent with census definitions of foreign born prior to the census of 1930. Only for 1920–30 and 1930–40 could we, and did we, use migration of immigrants and emigrants alone.

Age and Sex

The census data on age and sex of foreign-born population are quite detailed and present no particular difficulties in the application of the procedures employed here.

Undercounts and Errors

The starting point of this investigation is 1870. "The Census of 1870 was very deficient in the Southern States, and it has since been demonstrated by the census officials that the population in 1870 was approximately 39,818,449, instead of 38,558,371, as given in the report of the census."[25] Although this underenumeration occurred primarily in the South, the foreign-born population of 1870 may also have been underenumerated. The geographic distribution of the foreign born in the United States would suggest that, proportionally, the underenumeration for this class was less than that for the native population. Criticism of the 1890 census count of Italians indicated substantial underenumeration for this group.[26] This study corroborates Richard Mayo-Smith's conclusion as to probable underenumeration of the foreign born in the 1890 census.[27]

The general character of census data must always be kept in mind. For example, census enumeration of the population over the seventy-year period reflects changes not only in the nature of the instructions and training of enumerators, but also in the quality of the enumerators. Prior to 1900, the Census Bureau was not a continuing agency but was set up every ten years for the sole purpose of taking the decennial census. This meant complete changes in personnel, type of instruction, and kind of enumerators. There were no training periods for enumerators comparable to those for the censuses of 1930 and 1940. Assistant marshals who were appointed to do these jobs were selected on a political rather than competence basis. It is, of course, impossible to measure the magnitude of the errors introduced into the data by untrained enumerators.

Furthermore, the accuracy of information supplied by respondents probably improved as the educational level of the general population rose during this seventy-year period. Errors in reporting age, nativity, or other characteristics of the population obviously affected the census data. Thus, some foreign-born persons illegally in the United States probably were enumerated while some foreign born legally in the country were not or were returned as native born. Presumably a small number of native-born persons were identified erroneously as foreign born.

Migration Data

General Organization and Character

From 1866 until 1892, the Bureau of Statistics in the Treasury Department published annually the statistics of immigration based upon the returns furnished by the various customs districts of the United States.[28] For 1893, 1894, and 1895, the Bureau of Statistics continued to compile these data although the publication of migration statistics had been transferred to the Office of Superintendent of Immigration, Treasury Department, beginning with the fiscal year 1892. It was in 1892 that the Immigration Service was founded as a separate bureau, distinct from the Customs Service that previously had been enforcing the immigration laws.

This administrative change led to various modifications in the statistical reporting. The figures on the movement of aliens to and from the United States published by the Bureau of Statistics were apparently more complete than those of the Bureau of Immigration if only because the former included cabin passengers in its statistics.[29] For the years for which we have two sets of data, 1892–95, the Bureau of Statistics total exceeds that of the Bureau of Immigration by 208,000, or about 13 percent. We used the Bureau of Statistics data as long as they were available and, starting with 1895, used the Bureau of Immigration data.

Cabin passengers were first included with immigrants in 1904. Prior to that time, only aliens traveling as steerage passengers were classified as immigrants; the category of nonimmigrants probably included cabin passengers, but this is not certain.[30]

While the reporting of persons arriving in the United States has been required by law since 1819, official information on departures was not gathered until 1907. For this study, it was necessary to *estimate* departures of foreign born for 1870–1907 (see section Estimating Departures of Aliens, 1870–1907 below).

Beginning in 1908, data on migration of the alien foreign born are given for four classes: (a) immigrants—persons coming to the United States for permanent residence, (b) nonimmigrants—persons coming for temporary stay, (c) emigrants—persons who came as immigrants but are departing to take up residence abroad, and (d) nonemigrants—persons who have permanent residence in this country and who are departing for a temporary stay abroad, and also persons who came here as nonimmigrants and are returning to their permanent residence abroad.

Estimating Departures of Aliens, 1870–1907

For the period prior to 1908, the annual reports published data, furnished by courtesy of the steamship companies, on passengers departing. In order to estimate foreign born departing (assuming total coverage by the steamship companies of departures other than border crossings), it was first necessary to subtract the number of U.S. citizens from the total of departing passengers. For 1870–1900, the former were estimated by examining statistics of passenger arrivals, which indicate the number of arriving U.S. citizens, and by assuming, with regard to the citizens, that (a) average time spent abroad was one year, (b) their median age was thirty-five (in order to estimate mortality abroad), and (c) a small percentage (0.5 percent) remained abroad permanently. It will be recalled that this category comprises native and naturalized citizens. This method, admittedly crude, is somewhat more accurate than assuming that the number of departures of U.S. citizens is equal on the average to the number of arrivals.

The method just described was used for the period 1870–1900 and is restricted to emigration by water. For the decade 1900–10, a different procedure was followed. Estimates of emigrants for 1900–7 were obtained on the assumption that this class was comparable to recorded emigration for 1908–14. (After 1914, World War I and the quota acts of 1921 and 1924 introduced distortions that affected the trend.) We therefore applied the ratios of departures to arrivals, available for 1908–14, to the data on arrivals for 1900–7 (the ratios were 0.409 for males and 0.172 for females).

Scope of Data: Reporting Area

The acquisition of insular possessions, as well as changes in ports of entry in the United States, has affected the internal comparability of the migration statistics. Thus, starting with 1870, the statistics include Alaska as a port of entry of the United States.[31] Prior to 1892, arrivals are recorded only for water ports of entry of continental United States and Alaska. An important addition was made in 1894: immigrants to the United States who arrived by way of Canadian seaports were included. Honolulu, Hawaii Territory, became a port of entry in 1901 and San Juan, Puerto Rico, in 1902. In 1904, Ketchikan, Alaska, was made a port of entry, and land border ports of entry were established on the Mexican and Canadian borders. The Philippine Islands are shown as a port of entry in 1910, but statistics for this port are not included in the official totals. The migration data used in this report include, therefore, migration to and from the extracontinental territories described above. However, the lack of strict comparability over time and the inconsistency with the census coverage of foreign born have no appreciable significance.

Two other problems of scope are much more important. The first bears upon the number of ports for entry and for departure. The immigration data for 1870–92 are based on the statistics gathered at the various customs districts of the United States by customs inspectors. The annual reports prior to 1892 indicate considerable differences in number between ports listed for entry and for departure. For example, the Annual Report of 1870 shows forty-two customs districts as points of entry, but only twenty customs districts as points of departure.[32] Likewise the Annual Statement of 1880[33] lists thirty-nine customs districts for arriving passengers but only twenty-two customs districts for departing passengers.

Since departures were voluntarily reported by the steamship companies, the foregoing suggests understatement of emigration compared with immigration. But the differential bias is minor. In 1870 and 1880, customs districts are listed for arriving passengers that do not appear for departing passengers. The customs districts for which departures are given reported 85.7 percent of the recorded arrivals in 1870 and 78.1 percent of the recorded arrivals in 1880. Even as the figures stand, the possible underestimate of departures is not fatal. But it should be further reduced because departures may well be more concentrated in a few ports than arrivals, and in some instances, the statistics of departures by customs district may represent administrative consolidation. On balance, estimated departures may still be understated and therefore the true shortages of census enumerations of foreign born may be smaller than they appear.

However, the major problem is the flow across the land boundaries (not recorded until recently except for arrivals since 1894 via Canadian ports destined for the United States). Immigration from Canada and Mexico was inadequately reported for the decade 1870–80 since the reports do not reflect land border movements but refer only to entry by water. For the period 1880–85, the immigration statistics of the United States indicate that about 393,000 foreign-born persons came from Canada and 2,000 from Mexico. Approximately 380,000 aliens passed through Canada en route to the United States during the years 1885–90 and are not included in the reported statistics.[34]

Canadian immigration statistics indicate that for the period 1881–90, 527,000 persons came from the United States as the country of last residence.[35] According to the Canadian census, very few of this number could have been U.S. citizens.[36] Even a figure of five hundred thousand for foreign born who went to Canada from the United States is too high since *total* Canadian population increased only five hundred thousand between 1881 and 1891.

Data on foreign born entering the United States are incomplete for part of the 1890–1900 decade since they exclude aliens who landed in Canada and subsequently entered the United States.[37] For the calendar years 1890 and 1891, according to Canadian statistics, there were 104,000 and 105,000 such immigrants. The 1894 report included this group for the first time,[38] although the 1893 report states that in addition to 440,000 immigrants indicated as the official total, ". . . 28,108 immigrants arrived at Boston from Dominion of Canada . . . ."[39] With regard to border-crossers of Canadian or Mexican nationality, there are no data available in the migration reports for this decade. Border-crossing inspections were instituted in the United States in 1904.

Improvement in the statistics of border migration was gradual, increased by the need to police the borders after the Quota Acts of 1921 and 1924. An Immigration Border Patrol, operating on both the Canadian and Mexican borders, was created in 1924–25. Additional land border ports of entry were added after 1904, and more accurate migration data became possible. For this report, border-crossing net migration had to be estimated on the basis of the migration data and the censuses for 1870–1900, but for lack of data, this adjustment could not be incorporated in the continuous and detailed decade-to-decade analysis.

Minor Questions of Scope

Race. The migration statistics include all races, and nonwhites cannot be subtracted. Nonwhite net migration, however, is a small percentage of total in 1870–80, perhaps the most important decade for nonwhite immigration since the Chinese Exclusion Act became law in 1882: approximately 120,000 Chinese, almost all males, arrived in the United States. The censuses of 1870 and 1880 indicate an increase in Chinese foreign born in the United States of forty-one thousand; that is, there were 63,000 in the United States in 1870 and 104,000 in 1880.

Seamen. Foreign-born seamen who entered the United States and became part of the population are not included in the migration statistics. Statistics on the crews of foreign vessels entering and departing from the United States are available for 1870–76 and then were discontinued.[40] The annual reports of the Immigration Service since the early 1900s refer to the problem of deserting alien seamen.

Under the Quota Act of 1924, alien seamen are admitted as nonimmigrants but are not counted in the statistics for this group. Although all alien seamen reported as deserters did not actually remain in the United States, at least before 1924, this group does represent a net addition to the foreign-born population since 1870. There is no way of estimating the magnitude of this factor.

Miscellany. In addition to the illegal entrants and the unrecorded departures, there are groups for which statistical data exist, although not as part of the official migration statistics. For example, deportees (some of them "voluntary departures") may include persons who have been counted in censuses of the foreign born, yet their departures are not registered in the outflow statistics, whether of immigrants or of nonimmigrants. Prior to the 1920s, however, these classes were unimportant quantitatively. Special cases also exist of laborers imported into the United States during World Wars I and II, under emergency legislation, who are not included in immigration statistics.

All the groups covered in this section should have been accounted for, but no continuous data exist. Hence, as in the case of the far more important movements across the Canadian and Mexican borders, we can make adjustments only for some decades (see section Problems of Reconciliation below).

Distribution by Sex

Data on arrivals are given separately for males and females throughout the period. But no such information is available for total alien departures, which we estimated prior to 1908. We applied a constant factor of 0.828 to determine the number of *male* departures, a ratio estimated on the basis of the official data for 1908–14 and the sex distribution of the immigrant flows for 1900–7. The use of this constant ratio may have introduced errors into our estimate prior to 1908 and consequently affected the derived numbers of foreign-born males and females. But the preponderance of males among departures has been a constant characteristic of the out-migration streams during the periods for which data are available. Furthermore, about 75 percent of total departures of noncabin passengers for the period 1870–1902 were males.[41] Since departures of native-born U.S. citizens were not likely to be as heavily dominated by males as those of foreign born, these data tend to confirm the high level of the ratio used for the period prior to 1908. Nor do the Ferenczi data indicate any marked variations in the ratio.

Age Classes

Statistics on the age distribution of migrant aliens to and from the United States for 1870–1940 have varied considerably. For immigrants data are available for the following age-groups in the annual reports:[42]

A similar grouping is available for nonimmigrant arrivals since 1870 and for departing aliens since 1908. For naturalized citizens departing from the United States the age distribution data are very meager. Data for this class were first collected in 1918 and published each year until 1932; thereafter, information has appeared irregularly. No information on arrivals of naturalized citizens has been reported.

Obviously, the distribution of the migration data into five-year age-groups comparable to the census classification, especially for the period 1870–1924 when only three broad age-groups were given, is no easy matter. A study was made of the age characteristics of immigrants, based on detailed data from foreign sources for most of the period under discussion. The method of cumulative distribution was finally adopted to obtain the necessary age class intervals, and the results were checked against alternative sets of data to insure consistency.[43]

The age distribution of foreign-born persons leaving the country, first reported in 1908, is given in detail after 1925. It was possible, however, to develop evidence on the characteristics of departing aliens after 1908, for example, length of residence in the United States. These data suggest that the median age of departing aliens is significantly higher than that of arriving aliens. Two facts explain this difference: (a) proportionately fewer alien children under fourteen years of age and (b) proportionately more adults who are forty-five years old and

Period	Age–groups	Number of groups
1870–98	Under 15, 15–40, and 41 years and over	3
1899–1917	Under 14, 14–44, and 45 years and over	3
1918–24	Under 16, 16–44, and 45 years and over	3
1925–39	Under 16, 16–21, 22–29, 30–37, 38–44, and 45 years and over	6
1940–44	Under 11, 11–15, 16–20, 21–25, 26–30, 31–35, 36–40, 41–45, 46–50, 51–55, 56–60, and 61 years and over	12

over depart than enter the United States. In 1900–10, the middle decade of the period covered in this study, the median age of departing males was 28.9 years and of departing females, 27.8, while the median ages of the respective arrival groups were 26.6 and 23.7.[44]

The age distribution of departing aliens for years prior to 1908 was based on that reported for 1908–14. Here again the use of a constant base applied to a period of almost forty years may have introduced errors. But departures are, with some lag, reflections of arrivals, and the age distribution of arrivals has, on the whole, been relatively constant. Finally, in the earlier decades, when departures were small fractions of arrivals, errors in either the sex or age distribution of the former would have had limited effect on the sex and age distribution of the estimated foreign-born population at the end of a decade.

Biases in the Migration Data

It should be clear from the discussion above that the migration data, for most of the period covered in the analysis, are for a somewhat changing area of coverage and subject to serious biases. The major defect is the exclusion of movements across land borders and incomplete coverage even of arrivals and departures by sea. In addition to these difficulties, adequate data on sex and age of emigrants prior to 1908 are lacking.

Yet this recital of inconsistencies and gaps should not exaggerate their possible effects on the broad estimates of migration flows and survivals. Both arrivals and departures may suffer from undercount, but the absolute magnitude of the latter in the net balance probably did not constitute a large relative error in the decades when net immigration was substantial (i.e., prior to 1930), and in the later years, when immigration was more limited, the available data were much more complete. The deficiencies of sex and age data for departures prior to 1908 are of limited consequence since departures were until after 1900 small fractions of arrivals, since the unknown age structure of the former is determined in large part by the known structure of the latter and since deaths of the *net* balance of migration during a decade are small compared with deaths calculated for the initial census population of foreign born.

These comments are not intended to minimize the defects of the data or the consequent possible errors in the estimates, but rather to suggest a perspective in evaluating them.

Mortality Data and Methods

Data for 1900–40

For 1900–40 mortality data of the foreign-born white population, by age and sex, are based on the death registration area of the United States. This area has varied considerably because federal mortality statistics have depended upon agreement by the individual states. Thus, the "original registration states" of 1900 included only Maine, New Hampshire, Vermont, Massachusetts, Rhode Island, Connecticut, New York, New Jersey, Indiana, Michigan, and the District of Columbia.[45] This area represented 27 percent of the total population of the United States in 1900 and about 44 percent of the foreign-born white population. Ten years later, in 1910, the registration area comprised twenty states and the District of Columbia and constituted more than half the total population and close to 80 percent of the foreign-born white population.[46] By 1920, the death registration area included thirty-four states and the District of Columbia, representing 82 percent of the total population and 92 percent of the foreign-born white population.[47] In 1930, the death registration area of the country was complete except for Texas, which entered in 1933.

Obviously, until 1940, the death rates of the foreign-born white population are based on samples of varying size and representativeness. These samples of the foreign-born universe, however, are quite large and should yield fairly reliable age-specific rates between census dates. These rates should approximate mortality experience within a decade, provided that no special circumstance affecting mortality existed at the terminal points of the census period or during the interval between them. Except during 1910–20, when undue mortality resulted from the influenza epidemic of 1918 and possibly from casualties in the armed forces during World War I, this condition was satisfied.

Estimation of Mortality for 1870–1900

Adequate mortality data of the foreign-born white population for 1890 are not available;[48] and for the 1870 and 1880 decades, there is no information, official or otherwise, on age-specific death rates of the foreign-born whites.

Prof. Dorothy S. Thomas of the University of Pennsylvania has carefully examined the problem of estimating foreign-born white mortality in the United States for the period 1870–1900. The following quotation from an unpublished memorandum indicates the procedure she developed.

> In view of the faulty life tables available for the United States prior to 1900, there is no easy solution to the problem of estimating the trend and levels of foreign born mortality from 1870 to the turn of the century. Three possible procedures were considered:
>
> 1. To utilize the Massachusetts mortality data, for the whole period, with perhaps differential weights.
>
> 2. To estimate trends from census survival ratios for native whites[49] for the period 1870–1900 after adjusting them to a lower level for foreign-born whites by applying a correction based on the differences between survival ratios computed from Grove–Linder data for, say, 1900–1910.
>
> 3. To utilize "reliable" life tables from some other country for the earlier period, if it could be demonstrated that the foreign series followed the trends of the Grove-Linder series during some overlapping period in the twentieth century and if the foreign milieu and economic development were not too dissimilar from the American during this earlier period.
>
> The first possibility was rejected, partly because of its unrepresentativeness, partly because of its internal inconsistency.
>
> The second possibility was rejected, partly because of a desire to have independent estimates made by the life table procedure applied to both stock and flow for comparison with other procedures where *census* survival ratios were applied to *census* data alone. Moreover, census survival ratios are extremely unreliable indicators of *trends* during this early period, because of under-enumeration in both 1870 and 1890, which was greater at the former than at the latter date.
>
> In lieu of any better possibility, the use of foreign series was thoroughly explored. The longest, most consistent, and unquestionably the most reliable series available are the Swedish, but, unfortunately for our purpose, Sweden's socio-economic development during the late nineteenth century differed markedly from our own, particularly in respect to its late industrialization and slow urbanization. Even by 1900, less than 45 percent of its population was dependent on nonagricultural pursuits for a livelihood, and the proportion of its population living in towns and cities represented only 22 percent. Moreover, Sweden's gain in expectation of life exceeded that of most other European countries during the second half of the nineteenth century, i.e. there was a markedly more rapid rate of

decline in age-specific mortality. Following a suggestion of Dublin and Lotka, we decided that it would be "a fair presumption that the earlier English life tables would also represent approximately the conditions of mortality in the United States at the corresponding epoch" (Dublin, Louis I. *Length of Life: A Study of the Life Table*, Ronald Press Company, 1936, p. 45). It seemed appropriate to test this suggestion for application to the foreign-born series in view of the high degree of urbanization of our foreign-born population (and of the English population) and of the ethnic composition of our "old immigration" (i.e., the heavy weighting with British elements prior to 1890). Moreover, English life tables for the period with which we were concerned had been prepared under the expert guidance of Farr and of George King. We therefore computed 10-year survival ratios for the following official English life tables: 1871–1880, 1881–1890, 1891–1900, 1901–1910, 1910–1912, and 1920–1922.

Detailed comparisons of the English and foreign born survival ratios for each sex, age group by age group, indicate that the slopes are highly similar for the first decade of the twentieth century. For the second decade the English survival ratios flatten out for some ages while the American continue to rise, and vice versa. For all ages up to 70–74, and for both sexes, the English survival ratios were, for comparable periods, appreciably higher than were those for foreign born whites in the 1900 registration area. In view of the similarity of slope for the first decade of the twentieth century, and the relative constancy in the difference between levels, we lowered the English stationary population for each of the nineteenth century decades by applying to each age-sex group through ages 55–59 the ratio of the stationary population in the English tables of 1901–1910 to the stationary population in our foreign born tables of 1900–1910, and then computed survival ratios for the adjusted series. We accepted these as estimates of the trend in our foreign born series from 1870–1880 through 1890–1900. For ages 60 and over, we computed ratios as above, but extrapolated the adjusted English stationary population for 1890–1900 backward to 1870–1880, i.e. we assumed there was no trend in survival for these age groups during the two earliest decades. In order to obtain an indication of the extent of error of estimate, the English series were projected forward to 1910 by applying the correction ratios to the observed English values for 1910–1912. The discrepancy between estimate and observation was consistently a very slight one, except for the terminal age groups.

We know of no way in which we can adequately test the validity of our estimates, since the reason for making these estimates was that we had no series for the area, time period, and population groups which would show their actual patterns and trends of mortality.

> Our estimates do seem to make sense and, in general, to reflect the trend of increasing survival, which we believe occurred in highly industrialized countries during the late nineteenth century. On this basis, we can probably justify their use, except for the very first and the last two or three age-groups. There were so few foreign-born children under 10 years of age that the rates are unreliable, although the trend for this group is not unreasonable. Correspondingly, the estimated survival ratios for ages 55–59 (age at beginning of decade) through 70–74 (age at end of decade) are probably not too bad. The estimated ratios for ages 75 and over (age at end of decade) are, however, subject to wide margins of error, for this is an "open-end" age-group, the composition of which undoubtedly varied greatly from the nineteenth century English standard and varied greatly for the foreign-born white series from one decade to another during the twentieth century. It would probably have been better to have omitted the very young and the very old from all computations, but this could not have been done in a straightforward manner and would have required further estimates based on further insecure premises. Inasmuch as the numbers involved in initial and terminal ages are relatively unimportant for most of the period considered, no great distortion will result by use of our estimated ratios. With the aging of the foreign born over time, however, it is well to be on the alert for bizarre patterns of migration estimated on the basis of terminal ratios.

Calculating the Survival Ratios

To estimate the number of survivors of a given population by specified age-groups over a period of years, survival ratio tables, based on age-specific death rates, are necessary. The calculation of survival ratios depends upon the stationary population by single years of age as given in life tables, and life tables are based on the mortality experience of the population for a given time period. Such tables, based on the mortality experience of the foreign-born white population for the period 1870–1940, had to be prepared in the estimation process.

Various techniques have been developed for making life tables based on age-specific death rates. The Doering–Forbes method has been followed throughout this study.[50] Before their formulas could be applied, the age-specific death rates, given for the terminal points of each decade, had to be adjusted to reflect mortality throughout the decade. For 1930–40 when net immigration was extremely light, two life tables were prepared, for 1930–35 and for 1935–40. Average age-specific death rates were obtained for the first quinquennium by weighting the 1930 rates by three and the 1940 rates by one, for the second quinquennium by weighting the 1940 rates by three and the 1930 rates by one.

For 1900–30, however, net immigration was a substantial factor, and specific death rates for foreign born were available; consequently, three life tables were prepared for each decade. Each decade was split into three periods, for example, the 1920–30 into 1920–23, 1923–27, and 1927–30, that is, three-year, four-year, and three-year periods. Average age-specific death rates for these three periods, based on the actual terminal death rates of the decade, were obtained by weighting as follows: for the three-year period 1920–23, the 1920 rates were multiplied by seven and the 1930 rates by three; for the four-year period 1923–27, the terminal decade rates were simply averaged; for the three-year period 1927–30, the 1930 rates were multiplied by seven and the 1920 rates by three. For the period 1870–1900, survival ratios based on Dr. Thomas's approximations derived from English life tables were applied, as described in section General Outline of Method, above. Table B.2 shows the generally upward trend in five-year survival ratios for selected periods from 1870 to 1940.

Having determined the necessary age-specific death rates, we constructed abridged life tables, using the Doering–Forbes formulas to convert to a stationary population for specific age intervals. The tabulation on page 64 gives an example of such a life table.

In this tabulation, the data are given for ten-year age-groups, except for the age-groups 0–1, 1–4, and 85 and over. However, the age distribution of the foreign-born white population is given by five-year age-groups in the censuses. To compute survival ratios for the five-year age-groups, stationary population values (L_x) for single years were derived in the following manner. The stationary population by age-groups was plotted on an equal area basis.[51] The x-axis represents the number of years in an age-group, and the y-axis represents the frequency for that age-group, per year; the area formed by multiplying the height by the base is a rectangle corresponding to the frequency (L_x) for that age-group. By joining the midpoints of the upper bases of these rectangles, we drew an L_x curve on which approximately the same area was added to the rectangle to the left of the midpoint as was subtracted from the rectangle to its right. From this curve, yearly L_x values were estimated by taking the midpoint between two successive years. The estimates were adjusted by subtraction from or addition to the L_x values for age-groups given in the abridged life table. Part

Abridged life table of foreign-born white females, 1920–23

Age-group	Death rate m_x^{x+h}	Number alive at the beginning of age-group l_x	Stationary population L_x^{x+h}	Deaths d_x^{x+h}	Stationary population in year of age and all later years T_x
0–1	.0710	100,000	94,178[a]	7,100	5,573,656
1–4	.0141	92,900	368,578	5,197	5,479,478
5–14	.0026	87,703	865,775	2,251	5,110,900
15–24	.0043	85,452	836,535	3,597	4,245,125
25–34	.0057	81,855	795,868	4,536	3,408,590
35–44	.0068	77,319	747,766	5,085	2,612,722
45–54	.0115	72,234	683,064	7,855	1,864,956
55–64	.0244	64,379	573,788	14,000	1,181,892
65–74	.0545	50,379	395,906	21,577	608,104
75–84	.1179	28,802	181,202	21,363	212,198
85 and over	.2400	7,439	30,996	7,439	30,996
Check line			5,573,656	100,000	

[a]Doering–Forbes corrective factor of 18 percent was used.

Source: Based on 1920 and 1930 rates given by Forrest E. Linder and Robert D. Grove, *Vital Statistics Rates in the United States,* 1900–40, Bureau of the Census (1943), 186–87.

Yearly stationary population values, females, 1920–23

Year of age	L_x
20–21	83,798
21–22	83,448
22–23	83,048
23–24	82,648
24–25	82,348
25–26	81,687

of the life table for foreign-born females for single years, 1920–23, is given in the accompanying tabulation.

The next step in the computation was to prepare the *survival* ratios, which indicate the proportion of persons within a given age range expected to survive the next year of life. To find the survival ratio of persons in the age-group 20–21, the ratio L_{x+h}/L_x is used, that is, in the above case 83,448 ÷ 83,798, or 0.99582. This means that 0.99582 of the number of females between twenty and twenty-one years of age can be expected to reach the interval between twenty-one and twenty-two years of age.

Survival ratios for five-year age-groups were then calculated. Thus, the single years of the stationary population L_x had to be summed in series as follows:

$$L_{0-1} + L_{1-2} + L_{2-3} + L_{3-4} + L_{4-5} = L_{0-5}$$

$$L_{1-2} + L_{2-3} + L_{3-4} + L_{4-5} + L_{5-6} = L_{1-6}, \text{ and so on}$$

The proportion of persons in age-groups 0–5 expected to survive for one year is given by the ratio L_{1-6}/L_{0-5}; expected to survive for two years, L_{2-7}/L_{0-5}, and so on. This procedure was applied in the same way to all the five-year age-groups. To illustrate, the L_x's in the foregoing tabulation are summed from twenty to twenty-five years, giving L_{20-25} = 415,290, and from twenty-one to twenty-six years, giving L_{21-26} = 413,179. The ratio L_{21-26}/L_{20-25} = 0.99492 means that this proportion of the number of persons in the age-group 20–25 years can be expected to survive for one year. A modification of the method, using the *T* value (stationary population in year of age and all later years), was applied to the terminal age-group, for example, eighty-five years and over.

Effects of Possible Errors in Mortality Data

The mortality data for the foreign born may contain sizable errors, and their possible effects on our calculations should be considered.

First, we have assumed that English life tables for 1870–1900 adequately reflect trends in foreign-born white mortality in the United States. We have thus incorporated whatever defects the English series have. There is no way of knowing whether, by using these data, we have made an error and, if so, in what direction or in what order of magnitude. The method of surviving has, however, resulted in low estimates for the younger age-groups.

Second, the mortality data refer either directly or indirectly to the already resident foreign-born population. Yet we have to apply them to the net balance of arrivals or departures, the latter also largely composed of recent arrivals. If, as is possible, mortality for the same sex and age classes is greater among recent arrivals than among foreign born who have been in the country for some time, we are underestimating mortality and overestimating survivors at the end of the decade.

Third, in our calculations we average death rates given for successive points of time. This is a point of some importance in view of the erratic fluctuations in the rates. When the rates are averaged, such fluctuations may be at least partly ironed out.

Fourth, in the age structure of both resident and newly arriving foreign-born population, the very young groups—for which death rates are rather erratic and perhaps less adequate than for the adult groups—have comparatively little weight. Hence even sizable errors in the death rates for these groups would have little effect on the total estimated foreign-born population at the end of a decade.

Finally, and perhaps most important, deaths are a relatively limited variable, compared with the others in the estimating equation: resident foreign-born population at the beginning of a decade, and arrivals and departures during the decade. In all the decades before 1920 or even 1930, initial population and the migratory flows during the decades are overwhelmingly larger than the calculated deaths. It follows that fairly sizable proportional errors in the estimates of deaths can have only a very limited effect on the proportional errors in the final estimate of the foreign-born population at the end of a decade.

Problems of Reconciliation

In the systematic calculations carried through for each decade, certain specific gaps and defects in the data could not be corrected since the necessary data could be found only for some decades. These deficiencies are listed here, and an attempt is made to appraise their importance. Although the adjustments for these defects cannot be fully utilized in the continuous series discussed in Part II, they do bring into sharper focus the picture of the consistency (or lack of consistency) between the estimates (and hence migration and mortality data) and the census enumerations of foreign born.

Table 1.10 provides a full summary; a comparison of the enumerated totals and the estimated totals from the continuous systematic calculations described in the earlier sections (the top three lines), and then the various items for which discontinuous adjustments, with a rough breakdown by sex, can be made. In general, the census enumerations tend to run short of the adjusted estimates, confirming the repeated claim that the census underenumerates foreign-born residents in this country. Indeed, in only three of the fourteen comparisons is the enumerated total larger than the adjusted estimate and, in those, only slightly. However, the differences are not large, at most about 7 percent for males and much less for females.

The adjustments reduce the discrepancy between the estimated and enumerated totals. Because the nature of the adjustments reveals so clearly the gaps and inconsistencies in migration mortality and census data, a specific listing decade by decade is provided.

1870–80

Table 1.10 indicates that the census enumeration of 1880 for males is 118,000 less than the estimate, and the corresponding figure for females is 40,000 more than the estimate. Adjustment for special factors changes these differences to a shortage of thirty-three thousand for males and an excess of fifty-five thousand for females.

Net migration of alien seamen, which on the basis of reported statistics for 1870–76 was estimated for the 1870–80 decade at thirty thousand, is an addition to the estimate primarily involving males. The presumption is that these persons would have been counted as foreign born in the 1880 census. Statistics for arriving and departing foreign-born seamen were not included in the regular migration data of the United States.

The migration statistics embrace whites and nonwhites, but no breakdown by racial components is available. Information is given for country of birth or origin and also country of last residence of the foreign-born migrant, but these data do not yield an accurate subdivision by race. For 1870–80, however, census data on racial components of the foreign born can be used. Foreign-born Chinese in the United States increased forty thousand, and the remainder of the nonwhite foreign-born population increased to five thousand during this decade. Of this recorded increase, approximately forty thousand were males and five thousand were females—since these were included in the immigration data, they must be subtracted from the difference.

Emigration of foreign born from the United States prior to 1908 was estimated on the basis of passengers leaving this country by water, as reported to the Bureau of Immigration. On this basis, estimated alien male departures for this decade amounted to 528,000. These passenger data are incomplete for three reasons: (a) not all the steamship companies reported passenger departures, nor is it known how complete the reports were of those making them; (b) about twenty departure ports were listed in the annual reports for this decade compared with

Table 1.10 Reconciliation of estimates and census enumerations of the foreign-born white population of the United States, 1880–1940 (in thousands)

	1880		1890		1900		1910		1920		1930		1940	
Item	**Males**	**Females**	**Males**	**Females**	**Males**	**Females**	**Males**	**Females**	**Males**	**Females**	**Males**	**Females**	**Males**	**Females**
Estimate	3,640	2,998	5,306	4,183	5,144	4,561	7,504	5,826	7,819	6,379	7,622	6,618	6,007	5,534
Census	3,522	3,038	4,952	4,170	5,515	4,699	7,524	5,822	7,528	6,184	7,502	6,481	6,011	5,408
Difference (census – estimate)	−188	+40	−354	−13	+371	+138	+20	−4	−291	−195	−120	−137	+4	−126
Factors raising estimate														
Net migration of alien seamen	30	0	NA	NA	NA	NA	NA	NA	NA	NA	NA	NA	NA	NA
Unreported alien arrivals from Canada	NA	NA	239	129	405	270	NA	NA	NA	NA	NA	NA	NA	NA
Net emigration from naturalized foreign born	NA	NA	NA	NA	NA	NA	25	5	NA	NA	NA	NA	NA	NA
Mexicans not included in migration data	NA	NA	NA	NA	NA	NA	NA	NA	100	18	NA	NA	NA	NA
Negative migration deficit of nonwhites included in data	NA	NA	NA	NA	NA	NA	NA	NA	NA	NA	3	NA	NA	NA

Revised data on migration	NA	NA	NA	NA	NA	NA	NA	NA	NA	NA	18	10	NA	NA
Aliens deported	NA	NA	NA	NA	NA	NA	NA	NA	NA	NA	NA	NA	117	13
Factors lowering estimate														
Net migration of nonwhites	40	5	NA	NA	NA	NA	39	3	15	60	NA	36	NA	NA
Emigration underestimate	75	10	75	25	98	42	NA	NA	NA	NA	NA	NA	NA	NA
Mortality underestimated	NA	NA	NA	NA	NA	NA	NA	NA	55	30	NA	NA	20	10
Unreported alien departures to Canada	NA	NA	175	75	32	18	NA	NA	NA	NA	NA	NA	NA	NA
Net migration of U.S. possessions included in migration data	NA	NA	NA	NA	NA	NA	NA	NA	18	2	NA	NA	NA	NA
Underestimate of departures of naturalized citizens	NA	NA	NA	NA	NA	NA	NA	NA	45	15	NA	NA	NA	NA
Nonimmigrant students counted in census	NA	NA	NA	NA	NA	NA	NA	NA	NA	NA	NA	NA	8	2
Revised difference	−33	+55	−343	−42	+96	−72	+34	−6	−258	−106	−141	−111	−85	−127

NA indicates absence of data.

about forty entry ports; and (c) the passenger data do not include migration to Canada and Mexico.

We assumed (a) that underreporting for male departures was about 10 percent by sea, that is, on the basis of the passenger data and (b) that about two thousand net alien departures per year should be added for border migration. This yields a figure of seventy-five thousand for males. Female departures by sea amounted to 203,000 during the decade, and we assumed that underreporting for females would be half that for males, or 5 percent; we made no allowance for net border migration.

1880–90

The estimate, although larger than the census enumerated total, must be increased further because the data flow on the foreign-born immigration to the United States by way of Canada were discontinued after 1894. Using the reported statistics for the first quinquennium, we estimated that 393,000 foreign-born persons came from Canada during 1885–90 and were not recorded in the migration data. On the basis of the recorded data, we estimated that about 239,000 males and 129,000 females had survived until 1890; that is, mortality for this group was about twenty-five thousand.

Analogous to the foregoing factor, but decreasing the estimate, is the unreported movement by land of foreign born from the United States to Canada. Direct data are not available, but according to the Canadian immigration statistics and to the Canadian census of 1891, 527,000 persons came from the United States during the period 1880–90. Of this group, probably very few were native-born citizens of the United States. The decrease factor, estimated at 250,000 for the second quinquennium (175,000 males and 75,000 females), is less than half of the 527,000 and very likely understates the actual number of foreign-born departures.

Emigration by water was underestimated for 1890 for the reason given for 1880. The conditions of reporting departures were about the same as in 1870–80. The correction for emigration was about 10 percent for males and about 9 percent for females of estimated departures.

1890–1900

An exceptionally large factor for this decade is the unreported alien inflow from Canada. For 1894–1900, there are no official data of the number of foreign born who landed in Canada and crossed the land border into the United States. The estimate given here is based on information for this group recorded prior to 1894. Aliens of Canadian or Mexican nativity who crossed the border during this decade are included, as suggested, by comparing the U.S. censuses of 1890 and 1900 for these groups.

A crude allowance for the underestimate in emigration had again to be made. Of the adjustment of 140,000, or 8.8 percent of the estimated total emigration, 98,000 were allocated to males and 42,000 to females.

1900–10

This decade is the first for which adequate mortality rates for the foreign born were available and the one in which the official recording of emigration of aliens was initiated in the United States.

Net emigration of naturalized foreign-born citizens, an item that would decrease the estimated total, is not included in the migration data for 1900–10, which are for aliens alone. For 1910–20 (atypical because of World War I), official reports suggest an estimated deficit net migration of naturalized citizens of about sixty thousand. In the conservative estimate given here for 1900–10, only half of this amount was used.

On the other hand, net migration of nonwhites had to be adjusted. According to the censuses of 1900 and 1910, the nonwhite foreign born increased from 127,000 to 170,000. This increase was adopted.

1910–20

The most important factor for this decade was "Mexicans not included in migration data." Because of the manpower shortage in World War I, the U.S. government imported thousands of Mexicans under congressional enactment. These persons were not included in the in-migration statistics. The census of 1920 indicates an increase of 260,000 persons of Mexican birth, whereas net migration reported is only 142,000 for the decade.

Nonwhites were included in the migration data. There was a net migration to this country of fifteen thousand males and sixty thousand females after mortality had been taken into account.

Another factor of importance was the underestimate of mortality. Mortality for 1910–20 was estimated on the basis of age-specific death rates of the foreign-born whites in 1910 and 1920, the terminal points of the decade. In the fall of 1918 and continuing to the spring of 1919, there was a widespread influenza epidemic in the United States resulting in an unusually high national mortality. On the basis of the death rate for the entire country and the age and sex distribution of the foreign-born whites, an estimate of the foreign-born deaths was prepared for 1918–19. The figures in Table 1.10 are a conservative appraisal of the underestimate of foreign-born white deaths in those years.

During 1910–20, aliens going to some of the possessions of the United States were recorded in the total immigration statistics for continental United States. The net migration of aliens to these possessions was approximately twenty thousand.

Emigration statistics did not record the departures of naturalized citizens for the entire period. On the basis of departures of all citizens for the decade and of naturalized citizens in 1918–20 (these years were certainly not typical of such departures), we estimated that there was a net emigration of sixty thousand naturalized citizens.

1920–30

The migration data show fifty-eight thousand nonwhite male immigrants and sixty-one thousand nonwhite male emigrants. Since these data were included in the total migration statistics, after the mortality adjustment, about three thousand were added to the estimate for the end of decade. A further addition of eighteen thousand males and of ten thousand females was made to take account of a revision in the migration data reported by the Immigration and Naturalization Service.

For nonwhite female migrants, the immigration statistics include 49.5 thousand while the emigration data report only 13.5 thousand. The balance of thirty-six thousand is therefore subtracted from the estimate of foreign born for the end of decade.

1930–40

The annual emigration statistics do not include the number of aliens deported or those who left the United States voluntarily in lieu of deportation. Between 1930 and 1940, there were approximately two hundred thousand aliens in this special category, 90 percent of whom were males. Obviously, aliens who entered the United States illegally would not be registered in the immigration statistics. However, illegal entry is only one of many reasons for deportation or voluntary departure in lieu of deportation. The estimate shown includes only deportations.

The adjustment for mortality is based on an assumption made by Thompson and Whelpton in *Population Trends in the United States* (McGraw-Hill, 1933, p. 234) that about 2 percent of white deaths in the registration area were not registered in the period 1921–30. Presumably, a similar adjustment on the decrease side could have been made for the decade ending in 1930. There is no direct information on the reporting of foreign-born white deaths in 1930–40. However, since the foreign-born whites were more concentrated in large cities than was the native white population and since, in general, the registration of mortality is better organized and administered in the urban areas, the adjustment may be too large.

Under the provisions of the Immigration Act of 1924, twenty thousand students were admitted to the United States as nonimmigrants between 1930 and 1940. Census enumerators in 1940 were instructed to count them as part of the foreign-born population. It is estimated that of the twenty thousand admitted, about ten thousand left the United States. This group is entered as a lowering factor because they are not included in the statistics for immigrants.

As already stated, the reconciliation process depended on estimates in many instances, and no information was available on the age distribution for the special factors. Consequently, it would have been very difficult, even if at all possible, to use these factors in our direct calculations. Since they could not be used to revise the estimates by age-groups, they cannot be taken into account in the comparison in Table 1.2. Despite this qualification, the comparison does shed light on the consistency of census enumerations of foreign born with the migration and mortality data and is worthwhile since the census data are useful for analysis of the contribution of migration and the foreign born to the labor force of this country and to its population through the founding of families and raising of new generations.

As was to be expected, the relative disparities between the census enumerations and our estimates are larger for the specific age-groups than for the overall totals. But it is significant that the census enumerations are consistently larger than the migration survival estimates in the younger groups and consistently smaller in those adult groups whose rate of participation in the labor force is among the highest, that is, the groups from twenty-four to fifty-four or sixty-four years of age.

Table 1.11 **Census enumeration and estimated total of foreign-born white population, by sex and age, 1880–1940 (in thousands)**

Age-group	1880	1890	1900	1910	1920	1930	1940
				Total			
0–14 years							
1. Census	424	731	511	759	546	355	83
2. Estimate	254	399	319	754	526	215	46
3. Difference (1–2)	+169	+332	+192	+5	+20	+140	+37
15–24 years							
4. Census	907	1,439	1,481	2,104	1,455	1,124	374
5. Estimate	870	1,352	1,213	1,909	1,529	1,291	400
6. Difference (4–5)	+38	+86	+268	+195	−74	−167	−26
25–34 years							
7. Census	1,434	2,015	2,271	3,168	3,108	2,436	1,134
8. Estimate	1,636	2,394	2,249	3,235	3,106	2,501	1,157
9. Difference (7–8)	−203	−380	+22	−67	+2	−65	−23
35–44 years							
10. Census	1,502	1,731	2,144	2,712	3,166	3,448	2,312
11. Estimate	1,715	2,243	2,339	3,039	3,456	3,340	2,318
12. Difference (10–11)	−213	−512	−196	−327	−290	+108	−6
45–54 years							
13. Census	1,208	1,497	1,644	2,072	2,467	2,955	3,069
14. Estimate	1,193	1,539	1,591	2,049	2,540	2,988	3,147
15. Difference (13–14)	+15	−42	+52	+23	−73	−33	−78
55–65 years							
16. Census	684	1,003	1,188	1,329	1,624	1,974	2,387
17. Estimate	666	1,006	1,179	1,318	1,722	2,115	2,465
18. Difference (16–17)	+18	−4	+9	+3	−98	−141	−78
65 years and over[a]							
19. Census	402	707	975	1,210	1,348	1,692	2,059
20. Estimate	306	555	814	1,027	1,321	1,792	2,007
21. Difference (19–20)	+96	+152	+161	+183	+27	−100	+52
Males							
0–14 years							
22. Census	214	371	258	384	276	179	42

(*continued*)

Table 1.11 *(continued)*

Age-group	1880	1890	1900	1910	1920	1930	1940
				Total			
23. Estimate	121	188	147	398	263	126	25
24. Difference (22–23)	+93	+184	+110	−14	+13	+53	+17
15–24 years							
25. Census	458	734	728	1,176	716	552	181
26. Estimate	450	709	578	1,037	763	700	194
27. Difference (25–26)	+9	+25	+150	+139	−47	−148	−13
25–34 years							
28. Census	785	1,152	1,250	1,879	1,739	1,265	537
29. Estimate	907	1,388	1,181	1,920	1,732	1,323	535
30. Difference (28–29)	−123	−237	+70	−41	+7	−58	+2
35–44 years							
31. Census	818	969	1,230	1,564	1,812	1,926	1,187
32. Estimate	987	1,359	1,349	1,795	2,031	1,836	1,164
33. Difference (31–32)	−169	−390	−119	−231	−219	+90	+23
45–54 years							
34. Census	659	816	909	1,183	1,396	1,645	1,700
35. Estimate	632	821	843	1,119	1,401	1,653	1,729
36. Difference (34–35)	+27	−5	+66	+64	−5	−8	−29
55–64 years							
37. Census	378	533	631	712	896	1,057	1,309
38. Estimate	378	542	625	710	949	1,117	1,335
39. Difference (37–38)	−5[b]	−9	+6	+2	−53	−60	−26
65 years and over[a]							
40. Census	210	377	510	627	693	879	1,054
41. Estimate	166	299	422	525	681	868	1,025
42. Difference (40–41)	+44	+79	+88	+102	+12	+11	+29
Females							
0–14 years							
43. Census	210	360	253	375	270	176	41
44. Estimate	133	212	172	356	263	89	21
45. Difference (43–44)	+76	+148	+81	+19	+7	+87	+20

(continued)

Table 1.11 *(continued)*

Age-group	1880	1890	1900	1910	1920	1930	1940
				Total			
15–24 years							
46. Census	449	705	754	928	739	572	193
47. Estimate	420	643	636	872	766	591	206
48. Difference (46–47)	+29	+62	+118	+56	−27	−19	−13
25–34 years							
49. Census	649	863	1,021	1,289	1,369	1,171	597
50. Estimate	729	1,006	1,068	1,315	1,374	1,178	622
51. Difference (49–50)	−80	−143	−48	−26	−5	−7	−25
35–44 years							
52. Census	684	762	914	1,148	1,354	1,522	1,125
53. Estimate	728	884	990	1,244	1,425	1,504	1,154
54. Difference (52–53)	−44	−122	−77	−96	−71	+18	−29
45–54 years							
55. Census	549	681	735	889	1,071	1,310	1,369
56. Estimate	561	718	749	930	1,139	1,335	1,418
57. Difference (55–56)	−12	−37	−14	−41	−68	−25	−49
55–64 years							
58. Census	306	470	557	609	728	917	1,078
59. Estimate	288	465	555	608	773	998	1,130
60. Difference (58–59)	+18	+5	+2	+1	−45	−81	−52
65 years and over[a]							
61. Census	191	329	465	583	655	813	1,005
62. Estimate	140	256	392	502	640	924	982
63. Difference (61–62)	+52	+74	+74	+81	+15	−111	+23

[a]Includes population with age unknown.

[b]Less than −5 thousand.

Because of rounding, detail will not necessarily add to total.

The shortage of the census totals in the adult groups is not too surprising if the assumption that some foreign born pass as native born is at all true. Under conditions in which a native enjoys some social and economic advantages and in which at least some groups of foreign born desire to associate themselves closely with the life of their chosen country, a fraction of the resident foreign born very likely does report itself as native born. Furthermore, since it is simpler to report native birth and requires less additional information, there may well be a bias toward overreporting it—if only because census enumerators attempt to cover a maximum number of individuals within the time available for filling in interview schedules.

The excess of census enumerations in the younger groups is unexpected. The practice followed in the estimates of centering migration flows (at two points in each decade for 1900–30 and at one point in 1870–1900 and 1930–40) could hardly contribute much to this result. Although by this procedure infants and children of about three or four years of age and under are underestimated at the end of the decade, those in the age immediately above are overestimated. The explanation must lie in the possibility of greater undercoverage of children in the in-migration statistics, overestimate of young groups among the departures, exaggeration of the mortality rates for the young groups, and a tendency in the census to report young native-born children of foreign-born parents, particularly of relatively recent arrivals, as foreign born.

All these factors may be important, but we would discount the possible effect of errors in the estimates of departures since the proportions of the latter even among adult groups are rather low for most decades, and they would be particularly low for the very young groups. Nor would any error in mortality rates be likely to have a marked effect. The fact is that the census count for males under ten years of age is larger than the number of male immigrants in that age-group in all decades, if we assume that 10 percent of total immigration are under ten years of age at the time of entry—a fairly liberal allowance. In other words, the discrepancy is in the immigration and the census data, and only to a limited degree can it be assigned to mortality and emigration calculations. The discrepancy is actually even greater if, as has been generally claimed, census totals tend to underestimate the number of children under 5. The usual sources of shortages in immigration data—land crossings, illegal entry, and the extended stay of transients—are perhaps least important for the very young groups. It is impossible to state with any assurance which of the two major sources of the discrepancy, understatement in the immigration data or overstatement in the census data, is more important.

Appendixes

Appendix A

Notes on Earlier Research for Decades since 1870

Introduction

Lack of adequate statistical information hampered the conscientious efforts of early investigators concerned with the effect of immigration on the growth of American population. Despite their limitations, the analyses of such pioneers as Tucker, Chickering, and Jarvis are interesting in their treatment of technical problems and in the reasoning on which their conclusions are based.[52]

Immigration has had a long history in the United States. For the most part, however, it was seldom treated dispassionately even when an attempt was made only to ascertain the pertinent facts and their reliability. Books and innumerable articles were written to "prove" that immigration did not contribute to the population growth of this country because immigration depressed the fertility rate of the native population, that immigration, if it continued, would result in race suicide of the Nordic element, that immigration was a threat to "American" institutions, and so on. For this reason, much of the literature on the subject is almost worthless.

The Estimates by Mayo-Smith

Mayo-Smith studied the problem of immigration and wrote the first systematic treatise in the United States on the subject.[53] He was also concerned with purely statistical investigations of the foreign born. Of particular interest for this analysis is his article on immigration and the foreign-born population.[54]

Mayo-Smith's principal techniques and results may be summarized as follows:

1. According to the census of 1880, the number of foreign born in the United States was 6,679,943. Immigrant arrivals in 1880–90 amounted to 5,246,613. The total of 11,926,556 represents the number of foreign born in the United States if there had been no emigration and no deaths in this decade. According to the census of 1890, there were 9,249,547 foreign born. "This leaves us with 2,677,009 to account for by emigration and deaths" (ibid., 305).

2. Official statistics on emigration are not available. Emigration may be estimated on the basis of statistics of departing passengers

supplied to the government by the principal shipping companies. These data include U. S. citizens going abroad. To estimate foreigners departing, Mayo-Smith assumes that "the U.S. citizens who are among the passengers departing sooner or later reappear among passengers arriving in this country" (p. 306). Since the statistics on arrivals from abroad show the number of U.S. citizens, Mayo-Smith concludes that for a series of years, rather than for a specific year, a valid estimate of foreigners departing can be obtained.

3. Using the series for passengers arriving and passengers departing, and subtracting from each the number of U.S. citizens arriving, Mayo-Smith obtains a net immigration total for the decade of 4,414,337. Subtracting the net immigration estimate from the gross immigration total of 5,264,613 leaves a net loss by emigration of 832,276.

4. Having obtained an annual net immigration figure, Mayo-Smith assumes a probable death rate, applying this rate thus:

> Starting with the foreign-born population of the United States in June 1880, I have allowed a death rate of 15 pro mille, and at the end of the year have added the immigration of the year ending June 30, 1881. With this population I have continued, allowing a death rate of 15 pro mille, and adding at the end of the year the immigration for the year ending June 30, 1882. Continuing this process the survivors of the foreign born and of the immigrants should have been in 1890, 9,825,727. This still leaves a deficiency of 576,180. (p. 308)

5. In addition to this deficiency, Mayo-Smith mentions the immigration from Canada not shown in official returns from July 1, 1885, to July 1, 1890. According to a report of the Canadian Minister of Agriculture, 379,942 immigrants passed through Canada en route to the United States in 1885–90. Mayo-Smith applies a death rate of fifteen per thousand to this group and concludes that survivors in 1890 would amount to 368,186. Consequently, the total deficiency should be increased to 944,366 (p. 309).

6. Having completed this part of the analysis, Mayo-Smith proceeds to investigate the foreign-born data by nationality groups. His method, applied to specific groups (Irish, German, Hebrew, etc.), is similar to that for the total foreign-born population. Again he finds discrepancies between the census of 1890 and his estimates of population for specific nationality groups.

7. On the basis of his findings, Mayo-Smith suggests four reasons for this great deficiency: (a) the death rate among the foreign born was

greater than fifteen per thousand, (b) emigration was greater than that allowed for, (c) some foreign born might have declared themselves to be native born in the census, and (d) the enumeration of the foreign born at the *Eleventh Census* may have been defective (p. 309). He omitted a fifth reason—that his method may have contained errors that biased his results in one direction.

First, in estimating emigration of the foreign born, he assumed that all U.S. citizens departing from the United States return to this country sooner or later. This assumption is inaccurate for at least two obvious reasons: some U.S. citizens die while abroad and some take up permanent residence outside the United States. Also the U.S. citizens include some naturalized foreign born. Further, the number of departures is probably underreported by the steamship companies. Finally, more ports of arrival than of departure are listed in each annual report, and the information on emigration was furnished on a voluntary basis by the steamship companies.

Second, Mayo-Smith assumes a death rate of fifteen per thousand for the foreign born. Subsequent findings indicate that the death rate in 1890 was 19.4 per 1,000 for this population and in 1880, about 19.8 per 1,000.[55] If we take eight million as the average population of the foreign born in 1880–90, an underestimate of 4 per 1,000 in the death rate is equivalent to an underestimate of 320,000 in mortality. Although admittedly crude, this figure indicates the possible order of magnitude of the error in Mayo-Smith's mortality estimate.

Finally, Mayo-Smith's technique of estimating the surviving net immigration also introduces an error. He should have centered his net immigration data at the middle of each year instead of assuming that all the immigrants came in at the end of the year. Thus he neglected a half year of mortality on a total net immigration of 4,414,337 for the decade, roughly about thirty-three thousand at the death rate he used.[56]

The Estimates by Rossiter

We have already mentioned a second study related to the present analysis, William S. Rossiter's *Increase of Population in the United States, 1910–1920.* His estimate of net immigration for 1870–1910 and his appraisal of the foreign-born white count of the 1920 census are especially relevant.

Before turning to the problem of estimating net immigration after 1870, Rossiter observes with regard to the period 1820–70 that

> no data are available on which to base an estimate of the immigration which took place during the first half of the nineteenth century. It may be safely assumed, however, that the emigration up to 1850 was negligible; an examination of the census statistics and of the immigration statistics for the period 1850 to 1870, due account being taken of mortality, indicates that emigration between 1850 and 1870 was also negligible . . . . During the succeeding decades, however, considerable emigration took place, and it is therefore necessary to estimate it in order to secure an estimate of the net immigration.[57]

To expedite the analysis, Rossiter assumes that white emigration represented total emigration (nonwhite emigration was negligible) during this period. His method of estimation may be summarized thus:

1. The number of white immigrants during a decade is added to the number of foreign-born whites enumerated at the beginning of the decade.

2. Estimated mortality is deducted from the sum obtained in (1).

3. The foreign-born white persons enumerated at the end of the decade are subtracted from the result obtained in (2); the remainder represents the number of surviving foreign-born white emigrants (p. 199).

Rossiter's estimates of emigration can be accurate only under one of two conditions: (a) that the census data, immigration statistics, and mortality estimates are all correct or (b) that these three series, if incorrect, yield results in which the errors developed in this system of linear combination exactly cancel out. The first condition certainly doesn't hold, and the probability of the second is extremely slight.

In preparing his mortality estimate, Rossiter first estimates the mortality (for the ten-year period) of the foreign-born whites enumerated at the beginning of the decade. His technique requires a series of approximations, which take into account the advancing age of the foreign-born population and the further determination of increases in death rates by age. Thus Rossiter says as follows:

> It was estimated, therefore, after a careful inspection of the rates for each fifth year of age from 15 to 70, that the increase in the general rate for the entire foreign born population during a period in which the average age advanced by 5 would be about 30 percent.[58]

Since the general rate was 30 percent higher at the end than at the beginning of the decade, Rossiter assumes that the average rate for the decade was 15 percent higher than the rate at the beginning of the decade. He further assumes that the decrease during the decade in the total number to which the rate was applied was approximately one-fifth, and therefore the average was approximately nine-tenths of the number at the beginning of the decade. Thus, in order to obtain a decennial rate applicable to the foreign-born white population enumerated at the beginning of a decade, the normal rate should be increased by 15 percent to account for the effect of the advance in age, and the result should be decreased by 10 percent to account for the effect of the reduction in number. This would yield a net increase of only 3.5 percent in the decennial rate applicable to the number enumerated at the beginning of the decade.[59]

To estimate mortality among white immigrants during the decade, Rossiter multiplies the normal annual death rate for the foreign-born white population by five, assuming that immigration was distributed uniformly throughout the decade (i.e., the average length of residence for all immigrants during a decade was five years). Then this result ". . . was arbitrarily reduced by one-fourth to account for the lower average age of immigrants than of the entire foreign-born population."[60]

Finally, Rossiter combines these mortality results as follows:

A, foreign-born population (e.g., 1890)

Minus B, foreign-born mortality (1890–1900)

Equals C, foreign-born population in 1900 excluding migration.

D, total immigration (1890–1900)

Minus E, mortality of immigrants (1890–1900)

Equals F, surviving immigrants in 1900.

The difference between the sum of *C* and *F* and the census enumeration of foreign-born white in 1900 is the number of surviving emigrants at the end of the decade. The total number of emigrants departed during the decade is estimated by adding to this difference an estimate of mortality among the emigrants.

Various assumptions and arbitrary adjustments with regard to the mortality estimates made by Rossiter are open to criticism, of which

Estimates of net immigration to the United States, all races, 1820–1940 (in thousands)

Period[a]	Rossiter	Present	Period[b]	Willcox
1820–30	137	–	1820–30	152
1830–40	558	–	1831–40	569
1840–50	1,599	–	1841–50	1,542
1850–60	2,663	–	1851–60	2,208
1860–70	2,356	–	1861–70	1,852
1870–80	2,530	2,269	1871–80	2,109
1880–90[c]	4,273	4,492	1881–90	3,673
1890–1900	3,239	2,532	1891–1900	2,397
1900–10	5,558	5,285	1901–7	3,794
1910–20	3,467	3,197	1908–14	4,092
1920–30	–	3,085	1915–22	1,277
1930–40	–	104	1923–30	2,543

[a]Census periods.

[b]Fiscal years used in the *Annual Reports of the Commissioner of Immigration,* Bureau of Immigration and Naturalization.

[c]Mayo-Smith's estimate is 4,414,000.

– Indicates absence of data.

Willcox notes that his method probably exaggerated the outflow of aliens from the United States in 1850–1900,[63] a point corroborated by the results obtained by Rossiter and us for 1870–1900.

Rossiter was himself aware. His results are presented in section A Brief Comparison.

The Estimates by Willcox

Willcox, the dean of American demographers, has studied various problems with regard to immigration and has devised two methods for estimating net immigration.[61] One is as a percentage of gross. In examining the immigration data for 1907–14, Willcox found that net immigration was 61 percent of gross. He observes thus:

> In estimating net immigration during earlier years it is probably safe to assume that between 1900 and 1907 likewise it was about 61 percent of gross immigration. Before that it must have been greater. If one supposes that it was 65 percent for the decade 1891–1900, and that for each decade of the nineteenth century it

> was 5 percent above what it was in the next later decade, the series in Table 195 results. (pp. 390–91)

He does not indicate the basis for the linear aspect of his assumption, and if the nativity composition of immigration to this country in the nineteenth century as well as the conditions of transportation is true as reported, the return flow was definitely smaller in the earlier recorded period of immigration. Willcox's second method is an indirect one, requiring comparison between the proportions of the sexes among immigrants with those among the foreign born. He regards this method as less accurate, and it will not be discussed here.[62]

A Brief Comparison

The estimates by Mayo-Smith, Rossiter, and Willcox gave no sex or age distribution. However, the totals of net immigration obtained by the various methods are compared in the following tabulation.

Notes

1. See appendix A.
2. See., e.g., the statement by Walter F. Willcox, "There is, perhaps, no important or promising field of American immigration statistics so little worked as the attempt to relate the immigration statistics to the foreign born statistics" (*International Migrations*, vol. II (New York: National Bureau of Economic Research, 1931), 90). Commenting upon the failure of the government agencies issuing the two sets of data to establish agreement, Prof. Willcox adds, "In so large a field a private student cannot go far."
3. For the last period in the calculations, 1930–40, we felt it was adequate to center total net migration in the middle of the decade. The volume of migration was quite small and not very different in the first and second halves. For 1870–1900, we also centered net migration in the middle of the decade because the death rates used were rough, if reasonable, approximations, and refinement of the calculations by further splitting of the intercensal periods did not seem warranted.
4. Before the distinction was made by law, an alien arriving with a declared intention to visit could legally remain as a resident. Likewise, a departing resident alien could declare his intention to visit abroad temporarily and never return. On this and other intricacies of the data, see part III and discussion in Willcox, *International Migrations*, 8547.
5. The characteristics of the long swings will emerge more clearly in part II, section The Long Swings. Since there is no secure technique for describing these swings accurately, it is difficult to establish the precise dates of their peaks and troughs. The use of single-year dates in Table 1.3 may suggest greater precision than that is intended here. It may have been preferable to determine the peaks and troughs of the long swings from the data for quinquennia rather than single years. But this procedure would have complicated the calculation of average values for nonoverlapping periods. The

major conclusions suggested by Table 1.3 would not, however, be affected by such modifications in the dating procedure.

6. For 1897–1918, the ratio of arrivals to total population would become 7.9 percent and for 1838–61, 8.0 percent (8.4 percent reduced by 5 percent).
7. For a flexible description of movements underlying any discernible short-term fluctuations, the averaging procedure indicated should be followed for periods determined by the fluctuations observed in the specific series. Hence, the use in Table 1.4 of periods set by cycles in the net arrivals alone rather than by the specific cycles may not yield the best description of the underlying swings in total arrivals and in departures. However, specific cycles in total and net arrivals are fairly synchronous. Furthermore, it was desirable to derive movements in the departure series, which would assure the arithmetic consistency of total and net arrivals. This could be done only by using the same set of cycle periods for all three series.
8. See note 5 above.
9. *Annual Reports of the Commissioner of Immigration*, Bureau of Immigration and Naturalization, contain data on the period of residence of emigrants for years since 1908, and we can take the period 1908–14 as typical of "normal" nonwar and nonrestricted conditions. During that period, of some two million emigrants about 10 percent did not report length of residence. Of the 1.8 million who did, 77 percent had been in the country less than five years, and an additional 18 percent, from five to nine years.
10. These statements apply to gross immigration, emigration, and net immigration as well as to gross arrivals, departures, and net arrivals of all alien passengers. Panels A and B of Table 1.4 indicate almost complete agreement between the long swings in inflow and outflow of alien passengers and of immigrants in the decades for which we have data for both. We assume that a similar agreement existed in the earlier decades.
11. David M. Blank, *The Volume of Residential Construction, 1889–1950*, Technical Paper 9 (New York: National Bureau of Economic Research, 1954), Table 11, 42, and Table 18, 69.
12. The only exception is that labor force used to get gross national product *per worker* overlaps with urban population figures used as bases to "blow up" samples to totals in estimating the Blank Series on total residential construction. This, however, has little bearing upon the comparison.
13. In this connection, see also the rough correspondence between long swings in immigration and in the number of native born of native parentage noted below (Table 1.9 and discussion relating to it).
14. An index of thirty means that the series moved consistently with or against reference cycles in four out of six, seven out of eleven, or eleven out of seventeen cases.
15. In 1910, despite a large influx of net immigrants in the preceding decade, the median age of the foreign-born white population was over eighty-seven years. At the same time, the median age of the native-born white population was only slightly more than twenty-one years, and of the immigrating population, in the middle twenties.
16. The data on arrivals apply to immigrants alone; they and departures are taken from Imre Ferenczi, *International Migrations*, vol. I (New York: National Bureau of Economic Research, 1929), 390–92 and 472. The data

on composition of the foreign born are from Niles Carpenter, *Immigrants and Their Children*, Bureau of the Census Monograph VII (1927), 79. See also note 9.

17. The maximization of the number of resident survivors of the foreign-born initial population is due not only to the assumption that none left the country via migration but also to our estimate of deaths. We apportioned total deaths for each decade between the initial foreign-born population and the net balance of arrivals over departures on the basis of number without regard to age composition—primarily to avoid laborious calculations. Since the initial foreign-born population is significantly older than the net balance of arrivals over departures, the procedure underestimates the deaths of the former and overestimates the deaths of the latter.
18. A check is available, since Carpenter, *Immigrants and Their Children*, gives data for 1910 and 1920 of the distribution of foreign-born population by number of years in the country. Apportioning the nonreporting proportionately to those reporting, Carpenter shows the following percentages of foreign born in the country ten years or less: 1910—87.7; 1920—22.5 (see ibid., Table 35, 58). The 1910 figure in Table 1.7 is quite close to that in the census monograph; the 1920 figure is short because a substantial proportion of departures during 1910–20 was from the old resident, rather than the more newly arrived, foreign born.
19. A special category, officers and crews of foreign ships temporarily in a harbor, was exempted from the count of foreign born in 1920 (*Instructions to Enumerators, Fourteenth Census of the United* States, Bureau of the Census (1919), 19, par. 64).
20. *Instructions to Enumerators, Population and Agriculture, Fifteenth Census of the United States,* Revised and Supplemental Instructions, Bureau of the Census (1930), 1.
21. *Instructions to Enumerators, Population and Agriculture, Sixteenth Census of the United States,* Bureau of the Census (1940), 16: "Persons not to be Enumerated in Your District: 313d. Persons *from* abroad temporarily visiting or traveling in the United States and foreign persons employed in the diplomatic or consular service of their country. (Enumerate other persons from abroad who are *students in this country* or who are *employed here,* however, even though they do not expect to remain here permanently.)"
22. Ibid., 14, note 1: "78. *Citizens abroad at time of enumeration.* Any citizen of the United States who is a member of a family living in your district, but abroad temporarily at the time of the enumeration, should be enumerated as of your district. It does not matter how long the absence abroad is continued provided the person intends to return to the United States. These instructions apply only to *citizens* of the United States and not to aliens who have left this country."
23. *Instructions to Enumerators, Fourteenth Census of the United States,* Bureau of the Census (1919), Sec. 63, p. 19; (1950), Sec. 78, p. 14.
24. Sec. 14 (43 Stat. 162).
25. Carroll D. Wright and William C. Hunt, *The History and Growth of the United States Census* (Washington, DC: Government Printing Office, 1900), 57n.

26. See *Quarterly Publications of the American Statistical Association,* March 1896, 63.
27. "Immigration and the Foreign Born Population," *Quarterly Publications of the American Statistical Association,* March–June 1893, 304–20.
28. *Foreign Commerce and Navigation of the United States,* Annual Reports of the Bureau of Foreign and Domestic Commerce.
29. Willcox, *International Migrations,* vol. II, 651.
30. Before January 1, 1906, the alien arrival was counted as an immigrant, even though returning to the United States from a temporary visit abroad. See *Annual Report of the Commissioner-General of Immigration, 1906,* Bureau of Immigration and Naturalization (1907), 4, 5, 9; and Ferenczi, *International Migrations,* vol. I, 574.
31. *Commerce and Navigation of the United States,* Annual Report of the Chief of the Bureau of Statistics (1871).
32. Ibid. (For fiscal year ended June 30, 1870), 676–77, 712.
33. Ibid., 688–89, 735.
34. *Annual Report of the Superintendent of Immigration, 1892,* Bureau of Immigration, 30.
35. Ferenczi, *International Migrations,* 361.
36. *Census of Canada,* vol. 1 (1901), 482, gives Canadian population by birthplace. In 1881, there were 77,753 persons in Canada who were born in the United States; ten years later, in 1891, there were 80,915 such persons, an increase of only 3,000.
37. *Annual Report of the Superintendent of Immigration, 1892,* Bureau of Immigration, 30.
38. *Annual Report of the Superintendent of Immigration, 1894,* Bureau of Immigration, 3.
39. *Annual Report of the Superintendent of Immigration, 1893,* Bureau of Immigration, 3.
40. *Commerce and Navigation of the United States,* Annual Reports of the Bureau of Statistics(1870–1876).
41. Including U.S. citizens and presumably native born; see Ferenczi, *International Migrations,* 471.
42. *Historical Statistics of the United States, 1789–1945,* 22. Since 1945, age data have been reported by five-year groups comparable to that of the census, beginning with the class "under five years" and terminating with the open-end class "hundred years and over."
43. The following works were of value in this connection Gustav Sundbärg, *Bevölkerungsstatistik Schwedens: 1750–1900* (Stockholm, 1907), 160; *Annuario Statistico Della Emigrazione Italiana dal 1876 al 1925* (Rome, 1925), 528; J. Conrad, *Grundriss zum Studium der Politischen Oekonomie, Vierter Teil: Statistik* (Jena, 1902), 179–80; Ferenczi, *International Migrations,* for the following countries: Norway (p. 748), Sweden (p. 756), Denmark (p. 667), Germany (p. 698), Hungary (p. 719), British Isles (p. 642), Czechoslovakia (p. 661).
44. In 1910–20, when migration was considerably affected by World War I, the median age of male arrivals was 26.7 years and of departures 29.9; of female arrivals 23.0 and of departures 28.2. In 1920–30, only immigrant and

emigrant categories were considered because of the quota acts. The median age of male immigrants for this decade was 26.1 and for male emigrants, 36.1; the corresponding median ages for females were 24.8 and 33.9.

45. *United States Life Tables 1890, 1901, 1910 and 1901–1910,* prepared by James W. Glover, Bureau of the Census (1921), 66–67.
46. *Historical Statistics of the United States, 1789–1945,* 45.
47. *Mortality Statistics: 1920,* Bureau of the Census (1922), 3.
48. William S. Rossiter in *Increase of Population of the United States, 1910–1920,* Bureau of the Census Monograph I (1922), gives the death rate of the total foreign-born white population in 1890 as 19.4 per 1,000 (p. 200). See also C. H. Forsyth, "Trend of Longevity," *Quarterly Publications of the American Statistical Association,* December 1919, 495–501.
49. Dr. Thomas and Dr. Everett Lee are utilizing "census survival ratios" in a study of population redistribution. A census survival ratio is the ratio of the number in a certain age-group at one census to the number in the age-group ten years younger at the preceding census.
50. Carl R. Doering and Alice L. Forbes, "A Skeleton Life Table," *Proceedings of the National Academy of Sciences,* September 1988, 400–5. The basic formulas used in all intervals except the first and last are

$$L_x^{x+h} = \frac{l_x}{1/h + 1/2\, m_x^{x+h}},$$

$$d_x^{x+h} = m_x^{x+h} L_x^{x+h} \text{ where}$$

$$l_{x+h} = l_x - d_x^{x+h} \text{ where}$$

L_x^{x+h} = stationary population in the age-group x to $x + h$ years,

m_x^{x+h} = per capita death rate for this age-group,

l_x = number alive at the beginning of year of age,
h = the number of years of the age-group,
l_{x+h} = number of survivors of group l_x after mortality of h years, and
d_x^{x+h} = deaths in the cohort for the age-group.

51. Arthur Newsholme, *The Elements of Vital Statistics,* 3rd ed. (Macmillan, 1899), 265–69.
52. George Tucker, *Progress of the United States in Population and Wealth: As Exhibited by the Decennial Census* (New York: Hunt's Merchant's Magazine, 1843). Tucker discusses migration to the United States for the period 1790–1840 (Chap. X, pp. 80–88). He indicates difficulties with regard to the statistical data and notes the special problem of United States–Canadian border migration.
    Jesse Chickering, *Immigration into the United States* (Little and Brown, 1848). Chickering has much to say about the irregularity of the U.S. immigration statistics and the border migration problem, and he estimates the contribution of immigration to population growth. This small volume contains an appendix on immigration to the United States prior to 1820.

References to Edward Jarvis' work are contained in *Statistical View of the United States*, a compendium of the *Seventh Census*, by J. D. B. DeBow, Superintendent, Census Office (1854), 119–22. Jarvis was concerned with estimates of immigration and methods of estimating the mortality of immigrants for the period 1790–1850.

53. Richard Mayo-Smith, *Emigration and Immigration: A Study in Social Science* (Scribner, 1890), 316.
54. *Quarterly Publications of the American Statistical Association*, March–June 1893, 304–20.
55. William S. Rossiter, *Increase of Population in the United States, 1910–1920*, Bureau of the Census Monograph I, 200.
56. Mayo-Smith's technique is and so on. This procedure yields Mayo-Smith's estimate of 9,825,727 in June 1890.

Foreign born, June 1880	6,679,943
Times death rate	0.015
Equals mortality	100,199
Balance, June 30, 1881	6,579,744
Plus net immigration for year ending June 30, 1881	631,640
Equals foreign born, June 30, 1881	7,211,384
Times death rate	0.015
Equals mortality	108,171
Balance, June 30, 1882	7,103,213
Plus net immigration for year ended June 30, 1882	735,648
Equals foreign born, June 30, 1882	7,838,861

57. Rossiter, *Increase of Population in the United States*, 199.
58. Ibid., 201. Rossiter assumed that the average age of the group increased to about five years during the decade. The basis of the assumption is this: the younger element in the foreign-born population, e.g., ages ten to thirty, is hardly affected by death, whereas the older element is greatly affected; consequently in such a population distribution, the extreme older age range (i.e., maximum age) would remain virtually unchanged while the younger or minimum age-group would advance almost ten years. As an average for the entire group, five years is reasonable, especially since the distribution of the ages of the foreign-born population *is* approximately symmetrical.
59. Ibid.
60. Ibid.
61. Walter F. Willcox, *Studies* in *American Demography* (Ithaca: Cornell University Press, 1940), Chap. 20, "Immigration," 386–418.
62. Ibid., 391–92.
63. Ibid., 392.

Appendix B

Reference Tables

Table B.1 Annual arrivals and departures, all alien passengers, 1870–1945, and immigrants and emigrants, 1908–45 (in thousands)

Fiscal year ending June 30	Arrivals	Departures	Fiscal year ending June 30	Arrivals	Departures
All aliens					
1870	403	37	1900	519	134
1871	343	43	1901	563	275
1872	423	44	1902	731	345
1873	473	71	1903	921	389
1874	328	83	1904	841	311
1875	245	112	1905	1,060	398
1876	190	90	1906	1,166	469
1877	165	94	1907	1,438	671
1878	158	69	1908	925	715
1879	198	66	1909	944	400
1880	484	60	1910	1,198	380
1881	695	50	1911	1,030	518
1882	816	64	1912	1,017	615
1883	645	66	1913	1,427	612
1884	561	87	1914	1,403	634
1885	438	154	1915	434	384
1886	358	108	1916	367	241
1887	513	97	1917	363	146
1888	567	129	1918	212	193
1889	465	150	1919	237	216
1890	476	148	1920	622	428
1891	579	153	1921	978	426
1892	644	164	1922	432	345
1893	544	163	1923	673	201
1894	347	210	1924	879	217
1895	301	206	1925	458	226
1896	363	158	1926	496	228
1897	244	139	1927	538	254
1898	250	129	1928	501	274
1899	335	134	1929	479	252
1930	446	272	1940	209	166
1931	281	291	1941	152	88

(*continued*)

Table B.1 (*continued*)

Fiscal year ending June 30	Arrivals	Departures	Fiscal year ending June 30	Arrivals	Departures
1932	175	288	1942	111	75
1933	151	244	1943	105	59
1934	164	177	1944	142	84
1935	180	189	1945	202	93
1936	191	193			
1937	232	224			
1938	253	223			
1939	268	202			
Immigrants and emigrants					
1908	783	395	1930	242	51
1909	752	226	1931	97	62
			1932	36	103
1910	1,042	202	1933	23	80
1911	879	296	1934	30	40
1912	838	333			
1913	1,198	308	1935	35	39
1914	1,218	303	1936	36	36
			1937	50	27
1915	327	204	1938	68	25
1916	299	130	1939	83	27
1917	295	66			
1918	111	95	1940	71	22
1919	141	124	1941	52	17
			1942	29	7
1920	430	288	1973	24	5
1921	805	248	1944	29	6
1922	310	199			
1923	523	81	1945	38	7
1924	707	77			
1925	294	93			
1926	304	77			
1927	335	73			
1928	307	78			
1929	280	69			

Table B.2 Estimated five-year survival ratios of the U.S. foreign-born white population, selected periods, 1870–1940

Age-group	1870–80	1880–90	1890–1900	1903–7	1913–17	1923–27	1930–35	1935–40
Males								
0–4 to 5–9	.888927	.898520	.913575	.929759	.947067	.964023	.977270	.971729
5–9 to 10–14	.972661	.982556	.980895	.972322	.972570	.977277	.985806	.983653
10–14 to 15–19	.969304	.974964	.973743	.978466	.980867	.985361	.987780	.990384
15–19 to 20–24	.964094	.970186	.971088	.978391	.979273	.977870	.983796	.991006
20–24 to 25–29	.955639	.962356	.965834	.965055	.968034	.975752	.983136	.985017
25–29 to 30–34	.946793	.952117	.958671	.964807	.964740	.970973	.978350	.979422
30–34 to 35–39	.939223	.944452	.950135	.958535	.962281	.968702	.972338	.980294
35–39 to 40–44	.928306	.933878	.937921	.944172	.954666	.957500	.970562	.970473
40–44 to 45–49	.903645	.908211	.912001	.934526	.941201	.951823	.949020	.953721
45–49 to 50–54	.906731	.910604	.913060	.912291	.924948	.926916	.934050	.941949
50–54 to 55–59	.845288	.848178	.849757	.882737	.896801	.904193	.904366	.906552
55–59 to 60–64	.849397	.847682	.844569	.846887	.862543	.877377	.871000	.869135
60–64 to 65–69	.751538	.745214	.747647	.784737	.829742	.819593	.828673	.829399
65–69 to 70–74	.728460	.720692	.720983	.742787	.695065	.748238	.739315	.747204
70–74 to 75–79				.659605	.635497	.640625	.668170	.668001
65 and over to 70 and over	.596606	.588754	.588621					
75 and over to 80 and over				.390341	.463495	.465240	.458558	.455386

Females								
0–4 to 5–9	.896850	.908867	.920705	.932446	.950524	.965321	.980889	.980717
5–9 to 10–14	.975335	.986050	.982369	.978983	.976617	.984005	.987098	.989120
10–14 to 15–19	.972186	.978083	.976815	.982367	.983268	.984974	.990280	.991826
15–19 to 20–24	.964583	.969672	.972734	.977333	.981917	.982789	.987698	.989222
20–24 to 25–29	.955262	.960854	.965715	.971599	.972259	.976251	.984682	.977467
25–29 to 30–34	.948675	.952381	.960241	.964637	.967391	.974819	.983434	.983289
30–34 to 35–39	.938052	.941690	.949211	.962266	.969147	974092	.980446	.990913
35–39 to 40–44	.939298	.944304	.948021	.948898	.957080	.963756	.972802	.992636
40–44 to 45–49	.912062	.917270	.920240	.944269	.953496	.961280	.967912	.966883
45–49 to 50–54	.923049	.924544	.927812	.924408	.936980	.942985	.944535	.943121
50–54 to 55–59	.859585	.858831	.861668	.896393	.907619	.917593	.924210	.936677
55–59 to 60–64	.864559	.865165	.865483	.863567	.883637	.890882	.899606	.899149
60–64 to 65–69	.743626	.742616	.742491	.799651	.837077	.832258	.850783	.852204
65–69 to 70–74	.740759	.737443	.736866	.745267	.712195	.771327	.781283	.782860
70–74 to 75–79				.665361	.642921	.694663	.713931	.707020
65 and over to 70 and over	.598676	.593411	.592872					
75 and over to 80 and over				.406912	.477610	.446850	.468291	.473170

For the derivation of these survival rates, see the discussion in the text. For periods following 1900, they are based on the death rates shown in Forrest E. Linder and Robert D. Grove, *Vital Statistics Rates in the United States, 1900–1940*, Bureau of the Census (1943), 186–87. For the middle four-year period of each census interval from 1900 to 1930 (1903–7, 1913–17, and 1923–27), these death rates for successive census dates were weighted equally. For the first three-year period of each census interval from 1900 to 1930, the initial-year death rates were weighted by seven and the terminal-year death rates by three, and for the terminal three-year period, the weights were reversed. For the first quinquennium of 1930–40, the death rates for 1930 were weighted by three, and those for 1940 by one, and for the second quinquennium, the weights were again reversed.

Table B.3 Foreign-born white male population of the United States, January 1, 1920, and estimate for April 1, 1930

	Census	Estimated survivors	Jan. 1, 1920–Jan. 1, 1925		Adjusted estimate	Estimated survivors	Jan. 1, 1925–Apr. 1, 1930		Adjusted survivors	Estimated survivors
Age–group	Jan. 1, 1920	Jan. 1, 1923	Immigrants	Emigrants	Jan. 1, 1923	Jan. 1, 1927	Immigrants	Emigrants	Jan. 1, 1927	Apr. 1, 1930
All ages	7,528,322	7,133,124	1,535,310	598,729	8,069,705	7,516,797	842,235	267,701	8,091,331	7,622,409
Under five	22,857	8,864	18,000	3,000	23,864	4,620	12,000	1,000	15,620	5,327
5–9	85,774	47,072	50,000	17,000	80,072	34,194	23,000	3,500	53,694	28,489
10–14	167,152	116,849	142,000	32,000	226,849	107,704	62,000	3,500	166,204	91,933
15–19	259,270	201,719	225,000	42,000	384,719	254,983	163,000	9,000	408,983	247,913
20–24	456,988	333,741	230,000	50,000	513,741	403,139	167,000	21,000	549,139	452,012
25–29	792,088	581,074	258,000	56,000	783,074	556,083	180,000	43,000	693,083	590,438
30–34	946,818	837,161	232,000	69,000	1,000,161	807,347	85,000	50,000	842,347	732,124
35–39	1,008,667	950,181	185,000	86,000	1,049,181	983,254	51,000	46,000	988,254	874,696
40–44	803,195	902,281	75,000	82,000	895,281	983,781	34,000	30,000	987,781	961,225
45–49	744,423	753,817	28,000	40,000	741,817	828,694	29,000	16,000	841,694	903,712
50–54	651,546	676,904	25,000	29,000	672,904	684,611	18,000	16,000	686,611	749,527
55–59	503,789	555,800	24,000	26,000	553,800	597,435	11,000	8,000	600,435	613,104
60–64	392,629	419,954	21,000	24,000	416,954	472,411	6,000	8,000	600,435	613,104
65–69	275,400	304,913	17,000	21,500	300,413	334,508	1,235	7,000	328,743	368,444
70–74	194,732	204,240	5,310	16,000	193,550	219,587		5,701	213,886	238,165
75–79	124,170	128,881		5,229	123,652	126,377			126,377	139,854
80–84	56,701	65,781			65,781	74,540			74,540	71,997
85 and over	28,381	30,881			30,881	31,410			31,410	38,148
Unknown	13,732	13,011			13,011	12,119			12,119	11,416

Table B.4 Foreign-born white population of the United States, male and female estimated for census dates, 1880–1900 (absolute figures in thousands)

Item	1870–80	1880–90	1890–1900
Males			
1. Initial census figure			
a. Date	6/1/70	6/1/80	6/1/90
b. Number	2,942.6	3,521.6	4,951.9
2. Estimated survivors			
a. Date	6/1/80	6/1/90	6/1/1900
b. Number	2,385.1	2,784.8	3,933.1
3. Migration, intracensal period			
a. Date	6/1/70–6/1/80	6/1/80–6/1/90	6/1/90–6/1/1900
b. Arrivals	1,858.0	3,415.7	2,577.3
c. Departures	527.7	756.2	1,317.7
d. Net immigration (b–c)	1,330.3	2,659.5	1,259.5
4. Migrant survivors			
a. Date	6/1/80	6/1/90	6/1/1900
b. Number	1,255.2	2,521.2	1,211.1
5. Estimated survivors, end of census period			
a. Date	6/1/80	6/1/90	6/1/1900
b. Number (2b + 4b)	3,640.3	5,306.0	5,144.2
Females[a]			
1b. Initial census figure	2,551.1	3,038.0	4,170.0
2b. Estimated survivors	2,110.5	2,440.7	3,346.2
3. Migration, intracensal period			
b. Arrivals	1,141.5	2,120.1	1,546.4
c. Departures	202.8	287.0	273.7
d. Net migration (b–c)	938.8	1,833.1	1,272.6
4b. Migrant survivors	887.8	1,741.9	1,215.3
5b. Estimated survivors, end of census period	2,998.2	4,182.6	4,561.5

[a]Same dates as males.

Because of rounding, detail will not necessarily add to total.

Table B.5 Foreign-born white population of the United States, male and female, estimated for census dates, 1910–40 (absolute figures in thousands)

Item	1900–10	1910–20	1920–30	1930–40
Males				
1. Initial census figure				
a. Date	6/1/1900	4/15/10	1/1/20	4/1/30
b. Number	5,515.3	7,523.8	7,528.3	7,502.5
2. Estimated survivors				
a. Date	7/1/03	7/1/13	1/1/23	4/1/35
b. Number	5,160.6	7,103.6	7,133.1	6,780.4
3. Migration, intracensal period				
a. Date	6/1/1900– 7/1/05	4/15/10– 1/1/15	1/1/20– 1/1/25	4/1/30– 4/1/40
b. Arrivals	2,926.2	3,553.2	1,535.3	250.0
c. Departures	1,450.1	2,118.0	598.7	297.1
d. Net immigration (b – c)	1,476.1	1,435.2	936.6	–47.1
4. Adjusted survivors				
a. Date	7/1/03	7/1/13	1/1/23	4/1/35
b. Number (2b + 3d)	6,636.8	8,538.8	8,069.7	6,733.3
5. Estimated survivors				
a. Date	7/1/07	7/1/17	1/1/27	
b. Number	6,160.9	7,985.6	7,516.8	
6. Migration, second intracensal period				
a. Date	7/1/05– 4/15/10	1/1/15– 1/1/20	1/1/25– 4/1/30	
b. Arrivals	3,812.7	1,034.9	842.2	
c. Departures	2,106.2	858.1	267.7	
d. Net immigration (b – c)	1,706.5	176.8	574.5	
7. Adjusted survivors				
a. Date	7/1/07	7/1/17	1/1/27	
b. Number (5b + 6d)	7,867.4	8,162.5	8,091.3	
8. Estimated survivors, end of census period				
a. Date	4/15/10	1/1/20	4/1/30	4/1/40
b. Number	7,504.2	7,819.3	7,622.4	6,006.9

(*continued*)

Table B.5 (*continued*)

Item	1900–10	1910–20	1920–30	1930–40
Females[a]				
1b. Initial census figure	4,698.5	5,821.8	6,184.4	6,480.9
2b. Estimated survivors	4,375.9	5,500.3	5,851.5	5,935.8
3. Migration, first intracensal period				
b. Arrivals	1,232.1	1,914.4	1,171.4	321.1
c. Departures	288.5	640.5	196.5	169.9
d. Net immigration (b – c)	943.5	1,273.9	974.9	151.2
4b. Adjusted survivors (2b + 3d)	5,319.5	6,774.3	6,826.5	6,087.0
5b. Estimated survivors	4,947.4	6,343.1	6,384.5	
6. Migration, second intracensal period				
b. Arrivals	1,609.5	547.9	712.8	
c. Departures	451.0	236.7	113.7	
d. Net immigration (b – c)	1,158.5	311.2	599.1	
7b. Adjusted survivors (5b + 6d)	6,105.9	6,654.3	6,983.6	
8b. Estimated survivors, end of census period	5,826.2	6,378.8	6,618.3	5,533.6

[a]Same dates as for males.

Table B.6 Estimates of the foreign-born white population of the United States by sex, July 1, 1870–1939 (in millions)

Year	Male	Female	Total	Year	Male	Female	Total
1870	2.95	2.56	5.51	1905	6.41	5.13	11.54
1871	3.07	2.66	5.73	1906	6.72	5.31	12.03
1872	3.23	2.77	6.00	1907	7.10	5.50	12.54
1873	3.38	2.90	6.28	1908	6.98	5.61	12.59
1874	3.45	2.96	6.41	1909	7.19	5.71	12.90
1875	3.45	2.98	6.43	1910	7.61	5.85	13.46
1876	3.44	2.97	6.41	1911	7.72	5.97	13.69
1877	3.40	2.95	6.35	1912	7.73	6.08	13.81
1878	3.38	2.94	6.31	1913	7.73	6.08	13.81
1879	3.38	2.95	6.33	1914	8.32	6.48	14.80
1880	3.55	3.05	6.60	1915	8.11	6.45	14.60
1881	3.84	3.25	7.09	1916	7.98	6.41	14.39
1882	4.19	3.46	7.65	1917	7.93	6.37	14.31
1883	4.42	3.64	8.06	1918	7.76	6.27	14.03
1884	4.58	3.77	8.35	1919	7.58	6.18	13.76
1885	4.61	3.84	8.45	1920	7.46	6.19	13.65
1886	4.64	3.89	8.52	1921	7.58	6.36	13.94
1887	4.75	3.97	8.72	1922	7.44	6.34	13.78
1888	4.87	4.06	8.93	1923	7.55	6.41	13.96
1889	4.91	4.12	9.03	1924	7.77	6.55	14.31
1890	4.97	4.18	9.15	1925	7.71	6.53	14.24
1891	5.14	4.31	9.45	1926	7.67	6.52	14.19
1892	5.35	4.45	9.80	1927	7.66	6.51	14.17
1893	5.48	4.56	10.04	1928	7.62	6.51	14.12
1894	5.47	4.59	10.06	1929	7.56	6.50	14.05
1895	5.43	4.60	10.02	1930	7.49	6.48	13.96
1896	5.44	4.62	10.06	1931	7.34	6.39	13.73
1897	5.41	4.61	10.02	1932	7.15	6.25	13.40
1898	5.38	4.60	9.98	1933	6.96	6.11	13.07
1899	5.40	4.63	10.03	1934	6.80	5.99	12.80
1900	5.52	4.70	10.22	1935	6.65	5.88	12.53
1901	5.58	4.72	10.29	1936	6.50	5.76	12.26

Table B.6 *(continued)*

Year	Male	Female	Total	Year	Male	Female	Total
1902	5.70	4.76	10.47	1937	6.36	5.66	12.02
1903	5.91	4.86	10.77	1938	6.23	5.57	11.79
1904	6.12	4.98	11.10	1939	6.10	5.48	11.58

Because of rounding, detail will not necessarily add to total.

Notes

For the intercensal yearly estimates, migration data were available. But the mortality estimate for the decade as well as the discrepancy between the census enumeration and the estimated total had to be distributed annually.

For 1870–1900, annual mortality estimates are the sum of mortality of *foreign* born in the country at the beginning of the period and mortality of migrants during the period. Total mortality for each census period of the foreign born living in the country at the beginning of the period was centered at the midpoint of each period, and annual values were interpolated along a straight line.

Total mortality of the net migrants in each census period was distributed annually by the following procedure: (a) a percentage distribution of net annual migration, weighted by the number of years migrants were in this country (migrants of the first year of the period, weighted ten; of the second year, weighted nine, etc.), was applied to the total mortality for the period to yield the estimated total mortality during the period of migrants of each year; (b) these totals were divided by the number of years the migrants were in this country to yield average annual mortality for migrants of each year; (c) the average annual mortality estimates derived in step (b) were then added to yield the total annual mortality estimates for migrants (for the first year, this total was the mortality estimate for migrants of the first year; for the second year, it was the sum of the mortality estimates for migrants of the first and second years, etc.).

For 1900–40, annual mortality was estimated by the following procedure: For each segment of the decade for which mortality had been estimated (e.g., June 1, 1900–July 1, 1903, July 1, 1903–July 1, 1907, and July 1, 1907–April 15, 1910), the average annual mortality was calculated and centered at the midpoint of the given period. From the straight line connecting (or extending) these points, the average annual mortality in each year was estimated (column 3 of the following tabulation). The sum of these estimates differed only slightly from the estimate for the decade as a whole.

For the entire period, to adjust the annual estimates to the census enumeration, the difference between the lag of the ratio of the estimated number to the census count at the end of the decade and the log of one (the ratio at the beginning of the decade) was interpolated annually along a straight line. The antilogs yielded the ratio by which the estimated number at the beginning of each fiscal year was adjusted to bring it into line with the census enumeration. The estimates for July 1 were then derived by simple straight-line interpolation. The procedure is illustrated in Table B.7.

Table B.7 Calculation of estimates of foreign-born white males, July 1, 1900–10 (absolute figures in thousands)

Period	Preliminary estimate of number at beginning of year (1)	Net migration during year (2)	Mortality during year (3)	Preliminary estimate of number at end of year (1 + 2–3) (4)	Adjustment factor for (1) (5)	Log of column 5, lines 1 and 14 interpolated along straight line (6)	Final estimate of number at beginning of year (1 ´ 5) (7)	Change during year in (7) (8)	1/12 of (8) (9)	Estimated number on July 1 of given year (7 + 9) (10)
1. June 1, 1900–1	5,515.3	161.9	113.9	5,563.4	1.0000	0.00000	5,515.3	49.7	4.1	5,519.4
2. June 1, 1901–2	5,563.4	233.4	115.0	5,681.8	1.0003	0.00014	5,565.0	120.2	10.0	5,575.0
3. Dec. 15, 1901			115.0							
4. June 1, 1902–3	5,681.8	326.5	116.1	5,892.2	1.0006	0.00028	5,685.2	212.9	17.7	5,702.9
5. June 1, 1903–4	5,892.2	314.3	117.2	6,089.2	1.0010	0.00042	5,898.1	199.1	16.6	5,914.7
6. June 1, 1904–5	6,089.2	405.6	118.3	6,376.5	1.0013	0.00056	6,097.2	289.5	24.1	6,121.3
7. July 1, 1905			119.0							
8. June 1, 1905–6	6,376.5	421.3	120.3	6,677.4	1.0016	0.00070	6,386.7	304.1	25.3	6,412.0
9. June 1, 1906–7	6,677.4	476.6	123.6	7,030.4	1.0020	0.00085	6,690.8	355.8	29.6	6,720.4
10. June 1, 1907–8	7,030.4	41.4	126.9	6,944.9	1.0023	0.00099	7,046.6	(83.7	(7.0	7,039.6
11. Nov. 23, 1908			130.1							
12. June 1, 1908–9	6,944.9	323.2	130.2	7,137.9	1.0026	0.00113	6,962.9	195.7	16.3	6,979.2

13. June 1, 1909–Apr. 15, 1910	7,137.9	478.5	116.6	7,499.9	1.0029	0.00127	7,158.6	365.2	34.8a	7,193.4
14. Apr. 15, 1910	7,499.9				1.0032	0.00139	7,523.8			
15. Apr. 15, 1910, census	7,523.8									

[a]Column 8 divided by 10.5.

Column 1

Lines 1 and 15: census data.

Lines 2, 4–5, 8–10, and 12–14: From column 4.

Column 2

From unpublished worksheets. Data are adjusted to fiscal year beginning June 1. For example, line 1 is the sum of 12,590 (number for the month of June) and 149,331 (11/12 of 162,906, the number for the fiscal year July 1, 1900–1).

Column 3

Lines 3, 7, and 11: Calculated from Table B.5. For example, line 3 is the difference between the estimated survivors July 1, 1903, and the total number June 1, 1900, divided by the number of years covered (3 1/12) and centered at the midpoint of the period (December 15, 1901).

Lines 1, 2, and 4–6: Extrapolated from or interpolated between lines 3 and 7 along a straight line.

Lines 8–10 and 12–13: Extrapolated from or interpolated between lines 7 and 11 along a straight line.

Column 5

Line 1: Since the entry in column 1 is from the census, it requires no adjustment.

Lines 2–13: Antilogs of column 6.

Line 14: The ratio of line 15 to line 14 in column 1.

2

Israel's Economic Development

Simon Kuznets

This study briefly discusses several aspects of Israel's economic growth. The first two sections concern the overall and per-capita growth rates of the Israeli economy in comparison with other high-growth economies. These sections also deal with the increase in factor productivity. Section 3 ponders the possible contribution to Israel's brisk growth rate of mass immigrant absorption in the pre-1952 period. The final section briefly illuminates two different aspects of the contribution of Israel's import surplus to its economic growth.

Since I am not intimately versed in the range of economic data and analyses that exist in Israel, obviously my observation of the problems is basically illustrative and qualifies as a discussion proposal at best. A concluding impression that is largely self-evident although indispensable appears at the end of the study.

—Simon Kuznets

Growth of Product and Per Capita Product

Table 2.1 presents the growth rates of several aggregate values in the Israeli economy in overall, per capita, and per-worker terms. It also offers similar indices for the gross national product (GNP) or gross domestic product (GDP) of non-Communist countries that, like Israel, have attained—according to the international statistics—high rates of increase in per capita product.

Part A of Table 2.1 presents aggregate values relating to Israel: domestic uses including public consumption and gross domestic

I thank Dr. Gur Ofer and Dr. Yoram Ben-Porat of the Hebrew University of Jerusalem for their useful remarks on an earlier version of this study.

capital formation in addition to private-consumption expenditure. GDP representing the total income of productive players located in Israel (irrespective of their ownership) expresses domestic uses exclusive of the surplus of imports of goods and services over exports. GNP denotes total domestic product plus factor payments abroad (a negative value in Israel's case) and differs only slightly from GDP; its growth rates (in comparison with line 3) are 10.0, 9.0, and 9.2 percent, respectively (Table 2.1, p. 105).

Two special points deserve examination. First, the growth rates shown in Part A differ genuinely, if not perceptibly, commensurate with differences in the length of the period investigated and the aggregate values chosen. The differences relating to the period investigated are especially interesting and raise the problem of choosing the comparison period that is most justified from the analytic perspective.

Should the years 1950 and 1951, the first years for which data are available, be included or not? If data for 1948 and 1949 were available, would we include them in the series? As for the second question, the lack of appropriate estimates justifies what we know anyway: the 1948–49 period was definitively affected by the War of Independence, the establishment of state and institutional mechanisms, and the changes that existing mechanisms underwent when statehood was attained. The 1950–51 period was typified by immigration of such a magnitude as to have increased Israel's population from 1.04 million at the beginning of 1950 to 1.40 million at the beginning of 1952, a 35 percent increase in two years.[1]

Such growth rates did not recur later and one cannot find a parallel for such a phenomenon in economic history in the past two hundred years. For this reason, it seems preferable to discuss Israel's economic growth in the decade following the end of the mass immigration period, a time typified by the absorption and integration of the waves of immigration that arrived in 1948–51 but not by so startling a rate of population growth. In view of the foregoing remarks, the discussion that follows will focus, where Israel is concerned, on the period beginning in 1952, with attention to the fact that the inclusion of the period after 1966 causes a slight decrease in the growth rates of the aggregates: GDP, population, and labor force.

As for the aggregate magnitudes, we will devote the discussion to gross domestic (or National) product as the income of sources in Israel proper,that is, excluding at least the *direct* contribution of the import surplus. We emphasize the word *direct* because the reference

Table 2.1 Annual growth rates in past two decades, gross domestic product and other aggregate magnitudes, Israel and other non-Communist states (percent)

A. Israel, constant 1955 prices

	1952–54 to 1964–66 (1)	1952–54 to 1968–70 (2)	1950–51 to 1968–70 (3)
1 Private-consumption expenditures	9.2	8.5	8.8
2 Domestic uses	9.0	8.7	8.1
3 GDP	10.3	9.2	9.3
4 Population	3.7	3.4	3.9
5 Labor force	3.6	3.0	3.6
6 Per capita private-consumption expenditure	5.3	5.0	4.7
7 Per capita domestic uses	5.1	5.2	4.1
8 Per capita GDP	6.2	5.6	5.2
9 Per-worker GDP	6.3	6.0	5.5

B. Other rapid-growth countries according to UN sources: rates for 1950–68 (different period or base year marked in parentheses), Gross Domestic Product in constant market prices

	GDP (1)	Population (2)	Per capita GDP (3)
10 Israel	9.2	3.9	5.1
11 Japan (1952)	9.7	1.0	8.6
12 Taiwan (1951)	8.5	3.4	4.9
13 South Korea (1953)	6.3	2.7	3.5

(continued)

Table 2.1 *(continued)*

B. Other rapid-growth countries according to UN sources: rates for 1950–68 (different period or base year marked in parentheses), Gross Domestic Product in constant market prices

	GDP (1)	Population (2)	Per capita GDP (3)
14 Austria	5.2	0.4	4.8
15 Germany (Federal Republic)	6.2	1.1	5.0
16 France	5.1	1.2	3.9
17 Italy (1951)	5.6	0.7	4.9
18 Greece	6.4	0.8	5.6
19 Spain (1954)	6.1	1.0	5.1
20 Portugal (1953)	5.4	0.8	4.6
21 Puerto Rico (1950–61)	6.3	1.1	5.1

C. Other rapid-growth countries (AID sources): gross national product in constant market prices, other base year marked in parentheses

	Gross national product			Per capita gross national product		
	1950–60 (1)	1960–71 (2)	1950–71 (3)	1950–60 (4)	1960–71 (5)	1950–71 (6)
22 Israel (1952)	10.0	8.3	9.0	6.5	4.9	5.6
23 Japan (1952)	8.2	10.6	9.6	7.1	9.5	8.5
24 Taiwan (1951)	7.7	9.7	9.3	4.3	7.0	5.8
25 South Korea (1953)	4.9	9.3	7.6	2.1	6.8	5.0

26 Austria	6.2	4.8	5.5	5.9	4.4	5.1
27 Germany (Federal Republic)	7.8	4.6	6.1	6.8	3.5	5.1
28 France	4.5	5.8	5.2	3.6	4.7	4.2
29 Italy	5.8	5.2	5.5	5.2	4.4	4.8
30 Greece	5.8	7.8	6.9	4.8	7.1	6.0
31 Spain	5.0	7.3	6.2	4.2	6.3	5.3
32 Portugal	4.1	6.1	5.1	3.6	5.2	4.4

Part A: the data in Part A on GDP and its components, 1950–68, were culled from UN publications: Yearbook of National Accounts Statistics, 1968 and 1969, vol. 1, Individual Country Data, New York, 1969 and 1970.

Complementary data for previous periods were obtained from the United Nations Statistics Department.

The data series for 1950–59, presented here in constant 1955 prices, was extended to 1968 by attaching the series in 1959 to the next series, expressed in 1964 prices. The 1968–70 data, which were expressed in 1970 prices, were adjusted to 1968. The series were chained on the basis of data from Bank of Israel, Annual Report 1970 (Jerusalem, 1971).

The data on population and labor force in 1950–65 come from Nadav Halevi and Ruth Klinov-Elul, Israel's Economic Development (in Hebrew).

The data in Tables 3 and 13 were adjusted to estimates in the Bank of Israel, Annual Reports (with the exception of the population of eastern Jerusalem).

We assumed that the GDP estimates for the most recent years do not include the income of residents of eastern Jerusalem. (If they do include this income, they produce a mild upward bias in the estimated growth rate for 1968–70.)

Part B: all data except those for Puerto Rico were culled from UN publications: Yearbook of National Accounts Statistics, Volume II, International Tables, Tables 4A and 4B (New York: 1970).

The data for Puerto Rico, 1950–60, were obtained from a previous UN statistical yearbook.

The population growth rates were calculated by dividing GDP by per capita GDP.

Table 2.1 (*continued*)

The GDP data (quoted from the 1969 *UN Yearbook*, vol. II, 129) relate to GDP in market prices. The approach toward calculating product is the application of an exponential function to the data by the least-squares method.

The data on Puerto Rico were calculated as the average of the growth rates in 1950–60 (the GDP and population data for the entire decade were culled from the regular sources) and the growth rates presented in the 1970 *Yearbook*. For 1960–69, they are weighted by weights of ten and nine, respectively.

Part C: the data were culled from *Gross National Product: Growth Rates and Trend Data by Region and Country*, Agency for International Development, Re-W-138 (Washington, D.C., May 1972), Tables 1b, 1c, 1d, 1e, and 1h, 2–5.

The growth rates in multiannual periods are geometric means of the respective annual rates. The rates in 1950–60 (or a period bounded by a different base year) and for 1960–71 are shown in columns 1–2 and 4–5. The rates in columns 3 and 6 were calculated by weighting the rates obtained for partial periods by the respective number of years.

The AID dataset is based largely on UN data. However, it includes complementary data and corrections that do not appear in the UN *Statistical Yearbooks* for 1969 and 1970.

to domestic or national product (gross or net) instead of domestic (or total) uses does not dismiss the indirect effects of the import surplus. We will return to this matter below.

The second point relates to the comparisons in Parts B and C of Table 2.1. They include only countries that appear in international datasets in series covering periods no shorter than fifteen years, countries with populations of at least one million, and those that have rates of increase in per capita product (in at least one of the two parts, B or C) exceeding 4 percent per annum (≥4.2 percent).

Another constraint applies to the choice of countries. We deliberately excluded Communist countries due to their sociopolitical structure. The aggregate data calculated for such countries are not comparable with those of free-market economies unless they are modified and adjusted, as cannot be done within the framework of this study. The available data on non-Communist countries other than those in central Africa are rather significant. As for these African countries, we know that none of the forty or so sub-Saharan countries has attained rates of per capita product growth that approach those in Table 2.1. Therefore, the list of countries in Parts B and C of Table 2.1 is almost certainly a complete roster of non-Communist countries that have attained high rates of per capita product growth in the past two decades.[2] Among these countries, only Japan's rate of product growth surpassed Israel's. As for the increase in per capita product, Japan, Greece, and Taiwan outperformed Israel, and South Korea was only slightly behind. If we disregard minor differences, we may conclude by saying that among more than hundred economies around the globe, only a few attained growth rates exceeding or resembling Israel's.[3]

The characteristic features of the countries appearing in Parts B and C of Table 2.1 are thought-provoking. Although a comprehensive analysis obviously entails more thorough information, we may make several remarks:

The status of Puerto Rico is unique. Its direct access to the American market makes it a quasi-state among the states that comprise this advanced and massive economy. The other ten countries represent two different-sized groups.

The larger group includes the eight countries that are listed in each of the parts of Table 2.1 immediately after Israel. Nearly all of them were involved in World War II and were severely affected by the material and social outcomes of the war. This put them to complex processes of structural change in their political and social institutions, irrespective of whether they were among the "losers" in the war—Japan, Germany, Austria, and Italy—or among the "winners," if one may apply this term to France, Taiwan, South Korea, and Greece. The visceral physical destruction was accompanied by the shaking of the countries' institutional and sociopolitical underpinnings, a development that facilitated some adjustments that would have been impossible otherwise. This argument also appears to be valid for Greece, which was seriously battered in the war, although the extent of changes in its sociopolitical establishment is unclear. Even though high growth rates are saliently typical of the countries listed above, the devastation occasioned by the war and the subsequent changes hardly serve as sufficient reason for the vigorous growth rates that followed.

The two remaining countries, Spain and Portugal, are structured in the form of top-down dictatorial command economies. After World War II, they enjoyed, albeit belatedly, overt relations with West European countries. (Portugal is a member of *European Free Trade Association.*) In a certain sense, Spain and Portugal managed to make up the lag that had been occasioned by their civil wars and involvement with Fascist regimes before and after World War II. Unlike other European countries that appear on the list, and like Greece, these countries are undeveloped entities within the European communities even though their per capita product places them in the upper tier in comparison with undeveloped countries.

It is quite easy to draw parallels between Israel and other countries listed in Parts B and C. Israel, too, started out, at roughly the same time, by making a series of definitive changes in its political structure in order to sweep away erstwhile obstacles. The process was undoubtedly accompanied by the destruction of much physical capital in the War of Independence. Like most of the countries mentioned, Israel is poor in basic natural resources and bases itself largely on human capital.

However, another aspect manifested in Parts B and C, relating to countries not included on the high-growth list, should be borne in mind. As expected, the list excludes many developed countries that did not undergo major social and political changes during and after World War II. Furthermore, it does not include any country in the less-developed class (such as those of Latin America and several in Africa and Asia) that suffered no physical damage and did not even experience social changes after the war. The list we complied includes none of the less-developed countries that attained political independence after

World War II. After these countries achieved political independence and established new sociopolitical institutions, one might expect their total and per capita growth rates to accelerate impressively. It is true that some LDCs attained political independence belatedly and allow a much shorter period for discussion than that established in this article. Still, only a few LDCs that, like Israel, attained independence after World War II attained sufficiently vigorous rates of per capita product growth to allow comparison with the rates presented in Table 2.1. To be more precise, upon the attainment of independence and with emphasis on economic growth, many countries surpassed the rates of increase in product and per capita product that they had known in the past. The most important point in this context, however, is that Israel, despite resembling many of the aforementioned countries that had opportunities to create a domestic political establishment when they verged on political independence, is exceptional among these countries in its special combination of high rates of increase in both population and per capita product. Only very few countries, mostly in the developed class, posted rates such as or higher than Israel's. Thus, Israel's high growth rate presents an interesting analytical problem.

Factor Productivity

Lines 1–2 in Table 2.2 summarize the data on total factor productivity in the Israeli economy, which exist thanks to Dr. A. L. Goathon's meticulous research. The data were culled from Summary Table 22 in Goathon's book, with the exception of the uses of weights 0.3 and 0.7 for labor input and capital input, respectively. (These weights are also used for the other countries in the table and represent the respective weights for Israel according to Goathon. See note B in Table 22, p. 79.)

The increase in productivity, that is, the residual obtained after the contribution of labor and capital is taken into account, comes to 4.2 percent per year per person employed or seven-tenths of the increase in product per person employed (lines 1 and 2 in column 7). While such a rate of increase in productivity per worker is respectable by international standards, it would have been even higher had adjustments for changes in levels of schooling been made. Such changes would have contributed another 0.4 percent, bringing the total to 4.6 percent.[4]

The indicators on lines 1–2 prompt several questions if we wish to show that growth in factor productivity is affected by the efficiency

Table 2.2 Israel factor productivity, 1953–65 (annual percent growth rate, 1955 prices)

	GDP	Labor input (LI)	Capital input (CI)	CI	LI	CI+LI	Factor productivity
					Weighted		
	(1)	(2)	(3)	(4)	(5)	(6)	(7)
According to the data							
1. Total	10.8	4.3	11.0	3.01	3.30	6.41	4.13
1a. Log pct. of ratios (LR)	100			29	32	61	39
2. Per person employed	6.23	0	6.42	0	1.93	1.93	4.22
2a. Pct (LR)	100			0	32	32	68
Labor force as basis for labor input (LI)							
3. Total	10.8	3.5	11.0	2.45	3.30	5.83	4.70
3a. Pct. (LR)	100			24	32	55	45
4. Per worker	7.05	0	7.25	0	2.17	2.17	4.78
4a. Pct. (LR)	100			0	32	32	68
As in lines 3–4, with unproductive capital taken into account							
5. Total	10.8	3.5	8.5	2.45	2.55	5.06	5.46
5a. Pct. (LR)	100			24	25	48	52
6. Per worker	7.05	0	4.83	0	1.45	1.45	5.52

6a. Pct. (LR)	100			0	21	21	79
7. Per capita	6.85	−0.19	4.63	−0.13	1.39	1.26	5.53
7a. Pct. (LR)	100			−2	21	19	81
As in lines 5–7, with CI assigned greater weight							
8. Total	10.8	3.5	8.5	1.75	4.25	6.07	4.46
8a. Pct. (LR)	100			17	41	57	43
9. Per worker	7.05	0	4.83	0	2.42	2.42	4.53
9a. Pct. (LR)	100			0	35	35	65
10. Per capita	6.85	−0.19	4.63	−0.10	2.32	2.22	4.53
10a. Pct. (LR)	100			−2	35	33	67

Line 1, columns 1–3: A. L. Goathon, *Economic Productivity in Israel* (New York: Praeger, 1971), Table A-13, 205.

Unadjusted rates for the economy at large (used for comparison with other countries): from ibid., Table 22, 79.

Line 1, columns 4–7: obtained from columns 1–3 by weighting labor input at 0.7 and capital input at 0.3. Column 6 was derived by multiplying the ratios calculated from columns 4 and 5. Column 7 was calculated by dividing the ratios presented in columns 1 and 6.

Line 1a (and other lines marked "a"): percentages relating to logs of the ratios in columns 4–7. Given the multiplicative relation that exists among the growth rates (in percent), the division of the total growth rate between inputs and factor productivity should be performed by means of the logs of the ratios and not by adding the rates.

Line 2: obtained from line 1 by dividing all ratios expressed by means of the growth rates appearing on line 1, columns 1–3, by the growth rates in column 2 of line 1. The calculation was performed by assigning weights of 0.7 and 0.3 to per-worker LI and CI, respectively. The rate of increase in per-worker factor productivity is the denominator of the ratios.

Table 2.2 *(continued)*

Lines 3–4: here the labor input is the labor force and not the number of persons employed. On the growth rate of the labor force, see Goathon, Table 4, 17.

Line 4: obtained by dividing the appropriate columns on line 3 by the growth rate of the labor force.

Lines 5–7: the growth rate of capital stock (capital input) was obtained after the performance of an adjustment based on the assumption that the quantity of real (primary) unproductive assets in the base year was one-third of real asset stock that year. Another assumption is that from this year onward, the economy acquired no additional primary assets. For the argumentation underlying these assumptions, see the article proper.

Line 6: obtained by dividing the ratios expressed by the growth rates shown on line 5 by ratios based on the growth rates of the labor force. Line 7 uses the rate of population increase (which is also used in calculating line 10)—3.7 percent per year. See Goathon, Table 4, 17.

Lines 8–10: calculated by assigning capital input the weight of 0.5 instead of 0.3.

of individuals and institutions. First, should labor input be estimated on the basis of *the number of persons employed* or by *the entire labor force*? If the labor force represents all individuals who belong to society and are willing and able to engage in productive labor (a social group whose demand for a chance to work is acceptable in the public mind), and if some of this labor force is idled due to deficiencies in the organization of society's institutions (including a permanent deficiency in effective demand), then the lack of employment is proof of the inefficient use of productive sources. If so, the unemployed should be included in labor input; any increase in efficiency will be cited as proof of an *increase* in the productivity of society at large. Furthermore, if the labor force really is the appropriate estimator of labor input, then a *voluntary* reduction in hours worked would be reflected in the labor-input estimate. Moreover, an increase in a worker's output per hour worked (more than the increase per year worked) should be taken into account.

Although I have no data on the number of hours worked by employed persons during the entire period, I presume that the number did not increase and may even have contracted. A much more important variable is the difference between the size of the labor force and the number of persons employed. The Israeli economy managed to reduce the high unemployment rates that were prevalent at the beginning of the period; therefore, the rate of increase in the employed labor force, 4.3 percent per annum, far exceeds that of the labor force itself, 3.5 percent. I suggest that this decrease in unemployment rates is an indicator of progress in the use of productive sources and, accordingly, is one of the components of total factor productivity. (The same may be said about the increase in the rate of capital utilization.) Switching to the labor force as the basis for the measurement of labor input raises the growth rate of factor productivity to 4.7 percent per year and the respective rate per individual member of the labor force to 4.8 percent (lines 3–4 in column 7).

This brings us to the problem of capital stock. In lines 1–4, capital stock includes only productive fixed capital, to the exclusion of quantities in inventory and primary real property (land, mineral resources, and so on, i.e., capital formation that constitutes inputs invested in this property). Dr. Goathon explains the exclusion of stocks of raw materials and finished and semi-finished products in the following way: "Changes in the volume in stocks of the items listed above are strongly susceptible to temporary effects [whereas] fixed-capital formation is determined largely by long-term considerations" (p. 25). However, one may postulate that, in the long term, stocks have an effect on the periodic increase in output volume. For example, it is hard to imagine how the U.S. economy in 1960 could function if the capital stock available to it were, say, that of 1860. Obviously, the rapid increase in the output of the Israeli economy in the past twenty years was accompanied by a long-term upward trend in the volume of stock, and indeed, there is evidence that stock, parsed by types, did increase rapidly.[5]

The exclusion of primary natural resources raises the concern that the possible effect on the growth rate of capital stock is greater in this case. Addressing this point, Dr. Goathon terms the exclusion of natural resources "the only possibility consistent with the treatment of the National Accounts as a record of economic activity" (p. 27). This remark is somewhat discomfiting if we are indeed interested in the efficiency of the *human* contribution to output, as reflected in the ability to use personal and institutional knowledge and capabilities to maximize production by means of a given quantity of labor and physical capital. It has been argued, after all, that Libya is an efficient and productive country only due to its good fortune of being situated in a region awash in oil that is exploited, thanks to knowledge and resources not available in Libya. Furthermore, the efficiency of interest to us is the kind that reflects "the nation's propensity to economic progress" due to the impression that this national propensity reflects historical and institutional factors. Our understanding of these factors may be key in economic analysis and policy in the field of economic growth.

Be this as it may, there seems to be good reason to include natural resources in capital input. This way, the share of productivity that appears as a residual would reflect more directly the efficiency associated with institutional and individual capabilities. The difficulty here is that we have no data on the value of natural resources in Israel. However, data on the value of total assets and the share of primary sources in this total, in the early 1950s, are available for several countries. These estimates yield the ratio of primary sources to total physical capital in the possession of developers and government (with the exception of monetary metals, nonresidents' assets, and durable goods used for consumption, including dwellings). This ratio ranges from 16 to 18 percent in the United States, Belgium, and Luxembourg; 30 percent in Yugoslavia and South Africa; and 50 percent in India.[6] I chose a ratio of one-third for Israel, mainly for illustrative purposes, in the belief that it approximates the reality and, above all, due to the low level of productive capital at the beginning of the period investigated. This premise allows no intra-period increases in the stock of these resources.

Consequently, the rate of increase in total capital stock and, accordingly, in capital input is reduced considerably, whereas a corresponding increase, of up to 5.5 percent per year, takes place in total factor productivity per individual member of the labor force (line 6, column 7). In this case, we also calculate the productivity of the entire population, so that per capita factor productivity rises by 5.5 percent per year. It should be borne in mind that in this calculation, the increases in labor input and productive capital are added to a *fixed* stock of natural resources. As for the achievements in efficiency, under these conditions they *must* surpass those estimated under conditions in which natural-resources stock increases in proportion with productive-capital stock (as one realizes when one does not include natural resources in capital input).[7]

The last adjustment in Table 2.2 relates to the argument that the weights of 0.7 and 0.3 for labor and capital inputs, respectively, are effectively an underestimate of capital due to Israel's own policy considerations, and that a better approximation of the conditions of equilibrium in the factor-input markets would be attained at a weight of 0.5 for capital input (and 0.5 for labor input).[8] If we make this adjustment on the assumption that it "relates to capital including natural resources," total factor productivity would be reduced to 4.5 percent per year in both per-worker and per capita terms. This is still a high level, and it may even climb to 5 percent or more if we allow for changes in stocks, make an adjustment for the decrease in the level of schooling, and, perhaps, adjust for a small (voluntary) decline in the average number of hours worked.

Since the discussion thus far has been predicated on limited familiarity with the basic data and the estimates, it is susceptible to change. It does not stand to reason, however, that the main findings would undergo far-reaching changes or that the problems cited here would become irrelevant. Therefore, we may offer a brief presentation of the main findings:

First, the rate of increase in factor inputs in Israel resembles that in most developed countries in the West and apparently falls short of that in Japan and Taiwan. (See data below.)

Second, in Israel, as in other developed countries, per capita or per-worker capital stock made a perceptible contribution to the increase in factor inputs in unit terms (because hours worked per person usually declined). However, capital calculated on a unit basis, even when assigned the weight of 0.5, contributed less than one-third to the growth rate of GDP; the remainder represents the contribution of productivity obtained as a residual.

Third, we cannot infer that the increase in productivity is independent of the rapid growth of total and primary capital stock. Similarly, we cannot state that in the absence of an increase in per-worker or per capita capital, GDP would have increased at the rate of two-thirds of the increase that actually occurred. The absence of scale economies and other effects on the quantity of capital would change the picture. By the same token, we cannot infer that the results presented here would not have been obtained had we gone to the trouble of making adjustments. All we can say is that given the current weights, a unit investment of capital contributes one-fourth to one-third of the rate of increase in per-worker or per capita product.

Fourth, according to most analyses that offer conclusions that are presented in the study cited in note 7, about three-fourths of GDP growth should be imputed to per capita factor productivity. In other words, in Israel, as in other countries, the especially high rate of increase in per capita product is mainly the outcome of productivity growth. The increase in *per capita* factor inputs has only a small measured effect.

Fifth, the growth rates of per capita productivity and per-worker consumption are quite similar (4.5 percent in Table 2.3 and 5.3 percent in Table 2.1). In a sense, the per-worker output of consumer goods is a basic metric of productivity, since government consumption and capital formation are intermediates that *precede* the ultimate goal of economic activity—consumption by consumers. As long as one may assume that per-worker capital stock does not fall below a level that permits the production of the current supply of finished consumption goods, the ratio of output of finished consumer goods to the labor force (when one factors in voluntary hours worked) will be the purest indicator of productivity. It is not by chance that the rates of increase in total productivity, at least in democracies, approximate those of per-worker consumption (or per worker's hour of labor), assuming that the value of extra hours is included in final consumption.[9]

As we present this part of the discussion to the reader, we should note that we cannot provide a direct comparison between the adjusted indicators of factor productivity in Israel and those of other countries, because to do so we would have to reestimate and expand the estimates available to us, foremost for the developed countries in Europe and North America. The general conclusions, based on the close relation that exists between rates of increase in productivity and rates of per-worker and per capita product, provoke the thought that such a comparison would indeed show that Israel has a much higher rate of increase in factor productivity than developed countries in Europe (including those listed in Table 2.1).[10]

The comparison may show that countries such as Japan, Taiwan, and Greece posted a larger increase in total productivity. However, with the quality of the existing estimates taken into consideration, Israel's growth rates probably far surpassed those of other non-Communist countries with very few exceptions; these growth rates, coupled with extraordinary population growth, are exceptional in the global community.

The Effect of Immigration

Adjustment for Longevity in Israel

A typical characteristic of the Israeli economy is the combination of mass immigration in the three years preceding 1952 and a high rate of per capita product growth in the subsequent years, 1952–70. Was there a *positive* relation between the two?

One link in the factual chain relating to this question is provided by data on income of head of household or other economic unit of immigrants in Israel by year of immigration, that is, longevity in Israel, in 1957/58. The income data were adjusted for other relevant variables.[11]

The savings survey and its related data for 1957/58 are based on a sample of three thousand urban wage-earner households. The survey presents data on income per head of immigrant household sorted by continents of origin, Asia–Africa versus Europe–America, and by longevity in Israel. The income data are also adjusted to head of household's schooling and age. The income index for heads of household born in Asia–Africa who immigrated to Israel in subsequent years (1952–57) was forty-four as against one hundred among immigrants born on the same continents who had immigrated in 1932–38. For those who had arrived by 1931, the income index was 110. Similar indices calculated for immigrant households from Europe–America were 59 for those who had immigrated in 1952–57 and 100 and 109, respectively, for those who had immigrated in 1932–38 and 1931 or earlier. Juxtaposing the income of the "veterans" who immigrated in or before 1931 with those who came in 1932–38, we find that the ratio of the income of the less-veteran immigrants to that of the more-veteran ones is 42:100 among immigrants from Asia–Africa and 56:100 among those from Europe–America.

After adjustment for age and schooling is made, the labor income of head of household among veterans of Asian African origin is almost equal to that of those from Europe–America (ninety-seven and one hundred, respectively). Presumably, then, the attainment of veteran status obliterates all significant difference in head of household's income, after adjustment for age and schooling, among immigrants from different continents.

Raw comparisons of more recent immigrants' labor income with that of veterans (the data are presented in the table cited in note 11) elicit an index of forty-seven versus one hundred among immigrants from Asia–Africa. Conspicuously, however, the unadjusted income of veteran heads of household from Asia–Africa is 75 percent of that of veterans from Europe–America, and not 97 percent.[12]

These findings—along with raw data relating to the beginning population, classified by longevity in Israel and extent of immigration during the adjustment period—underlie the calculations that are presented for illustration purposes in Table 2.3. This is because to establish proof, one must include more up-to-date data and investigate the problem more thoroughly and because the assumptions must be checked. The premises are realistic only in the sense that they use parameters that were derived from observation data obtained from at least one sample.

In Table 2.3, we assume that a recent immigrant attains veteran status after twenty years in the country. The point of departure, then, is the structure of Israel's Jewish population in 1952–53, which serves as a beginning population for our purposes. Half of this population was composed of immigrants who arrived in 1948/51 and one-fourth of it is thought to have amassed ten years' longevity on average (i.e., these are immigrants who reached Israel during the twenty years preceding 1948, with a gross correction for the mortality factor). The remainder are veterans including natives, immigrants with more than twenty years' longevity, and offspring who reached head-of-household age. We attribute to the three groups—recent immigrants, longer-tenured immigrants, and veterans—head of household's labor income on the basis of indices calculated by G. Hanoch. The index of forty-two among recent immigrants reflects the premise that most of them are from Asia–Africa (according to an alternate premise based on a weighted average of forty-two and fifty-six, we obtain an index of forty-five); multiplying by two hundred elicits the result that appears on line 1. Column 2 reports 112. (An alternative premise that takes into account the proportion of immigrants from Asia–Africa in this population group would yield only slightly lower results.) We assume that these immigrants are halfway between the initial immigration stage and veteran status; thus, the record in line 2, column 2, reports the income of those who are halfway between 112 and 200, that is, 156. Finally, veterans' income is set at two hundred.

These calculations (columns 1–3, Cases I and II) prepare the ground for the adjustments that will be made in their aftermath. In Case I, we assume first that the population is constant (or, alternatively, that the group structure of the beginning population does not change) and, second, that the process of an immigrant's becoming a veteran is completed twenty years after his or her arrival. This allows us to calculate the income per head of economic unit or product in the beginning and ending years. Under these assumptions, the head-of-unit income among the entire population would have increased by 2.14 percent per year during the period *without* an increase in income per veteran. If we were to allow an increase in veterans' income, the effect of the adjustment would be additive: an increase of 3 percent per year in income per veteran. Under the foregoing assumptions, this would mean a growth rate of 5.14 percent in income per head of unit among the entire population.

In Case II, we made another correction relating to the extent of immigration during the period investigated and to natural increase. (We assigned a 1.7 percent annual rate of increase to each of these factors, thereby adjusting the data to the total average increase of the population, which was 3.4 percent; see Table 2.1, line 4, column 2.) Another assumption is that current immigration originated mainly in Asia–Africa; accordingly, the appropriate income index is forty-two relative to the index of veterans' income, which is set at one hundred. We further assumed that adults added by means of natural increase would be considered veterans. (This group would also include immigrants and native-born after adjustment for age and schooling level.) Assuming linearity, we set the income of heads of unit who belong to

Table 2.3 Illustration of effect of longevity in Israel on labor income of head of economic unit

	Beginning year			Ending year		
	N (1)	Head of unit's income (2)	Total income (3)	*N* (4)	Head of unit's income (5)	Total income (6)
Case I: constant population, adjusted to age composition and schooling level of head of economic unit						
1 Recent immigrants	50	84	4,200	50	200	10,000
2 Veteran immigrants	25	156	3,900	25	200	5,000
3 Veterans	25	200	5,000	25	200	5,000
4 Total	100	131.0	13,100	100	200.0	20,000
Case II: immigration and natural increase take place during the twenty-year period (Rate of increase = 1.7 percent per year of beginning population)						
5 Recent immigrants	50	84	4,200	50	200	10,000
6 Immigrants arrived during period	0	0	0	40	142	5,680
7 "More veteran" immigrants	25	156	3,900	25	200	5,000
8 Veterans	25	200	5,000	25	200	5,000
9 Natural increase	0	0	0	40	200	8,000
10 Total	100	131.0	13,100	180	187.1	33,680

Case III: including adjustments for differences in head of unit's schooling level and age						
11 Recent immigrants	50	70.5	3,525	50	150	7,500
12 Immigrants arrived during period	0	0	0	40	110	4,400
13 "More veteran" immigrants	25	150	3,750	25	200	5,000
14 Veterans	25	200	5,000	25	200	5,000
15 Natural increase	0	0	0	40	200	8,000
16 Total	100	122.75	12,275	180	166.11	29,900

Case I: annual rate of increase in per capita income and total income—2.14 percent.

Case III: annual rates of increase: 1.52 percent in per capita income and 4.55 percent in total income.

The method used to calculate the parameters in this table is discussed in the study proper.

current immigration halfway between 84 and 200, that is, 142 (Table 2.2, line 6, column 5) and income per native-born adult head of unit (natural increase) at 200. By adjusting various categories of immigrants who are en route to becoming veterans and assuming that ongoing immigration is 1.7 percent per year continually and that natural increase occurs at a similar rate, we obtain an increase of 1.80 percent per year in head of unit's income across the entire (twenty-year) period. This adjustment is additive, that is, it may be added to any rate of increase in income attributed to the veteran population. Since this case allows an increase in Israel's Jewish population, the growth rate of total product comes to 5 percent, thanks to population increase and the fact that both "more-veteran" and "less-veteran" immigrants steadily converge with veterans in terms of their income level.

In Case III, we allow the assumption that the age and schooling level of heads of unit are equal among different population groups and that the income of immigrant (and veteran) heads of unit of Asian–African origin is one-fourth lower than that of veteran immigrants of other origin. By so doing, we mitigate the effects of integration and absorption of immigrants from Asian–African origin on the increase in head of unit's income. Although this approach is more realistic, it disregards, in a sense, the fact that some recent immigrants (those who immigrated in 1948–51) and a large proportion of more recent immigrants are not of Asian–African origin. (This would increase the income appearing in columns 2 and 5 in Case III.) In any event, this assumption induces two increases: of 1.5 percent per year in head of unit's income during the entire period and more than 4.5 percent in total product.

Obviously, these kinds of calculations have many limits. The parameters relating to head of household's income—in a specific annual sample of wage-earner households—and the evidence in note 12 show how widely the relative differences in income vary among groups of immigrants and how inconsistent they are. The approximate *path* of convergence of income between immigrant heads of unit and veterans was obtained, practically speaking, by means of (linear) assumptions and empirical data. Furthermore, the samples in our possession are limited to urban households; there is no reason to be sure that they accurately reflect the income of employed persons—immigrants and veterans—who belong to other population groups. In parsing the population into veterans, recent immigrants, and long-tenured immigrants, we made no correction for the non-Jewish population. Also, we did not take mortality by age and sex into account; presumably, the mortality rates of adult veterans and immigrants who arrived in earlier periods surpassed those of other immigrants. This may have had an effect on the final distribution of the population by subgroups and by longevity in the country. Finally, the use of differences in income among different longevity groups, which were obtained from cross-sectional studies at the beginning of the investigation period, is problematic.

The problem originates in the wish to use these data to profile the development, during the period investigated, of the relative income of immigrants as their longevity in Israel grows. It is certain, in view of the income data, that the timing of changes in the findings obtained from the 1957/58 sample reflect differences between population groups that are differentiated by longevity; they trace to the accumulation of historical events preceding the year in question. This, however, does not make it certain that the historical process will recur in the period from the early 1950s to the early 1970s. Sometimes the meaning of findings in a cross-sectional study that are translated into historical trend data may lose its validity or turn in the opposite direction.

This risk exists because cross-sectional studies fail too often to shed light on important variables or, in cases where important variables are conditioned on other variables, on the effect of the former or the disappearance of the latter.

For these and other reasons, the foregoing calculations are merely food for thought and may in this sense be misleading. The general conclusions, however, assure a formulation that will conduce, to the extent possible, to a partial explanation of Israel's high rate of economic growth and of the *differential* trends in productivity and consumption per head of unit that exist in its population.

The first conclusion relates to the possible effect of the large share of recent immigrants in the 1952/53 population, at the beginning of the period investigated, on the growth rate of per capita product. The better integrated and absorbed immigrants are, the larger the potential increase in income and productivity. Assuming that the arrival and absorption of more-recent and less-recent immigrants does not reduce product per head of unit in the veteran population, then the immigrants' integration and learning process may contribute to the annual increase in per capita product among the population at large—an increment that may be added to any rate of increase in the per capita product of the veteran population. In a calculation such as that performed in Case I, one may separate the 5.1 percent annual rate of increase in per capita product into two rates: 3 percent per head of unit among veterans, 7.7 percent in product per head of unit among recent immigrants, and 4.4 percent among longer-tenured immigrants—all of which assuming that the differentials parsed by longevity, obtained from the cross-sectional study, are convertible into a long-term trend that indicates the convergence of recent immigrants with veterans.

The second conclusion is that the analysis also applies to the increase in consumption per head of unit if the expected relation between income and per capita consumption exists. The rapid learning process of the immigrant population, which induces an even faster increase in productivity, would probably be accompanied by adjustments in consumption due to the convergence of head of unit's consumption with that of veteran immigrants. The parameters that determine consumption are almost certainly different from those of income, and the timing of the changes in consumption and product may also be different; this creates problems if and when the immigrants' consumption has to be increased *before* their productivity grows meaningfully.

The general analysis and the conclusions offered, however, may explain the rapid growth of per capita private consumption in Israel. A much faster upturn in recent immigrants' per capita private consumption may indicate a more modest increase in veterans' per capita consumption than that indicated by the overall data. More important, the existence of a relatively large subgroup of immigrants in the population may help to accelerate the growth rates not only of per capita product but also of per capita consumption.

Again, all the foregoing remarks should be considered guesses. The serious question that they raise, however, about the relations among the absorption of immigrants (and, of course, of other population subgroups such as non-Jews), aggregate growth rates, and differential trends in per capita productivity and consumption, is of definitive importance in understanding the growth process of the Israeli economy. The focused use of appropriate samples of household income and expenditure surveys among population subgroups, coupled with data from other sources (e.g., population censuses), creates a meaningful opportunity to explore this question thoroughly.

The Import Surplus

Even though we noted above (in Section Factor Productivity) that the vigorous growth rate of capital stock (and input) in Israel was accompanied by an especially high rate of increase in factor productivity per worker or per capita, one should not belittle the contribution of capital formation to growth. In a certain sense, the differences among population subgroups that are differentiated by longevity in the country, as discussed above, and the convergence of income or product of head of household, are related to and dependent on a supply of capital that increases persistently but unevenly. Needless to say, the large and annual capital inflow that is one of the most conspicuous characteristics of Israel's growth process contributed to growth in capital supply and to consumption originating in growth of productivity. In this context—that of capital inflow—two problems arise. One is whether other countries have had import surpluses of this kind or of similar magnitude relative to the aggregate magnitude of product in the past two decades, and, if there are such countries, what may one say about the properties of such a group? Second, how may one estimate the quantitative effects of the import surplus on the growth rate of total product and per capita product in the Israeli economy?

Table 2.4 presents several summary indicators that may yield a guideline of sorts as a preliminary to a more thorough and broad analysis of the problem. Obviously, the data in Table 2.4 do not illuminate the main factors behind the formation of import surpluses in the few countries in which we encounter them. Furthermore, these data (or others) do not offer a basis for the estimation of the immediate and direct effects of import surpluses on these economies' growth rates. However, the comparative data in Table 2.4 do suffice to instigate an initial trend of thought.

Lines 1–5 summarize the main data on Israel's import surplus: the rapid increase in exports but the even larger share of imports during the entire period, and the existence of an average import surplus—19 percent of GNP—in 1952–66.

The other countries in Table 2.4 were chosen on the basis of the following criteria: countries listed in Part B of Table 2.1 (i.e., the criteria used in their selection are also valid in the case at hand); the same countries (Part B of Table 2.1) excluding those with growth rates (of product, not of per capita product) of 6 percent or less; and finally an especially important criterion: countries that have a high share of

Table 2.4 Import surplus, gross capital formation, and change in capital/output ratio—Israel and other countries (Current prices except capital/output ratios; per capita Gross National Product in 1958, USD as figure in parentheses): Percent of GNP

	Exports (1)	Imports (2)	Net flow of factor payments (3)	Import surplus (4)	Gross domestic capital formation (5)	GNP growth rate (6)	Capital/ output ratio growth rate (7)
Israel 1950–66 (790)							
1 1950–51	3.5	22.0	–1.5	–20.0	33.5	N/C	N/C
2 1952–56	10.8	32.2	–1.6	–23.0	30.4	N/C	N/C
3 1957–61	13.0	27.2	–2.0	–16.2	28.4	N/C	N/C
4 1962–66	20.4	35.8	–1.4	–16.8	28.6	N/C	N/C
5 1952–66	14.7	31.7	–1.7	–18.7	29.1	10.3	2.8
Countries appearing in Table 2.1, Part B							
6 Japan, 1952–68 (350)	10.6	10.5	0.1	0.2	32.2	9.7	3.3
7 Taiwan, 1951–68 (114)	13.4	18.4	0	–5.0	18.7	8.5	2.2
8 South Korea, 1953–68 (141)	5.1	14.5	1.1	–8.3	14.9	6.3	2.4
9 Austria, 1950–68 (752)	22.5	23.3	0	–0.8	25.5	5.2	4.9
10 West Germany, 1950–68 (1015)	19.7	17.3	0	2.4	24.8	6.2	4.0
11 France, 1950–68 (1107)	14.1	13.6	0	0.5	22.5	5.1	4.4
12 Italy, 1951–68 (617)	13.7	14.0	0.2	–0.1	21.4	5.6	3.8
13 Greece, 1950–68 (385)	9.6	19.1	1.7	–7.8	21.0	6.4	3.3
14 Spain, 1954–68 (349)	8.9	10.5	0	–1.6	22.9	6.1	3.8

15 Portugal, 1953–68 (246)	19.8	25.0	0.1	–5.1	17.1	5.4	3.2
16 Puerto Rico, 1950–68 (660)	44.9	64.9	0.9	–18.8	23.4	6.3	3.7
Other countries with GNP growth rates exceeding 6 percent							
17 Jamaica, 1950–68 (370)	32.2	37.2	–2.4	–7.4	20.4	7.2 (1950–66)	2.9
18 Brazil, 1950–67 (169)	7.6	7.6	–0.9	–0.9	17.3	6.2	2.8
19 Mexico, 1950–67 (302)	12.7	13.2	–1.2	–1.7	14.9*	6.2	2.4*
20 Venezuela, 1950–68 (775)	34.5	24.5	–10.5	–0.5	25.9	6.7	3.5
Other countries with large import surpluses (in percent of GNP)							
21 Ireland, 1950–68 (578)	30.7	38.4	3.3	–4.4	18.0	2.6	7.2
22 Malawi, 1954–68 (<50)	–13.5		–0.6	–14.1	14.9	3.1 (1954–63)	4.8

N/C, not calculated.

*Not including changes in stocks.

All data except rate of increase in Israel's GDP (taken from Table 2.1) are culled from *Yearbook of National Accounts Statistics,* 1969, vol. II, International Tables (New York: United Nations, 1970).

The data on apportionment of GNP among uses (for columns 1–5) were taken from Table 2.2; per capita income in USD was culled from Tables A4 and B4.

Table 2 in the source presents annual GNP data in percent in current prices. The values in the Table for arithmetic average are of the respective rates for the periods at issue.

The changes in capital/output ratios (ICORs) in column 7 are calculated as follows: the share of gross domestic capital formation (column 5) is expressed in percent of GDP (by using the data on net flow of factor payments in column 3) and is then divided by the growth rate of gross product. In calculating this ratio, it is important to note that the share of gross domestic capital formation in GNP will be calculated from GNP in constant prices and on the same basis as the calculation of GNP from which the growth rates were derived. We assume, however, that the relative differences are hardly affected by the transition to GNP in constant prices; this is because in many countries such a transition is not possible due to lack of appropriate data.

Where a zero appears in column 3, the source described is insignificant in size.

import surplus in product (at least 5 percent). The use of multiple criteria (when discussed separately and not in the aggregate) reflects the need for data in order to focus the discussion on several questions.

First, which countries other than Israel had high shares of import surplus in product throughout the entire period? The following countries satisfy this condition: Taiwan, Greece, Portugal, Puerto Rico, South Korea, Jamaica, Malawi, and even Ireland, which were included in Table 2.1.

If we also had to examine countries that are covered by data for shorter periods (excluding countries with populations of less than one million), we would include (from the source cited in Table 2.4) Algeria in 1950–59, Tunisia in 1960–68, Chad in 1961–63, Dahomey in 1963–66, Jordan in 1959–68, and Lebanon in 1964–67. These countries had import surpluses of 9.4, 12, 10, 14, 19 percent, and nearly 17 percent of GNP, respectively. All the high-import-surplus countries are relatively small. (South Korea is the most populous.) All are closely tied to a major economic power—Ireland with Great Britain, the former French colonies with France, and, very conspicuously, Puerto Rico with the United States—or are related to a certain group of countries (e.g., Greece and, to some extent, Lebanon). Israel, like the other countries in this cohort, is closely connected with groups of other countries and, especially, with Diaspora Jewish communities, which are situated in free and economically developed countries. However, Israel's per capita income is much higher than that of any other country that has a large import surplus, with one outlying exception that proves the rule: Puerto Rico.

Another conclusion that our observations allow—ostensibly an obvious one—is that a large import surplus does not necessarily assure a high rate of increase in per capita product. The cases of Malawi and many countries in Africa and elsewhere demonstrate this; practically speaking, their economic condition is typical of colonial dependency irrespective of their formal political status. In the 1960s, Tunisia had a 12 percent import surplus and annual growth rates of less than 4 percent in total product and 1.6 percent in per capita product.

The best way to resolve the discussion of the effects of the import surplus on the Israeli economy, it would seem, is by distinguishing between a time of all-out crisis and steady adjustment factors. The reason for this differentiation is self-evident: the method of analysis that we would use to estimate the contribution of Israel's import surplus to its economic growth, not to speak of the quantitative aspect, would plainly be different in each of the types of situations that these two terms capture.

We shall describe times of crisis and all-out effort as historical states of emergency that menace a state's security and very existence. In such cases, the ability to control foreign sources, manifested in the import surplus, may take on life-and-death importance. Alternatively, it may affect postcrisis development with no systematic relation to the size of the import surplus per se. In Israel's brief history, one may find quite a few examples of such situations. The country's import surplus during the War of Independence, composed in particular of weapons and other military gear (or services that were vital at the time) had direct outcomes that transcend any economic calculus. Identifying some of the factors that are corollaries of armed conflict (border changes, etc.) and estimating their economic results may overshoot the abilities of socioeconomic analysis. Presumably, the import surplus in 1949–51 and several subsequent years largely reflected the essential all-out effort to absorb mass immigration. Had the integrity and viability of the Israeli economy failed the test at this time, there would have been acute adverse repercussions for subsequent economic growth. Israel has known plenty of moments of crisis in its brief history. It is mired in a continual confrontation with a hostile environment. It was forced to offer asylum to Jewish migrants who had reached the country in ways that were not the outcomes of decision. Had Israel refused to receive them, it would have endangered their future prospects in their countries of origin; furthermore, an expected change in policy might have thwarted the possibility of their emigration. Finally, the Middle East became a focal point of tension and international conflicts, with political changes and combinations of circumstances beyond Israel's control. Arguably, then, moments of crisis are not exceptional in Israel's experience; instead, they are its regular fare.

In view of the foregoing, let us sum up as follows: estimating the contribution of the import surplus to Israel's economic growth entails systematic analysis of the various crises and examination of the properties of each crisis in terms of the effort required and the goods and services that were supplied at the time by means of the import surplus. Our job in such a case is to note the contribution of the import surplus to resolving the crisis in consideration of the contribution of other domestic factors to the same outcome.

Although I believe this role deviates from that of the economist, it certainly deserves thought. After all, it would facilitate estimation of changes in the contribution of domestic sources and the import surplus to growth, the import surplus reflecting, in general contours, all or some of the external sources that were available to Israel's economy and society. Furthermore, in such an analysis the import surplus should be viewed not only as a factor that helps a country to *surmount overt crises* but rather and also as a factor that helps to *inhibit covert ones.*

Steady adjustment factors[13] relate to the contribution of the import surplus to growth under nonemergency conditions. By implication, at a time of stability, when the political, social, and economic framework functions properly and is not threatened by a crisis, the import surplus may serve the economy as an appropriate response. Even if we agree that this premise is altogether unrealistic in Israel's case—even in 1953–66—we still have to answer the question of how to estimate these factors, if only by approximation.

To answer this question simply, let us use the capital-formation rate, the growth rates, and changes in incremental capital/output ratios (ICORs) in Israel and other countries listed in Table 2.4. However raw the data in our possession are and however simplistic the method of analysis may be, the results at least provide food for thought.

Column 7 shows that the Israeli economy is typified by relatively modest rates of increase in ICOR. We find lower growth rates (with the exception of Mexico, which omits changes in stocks from its capital-formation data) only in Taiwan and South Korea, less-developed countries in which one would expect to find meager ICOR growth rates. We find sluggish rates resembling Israel's in Jamaica and Brazil. The other countries (even Greece and Puerto Rico) have much higher ICOR growth rates. Israel's low rates indicate that the country attained its high rates of increase in product by pledging a relatively modest share of GDP to capital formation. The rates of increase in ICOR that are needed to perform the following calculations may be derived from the share of gross domestic capital formation in domestic uses, which comes to 24.5 percent (29.1 / 118.7 × 100), and the rate of increase in total domestic uses, which works out to 9.0 percent per year (see Table 2.1, line 2, column 1). The rate obtained, 2.72, is not far from 2.8, the rate of increase in ICOR that appears in Table 2.4, line 5, column 7.

Now let us rephrase the question. If we assume that there is no long-term import surplus and that the Israeli economy has adjusted to the consequences of this—i.e., a 16 percent decrease in domestic uses (from 118.7 to 100)—how would gross domestic capital formation and the rate of increase in the relevant ICORs be affected? All of this assumes that the aforementioned adjustment takes place under conditions that are *not* internal or external emergencies, meaning that there are no serious problems other than those related to the lack of an import surplus. We discuss this problem in terms of the increase in ICORs for total domestic uses and the share of gross capital formation in domestic uses. According to the foregoing assumption, domestic uses and GDP are one and the same.

A partial answer to the question about the ICOR may be obtained from column 7 in Table 2.4. Assuming that product and population are growing, one would expect lower ICORs in countries that have smaller per capita product. Although there is no clear overlap, when one assumes a lower level of total domestic uses and per capita domestic uses—and, accordingly, a smaller extent of capital formation—while the rate of increase in the labor force does not change, one may expect changes in the ICORs to tend to be lower. We set the new ICOR at 2.65, slightly under the observed ratio (2.72).

How will the rate (as opposed to the absolute size) of capital formation be affected by our assumption of a lower level of domestic uses? One may adduce the answer from Table 2.4, column 5. It appears that the capital-formation rate will be lower because low-income countries (in terms of total per capita uses) have lower rates of capital formation. The data also show, however, that by reducing total domestic uses by 16 percent—which would still leave Israel with a rather high level of per capita domestic uses—one would expect a decline of no more than 2–3 percent in the rate of gross domestic capital formation. By implication, after the maximum reduction, the share of gross domestic capital formation in total uses (and in GDP) will be 21.5 percent. This outcome, together with an ICOR of 2.65, will induce an 8.1 percent annual rate of increase in total uses (or GDP) in the 1952–66 period. Since the rate of population increase during that time was 3.7 percent, the annual rate of increase in GDP or total per capita uses comes to 4.3 percent—still vigorous by international standards.[14]

Assuming the lack of an import surplus has farther-reaching effects than one can see at first glance. It means a 16 percent decrease in total per capita uses in the base year, a decline in the per capita capital formation rate from (0.245 × 100) to (0.215 × 86)—a one-fourth decrease—and a smaller downturn in per capita consumption (private and public). Furthermore, the decline in the annual growth rate of per capita domestic uses (for the 1952–66 period) from 5.1 percent

(Table 2.1, line 7, column 1) to 4.3 percent means that per capita domestic uses in 1966 will be one-fourth lower than the level actually attained—quite a meaningful decrease. As for GDP, the calculations do not show a decline in its level in the base year. However, the per capita growth rate slumps from 6.2 percent per year (in 1953–66; see Table 2.1, line 8, column 1) to 4.3 percent, meaning that per capita GDP in 1966 will be one-fourth less than it actually was.

The foregoing calculation is simple and logical but rather raw. If it seems unreasonable, it creates this impression due to a fallacious element in the main assumption: a political and international situation in which Israel is safe from harm, receives limited and controlled immigration (without crises), and has plenty of time to adjust to getting along without an import surplus. Still, however unrealistic this premise is, this calculation (or a more refined version of the same) may be valuable because, in contrast to an approach that takes crises into account, it establishes a lower bound, so to speak, of the contribution of the import surplus to Israel's growth rate. Although I admit the calculation is raw, I doubt that a more complex regression analysis would elicit much different or more reliable results.

As matters seem at the present writing, we credit the import surplus with adding 2 percentage points to the rate of increase in per capita GDP—or perhaps even less if we assume a lower ICOR and a slower rate of capital formation. At what point in the range between the crisis-and-all-out effort approach and the steady-adjustment-adjustment approach should we position the contribution of the import surplus? This is a question of judgment that cannot be answered here but that definitely provides food for thought that may make us wiser.

Concluding Remarks

The discussion in this study revolved mainly around the vigorous growth rate of total product, per capita product, and factor productivity in Israel in 1952–66. (The discussion is also valid for the period up to the early 1970s.) The analysis was based on comparing Israel's achievements in economic growth with those of several other non-Communist countries; the comparison was performed mainly in regard to aggregate economic magnitudes.

Several ideas were bruited: the increase in total productivity may have been greater than that elicited by conventional indicators, the mass immigration in Israel's early years made a weightier contribution to the increase in productivity, and the contributions of capital and even of the import surplus, under noncrisis conditions, were smaller than they appeared to be. In any event, I wish to qualify my remarks in two ways *in addition* to the limits already mentioned, which concerned the unavailability of basic data relating to Israel and other countries.

The first qualification is that one cannot possibly draw conclusions about the correspondence with needs, let alone the optimization, of the various aspects of Israel's economic growth, due to the lack of a partial analysis and of nonaggregate data. Although the growth rates measured are rather high indeed, two questions were not taken up in the discussion: are the structural aspects and the distribution of the growth rates the best ones possible, and was the potential illuminated by the aggregate magnitudes put to optimal use? There is no country that utilizes its entire economic potential or attains full optimization in its structural aspects and the distribution of its growth process, even if it could implement the appropriate programs irrespective of the political and institutional conditions that underlie its process of economic growth. However, by examining and analyzing *special* secondary problems, culled from the lengthy list of problems, we may draw some basic conclusions. Even though a primary debate such as the foregoing does not explicitly acknowledge the emphasis of this qualification (which is suited to any economic analysis that addresses an observed period in economic history), it cannot hurt to speak of it again.

The second qualification is much more important. It has to do with the lack of any attempt whatsoever to analyze and explain Israel's high growth rates of productivity and per capita income outside of noting the possible effects of mass immigration at the beginning of the period and the contribution of the growing capital stock and the import surplus. This leaves us with a broad domain of as-yet-unanswered questions. How was Israel able to attain such a high rate of increase in factor productivity even given its extent of immigration, the structure of its population, and the size of its import surplus? Many other countries, mostly undeveloped, that have large import surpluses and high population growth rates post rates of increase in per capita product and, accordingly, in productivity, that do not even begin to approach Israel's (except for aberrant cases such as Taiwan). In contrast, several developed countries that have high rates of capital formation and low rates of population increase have managed to attain growth rates of per capita product and productivity resembling Israel's.

To get to the root of the problem, an attempt should be made to identify aspects of Israel's social and institutional structure in recent decades that enabled the Jewish population of Palestine to attain the sort of political independence that paved the way to rapid economic growth and rapid utilization of the potential of the material and economic technology that has been amassed amid modern economic growth around the world. An attempt should also be made to detect the externalities—desirable and undesirable—that underscored the accelerated actions that were taken for the attainment of rapid economic growth as an essential basis for the steadily progressing fortification of a strong country that could withstand external threats.

From offhand observation, it seems to me that many of Israel's ideological and institutional aspects were tailored, at a fundamental level, to the conditions of rapid economic growth. Obviously, Israel's domestic political stability and national unity stand in conspicuous contrast to the historical experience of many countries that attained economic independence long ago. Is the selected and special nature of the veteran immigrants, especially those whose arrival preceded the rescue immigration in the 1930s, closely related to the ideological background of those who became the key group in the Israeli society and state?

The 1930s immigrants and some who came later boasted high levels of schooling. Many institutional innovations that the Jewish community in Palestine introduced in its attempts to fulfill its ideological goals persisted even after statehood was attained and were vastly important in the attainment of a higher rate of economic growth. Finally, the secret of Israel's rapid economic growth resides in the pressures that were brought against the country by its hostile surroundings.

When we introduce these ideological and institutional factors into the discussion, the economic tools lose some of their acuity. However, these tools may be useful, when coupled with thorough knowledge of the structural aspects of the Israeli economy; the ideological legacy of the pre-statehood Jewish community; the institutional innovations that were introduced at that time and that continued to exist later, if perhaps in a slightly different format; and the special influences and encouragement that were lavished on economic growth due to the situation of continual enmity in which the State of Israel is embroiled.

Notes

1. The source of data on Israel's population is M. Sicron and B. Gill, *Jewish Population by Sex, Age, and Country of Birth (1931–1954)*, Special

Publication 37 (Jerusalem: Israel Central Bureau of Statistics, 1955), Table 1.

2. There is one group of rapid-growth countries that we would exclude from the discussion even if we had long-term data about them: those that, due to abundant natural resources that others organized and exploited, enjoyed high growth rates only due to the royalties they were paid. Were it otherwise, these countries would be mired in backwardness and economic stagnation. For example, the UN data on Libya that appear in Part B (Table 4B, p. 131) indicate that this country experienced 27.3 percent annual growth of GDP in 1962–68, corresponding to 22.8 percent per capita growth. Even if we assume no increase whatsoever in per capita product from 1950 to 1952, the annual average in 1950–68 would come to 7.1 percent. The reasons for our exclusion of such economies from the discussion are self-evident. Furthermore, this group of economies is small and its exclusion has no significant effect on the arguments presented below.
3. In 1965, there were 106 non-Communist countries with populations of at least one million. (See my article, "The Gap: Concept, Management, Trends," in *The Gap between Rich and Poor Nations,* ed. Gustav Ranis, Proceedings of a Conference Held by the International Economic Association at Bled, Yugoslavia (London: Macmillan, 1972), Table 1.3, 37).
4. This figure is quoted from a summary by Michael Bruno based on research by Yehuda Manzly. The findings of this study are presented in "Measuring Productivity and Sources of Growth of Private Product, 1950–1967," *Bank of Israel Survey* 35 (November 1970). I base myself mainly on Bruno's summary, which appears in his article, "Economic Development of Israel," in Charles A. Cooper and Sidney S. Alexander, *Economic Development and Population Growth in the Middle East* (New York: American Elsevier Publishing Co., 1972), note 7, 96.

   The adjustments relate to the private sector only and Y. Manzly's study introduces an explicit adjustment to the schooling factor for 1962–67 only. (As for the occupational composition from 1956 onward, see Table 8, p. 66.) Thus, the adjustment is rather crude. These data are supported to some extent by another interesting study: Joseph Baruch, "Changes in Labor Input Quality in Israel, 1950–1961," *Bank of Israel Survey* 25 (April 1966): 32–34. Table 2 on p. 24 shows that the general schooling index declined from 94.3 (1950 = 100) in 1952 to 93.3 in 1961. A more meaningful statistic for our purposes may be the decrease in per capita education inventory among males—from 95.1 in 1952 to 91.7–91.9 in 1958–61 (see Appendix, Table A90, pp. 42–43.)
5. Nadav Halevi and Ruth Klinov-Elul *(The Economic Development of Israel.* New York: Praeger, 1968*)* include a series of stock data culled from an earlier version of Dr. A.L. Gaathon's book (see Table 44, p. 125; *Capital Stock Employment and Output in Israel, 1950-1959. Jerusalem: Bank of Israel, 1961*). This table, showing fixed capital and stock data for 1950–66 in 1955 prices, indicate that stock increased at a rate resembling that of the strong growth rate of fixed capital and even surpassed it slightly. The National Accounts data (in 1955 prices) show that the share of fixed-capital formation in GDP ranged from 28 to 38 percent in the period from 1952–54

to 1964–66, with no clear trend. The rate of change in stock as a share of GDP came to 2 percent in 1952–54 and 1.6 and 1.3 percent in 1961–63 and 1964–66, respectively. Even though the rate of increase in stock was slightly lower than that of fixed capital stock, its inclusion in capital input would not have affected the total growth rate perceptibly. If it were indeed possible to deal properly with the rates of capital formation, the rate of increase in capital input, including stock, would prove to be only slightly lower than that obtained on the basis of fixed capital stock.

6. See R. Goldsmith and Christopher Saunders, eds., "The Measurement of National Wealth," in *Income and Wealth, Series VIII of the International Association for Research in Income and Wealth* (London: Bowes and Bowes, 1959), Table III, 17–18. This source includes only countries for which complete data on both productive assets and primary assets existed. The reported rates of primary assets are high because they are based on estimates in current prices. Over the years, as economic growth takes place, the relative prices of primary resources, foremost land, presumably increase. Obviously, the current rates would have been much lower had they been calculated in terms of the prices that prevailed at the beginning of the period.

7. This argument is also used for international comparisons and the apportionment of growth sources down the lengthy path of modern economic growth. For an illustrative analysis of the known effect of the inclusion of *nonproductive* capital in productivity calculations over lengthy periods of time, see my book, *Economic Growth of Nations, Total Output and Production Structure* (Cambridge, MA: Harvard University Press, 1971), 61–70.

8. See reference to M. Bruno's article in note 4 and the use of these weights in Halevi and Klinov-Elul, *The Economic Development of Israel*. New York: Praeger, 1968, Table 45, 127. This adjustment brings two problems to the fore:

Assuming that the equilibrium rates of return to capital in Israel are higher than actual market rates and higher than those in most of the countries (especially the developed ones) with which we wish to compare Israel in terms of productivity growth, should we use these *national* rates in setting weights for the increase in factor inputs in calculating *productivity* for cross-country comparisons? If we do so, we will be subtracting from the productivity obtained as a residual the productivity of capital, which is especially strong in Israel as in several other countries, most of which are undeveloped. I elucidate this by offering an analogy: when we compare different countries' rates of increase in product, we would like to make an adjustment in order to do away with the overestimation of industrial goods relative to agricultural ones, especially in countries where price ratios are distorted due to deliberate economic policy. In these countries, the high growth rate of the manufacturing sector is overweighted in calculating the growth rate of total product. Similarly, when cross-country comparisons are performed, should we not make an adjustment for the overestimation of capital and prefer the use of an international set of weights for capital and labor inputs over a national set? The general upshot of this problem is that the calculation depends on the relevance of productivity obtained as a residual for the analytical uses that we wish to make of this index. Thus, for certain purposes, the international weights for factor inputs (market weights or equilibrium weights) may be more relevant.

The second problem has to do with the relation between the weights of factor inputs and those of added value (or derived income) in estimating total product. Is the higher rate of return on capital, which represents the distorted setting of a value smaller than that prevailing in the markets, also manifested in the prices that are used to estimate GDP—so that assigning greater weight to the capital input would effectively raise the weights (which are used to calculate sectoral growth rates) of especially capital-intensive sectors? Exactly what are the factor-input weights that are embodied in the added-value weights (or the derived-income weights) and that underlie the estimate of GDP (or some other aggregate magnitude) that is used for the calculation of productivity?

It is impossible to delve into these problems in this study; the appropriate literature may offer an answer to the second question. However, the questions are intriguing enough to be mentioned here.

9. The value of per-worker final consumption per hour (or year) worked as the correct indicator of an economy's total productivity would increase if it were possible to subtract the components that constitute intermediates and are included in the regular category of household-consumption expenditure, and if it were possible to add the services that government provides consumers, which are now included in government consumption. This remark brings us back to the problems associated with the use of conventional National Accounts indicators in determining a yardstick for economic growth and long-term changes—matters that are being extensively debated at the present writing.

10. Gaathon (Table 22; see note 5 for citation) compares Israel's productivity growth rates in 1950–65, without making the adjustments proposed above, with productivity growth rates in the 1950s in ten countries, eight of which (apart from Canada and Yugoslavia) belong to the class of developed European countries. The comparison shows that Israel's productivity growth rates were lower only than those of West Germany and Italy and equal to that of France. If the investigation period in Israel is changed to 1953–65 and the reference for West Germany and Italy is changed to the 1960s, Israel emerges with the highest rate of productivity increase among the countries in the group, even without the aforementioned adjustments. It should be borne in mind, however, that the table does not include Japan, Taiwan, and Greece.

11. See Giora Hanoch, "Income Differentials in Israel," *Falk Project for Economic Research in Israel, Fifth Report, 1959 and 1960* (Jerusalem: August 1961), Table 22, 100.

Subsequent studies that sort the income of immigrants and native households by longevity in Israel, country of origin, and other variables are Central Bureau of Statistics and Bank of Israel, *Savings Surveys 1963–1964,* Special Publication 217 (Jerusalem: CBS, 1967) and *Household Expenditure Survey 1968/69,* Part A, Special Publication 330 (Jerusalem: CBS, 1970).

These studies do not provide a full adjustment of head of household's income to age and level of schooling.

I discuss these data in general terms later in this study. Obviously, to put these data (and other data in Giora Hanoch's study) to appropriate use, we would have to return to original data that were not published. Since this burdensome task would overtax my strength, my main purpose in using Hanoch's data in the discussion is more for illustration than for basic analysis.

12. Importantly, the foregoing parameters relate to the *labor* income of heads of household. Be this as it may, ibid., Tables 8–9, 68–69, presents comparisons of household personal income over a three-year period. In 1957/58, the ratio of more recent immigrants' personal income that of veterans was 50:101.5, 48 among immigrants from Asia–Africa, and 49:105.5 among immigrants from Europe–America. These findings approximate those cited above, which were based on head of household's *labor* income.

The following data were obtained for the 1956/57 sample (Household Income and Expenditure Survey): the ratio of personal income per immigrant household to that of veterans was 75:103.0 or 73 among immigrants from Asia–Africa and 71:100 among immigrants from Europe–America—perceptibly higher than the ratios found in the 1957/58 savings survey. The data from the 1954 sample (in which recent immigrants were defined as those who had immigrated between 1951 and 1954), the ratio (among immigrants from all continents) was 60:104.5 or 57:100. I admit that the higher rates in 1956/57 relative to those of 1957/58 are somewhat perplexing.

In a survey conducted in 1963/64, the parsing of years of immigration distinguishes among those who had arrived before 1947, those who arrived in 1948–54, and those who immigrated in or after 1955. The index of gross income per wage-earner household for immigrants from Asia–Africa (with the income of veterans who immigrated before 1948 equaling one hundred) was ninety-three among 1948–54 immigrants and seventy-five among those who immigrated in 1955 and after. (See source cited in note 11, Table 18, 42.) One may compare these data with the grouping in the 1957/58 survey (averaging of personal income per household among all population groups that immigrated before 1947 and indexing the result at one hundred). The indices obtained are seventy-five for the 1948–51 period and fifty-three for 1952 and afterwards. The data allow us easily to discern the trend of the immigrants' absorption over time. The data on income per wage-earner household in 1968/69, sorted by years of immigration, are identical to those obtained from the 1963/64 sample. The indices calculated for that point in time are seventy-eight among 1948–54 immigrants and sixty-three among immigrants who arrived in 1955 or later. Both indices are lower than those for 1963/64 even though they "converge" somewhat relative to 1957/58. (Ibid., Table 19, 74–75.) The respective indices for immigrants from Europe–America are eighty and fifty-six in 1963/64 and seventy-nine and sixty-eight in 1968/69 as against seventy-three and forty-eight, respectively, in 1957/58.

Obviously, given the changes in the sorting of immigrants by years of immigration and the average longevity in Israel of the different population groups in the survey year, any insight that one may glean from the surveys in our possession must be thoroughly examined before appropriate comparison can be performed. For illustration purposes, it suffices to observe that the veteran and immigrant indices converged somewhat over time and that the extent of the convergence increases in tandem with longevity in the country. For the analysis at hand, one might settle for adjusting head of household's income to age and schooling level. Such an adjustment, however, is too complex to perform within the ambit of this study.

13. I refrain from calling these factors "long term," even though essentially this is what they are because emergencies that entail all-out efforts may have long-term outcomes even if they themselves are temporary. Accordingly, an import surplus that serves to alleviate tension and crisis in the short term sometimes has long-term effects.
14. An alternative way of doing the calculation, based on the coefficients in Table 2.2 and pertaining to the relative contribution of labor and capital inputs and factor productivity, elicits data on capital stock for the various countries. However, the current data on capital formation are more complete and available.

3

Immigration of Russian Jews to the United States: Background and Structure

Simon Kuznets

Introduction

This chapter deals with the background of the mass immigration of Jews from Tsarist Russia to the United States. The movement began in the early 1880s, reached a crest in 1906, remained high up to World War I, was reduced sharply by that war, and then, except for a short period of substantial flows in 1920–24, dwindled to a trickle. The sharp reduction since the twenties reflected not only the severe restrictions on immigration in the United States but also the rigid barriers to emigration in the major successor states of the Russian Empire. Our discussion will relate to Jews in Tsarist Russia[1] and to the background of their immigration and the propelling forces during the three and one half decades from the beginning of the 1880s to 1914. However, some attention will be paid to other groups of Jewish immigrants to the United States and to other periods.

We begin with a brief account of the volume and time pattern of immigration of Russian and other Jews to the United States in the years 1881–1914. Some attention is given to earlier and later years in order to place the mass migration in proper perspective and particularly to permit us to consider the factors that could account for the migration patterns indicated (and paralleled in some respects by the migration flows of other groups to the United States). Next we review the historical background of Russian Jewry, which may help to explain both its social and its economic characteristics and the factors that impelled its migration, primarily to the United States. Since this migration was selective (all migrations, particularly long-distance ones, are), we compare the specific characteristics of Jewish immigrants to the United States, most of them from Russia, with the relevant characteristics of Jews in Tsarist Russia, and with those of non-Jewish immigrants to the United States over the period in question. We conclude with brief reflections on broader questions raised by this detailed, and statistically oriented, discussion.

Immigration—Volume and Time Pattern

Table 3.1 summarizes the data on immigration of Jews into the United States from Tsarist Russia and from the two other major countries of origin, Austria-Hungary and Romania, for the period 1881–1914.[2] The United States immigration data distinguish Jews for the first time in 1899—when the category designated "Hebrews," based largely on linguistic considerations (Yiddish mother tongue), was introduced. Unofficial data from the reports of Jewish immigrant aid organizations provide the basis of the estimates for 1881–98. The details of the estimation are given in the notes to the table. However, some general characteristics of the data are worth noting here to permit a better understanding of the significance, and possible limitations, of the estimates.

First, even the United States immigration count of "Hebrews" beginning with 1899 and discontinued in 1943 falls short of the total of Jewish immigrants. The data relate to steerage passengers alone and may even exclude some of those who were assimilated Jews reporting a language other than Yiddish as mother tongue.[3] No adjustment for such possible omissions is practicable, but it probably was not significant for Jews from Russia or Eastern Europe.

Second, and more important, the distribution of the total of Jewish immigrants between those from Eastern Europe and those from other countries, particularly from Western or Central Europe or Canada, had to be adjusted. Eastern European Jews immigrated into the United States via ports in Germany, Great Britain, and eventually Canada where many may have stayed for a year or more before migrating for permanent settlement in the United States. The official "data prior to 1906 cover countries from which the aliens came; data for the years following, countries of last permanent residence."[4] But even the latter may have been a transition residence. Internal evidence on this point is striking: the number of Hebrew immigrants reported from the United Kingdom (fewer than six hundred per year for 1899–1904) rose to over fourteen thousand in 1905 and averaged over five thousand per year in 1906–10, the period of huge migration of Jews from Tsarist Russia; and the rise in the reported flow of Hebrew immigrants from Canada was similarly striking.[5] Since we are concerned with establishing the weight of Russia in total Jewish immigration into the United States, it seemed best to make an adjustment, rough as it is, for this distortion. We assumed that the shares of countries other than the major three (Russia, Austria-Hungary, and Romania), for which transition passage could be expected, were limited to the levels prevailing in years of moderate immigration and hence did not involve lengthy stopovers on the way to the eventual destinations. This limit was set roughly at 2 percent (somewhat above that observed for 1899–1902), and the residual was allocated proportionately among the three Eastern European countries.[6]

Finally, all the data used here refer to gross immigration, either aliens or immigrant aliens admitted, without correction for the return flow. Figures on the latter are available only beginning with fiscal 1908, and they are summarized in Table 3.1 for 1908–14. Partly because of the limited time coverage of the departure data, partly because of the limited detail that they provide on the characteristics of the people involved, we shall have to use gross immigration as an approximation to net.

We can now summarize the findings in Table 3.1 on Russian-Jewish immigration, largely for 1881–1914 but with some consideration of the record for the earlier and later periods.

The table begins with 1881 because there is no acceptable basis for making estimates for earlier years. Yet this lack of an acceptable basis may, in turn, reflect the fact that in these earlier years the influx of Jewish immigrants was relatively limited and did not elicit the kind of organizational activity and the resulting data supplied by the Jewish organizations beginning in the 1880s. The indirect data do in fact suggest that the number of Russian-Jewish immigrants could not have been large before the 1880s.

These indirect data cover admissions of all immigrants from Russia and Poland and the number of foreign born by country of birth in the decennial censuses. Data on immigrant admissions from Russia and Poland show for 1820–70 a cumulative total of less than four thousand from the Russian Empire and about the same from Poland—this over a period of half a century.[7] These few thousand probably included some Jews but not many.

Table 3.1 Jewish immigration to the United States, by country of origin, 1881–1914 (fiscal years ending June 30, absolute figures in thousands)

A. Gross immigration, total and Jewish, 1881–1914

		Jewish				
	Total (1)	Total (2)	Tsarist Russia (3)	Austria-Hungary (4)	Romania (5)	Other (6)
Gross immigration, total for period						
1. 1881–89	4,790	204.3	139.5	53.1	7.6	4.1
2. 1890–98	3,383	366.6	279.1	73.4	6.9	7.2
3. 1899–1902	1,898	214.0	136.8	53.9	20.9	2.4
4. 1903–7	5,082	615.2	482.0	93.9	27.4	11.9
5. 1908–14	6,710	656.5	519.7	106.3	17.3	13.2
6. 1881–1914	21,863	2,056.6	1,557.1	380.6	80.1	38.8
Average per Year						
7. 1881–89	532	22.7	15.5	5.9	0.84	0.4
8. 1890–98	376	40.7	31.0	8.2	0.79	0.8
9. 1899–1902	475	53.5	34.2	13.5	5.2	0.6
10. 1903–7	1,016	123.0	96.4	18.8	5.5	2.4
11. 1908–14	959	93.8	74.2	15.2	2.5	1.9

Portions and percentages		Jewish as percent of total	Percentage distribution of Jewish immigration			
12. 1881–89	100	4.3	68.3	26.0	3.7	2.0
13. 1890–98	100	10.8	76.1	20.0	1.9	2.0
14. 1899–1902	100	11.3	63.9	25.2	9.8	1.1
15. 1903–7	100	12.1	78.3	15.3	4.5	1.9
16. 1908–14	100	9.8	79.2	16.2	2.6	2.0
17. 1881–1914	100	9.4	75.7	18.5	3.9	1.9
B. Departures of emigrants, 1908–14						
	Non-Jewish	**Jewish by origin**				
		Total	**Tsarist Russia**	**Austria-Hungary**	**Romania**	**Other**
	(1)	**(2)**	**(3)**	**(4)**	**(5)**	**(6)**
18. Departures, absolute	1,947	46.8	28.1	11.3	0.7	6.7
19. Percentage distribution of Jewish departures		100.0	60.0	24.2	1.5	14.3
20. Admissions, distribution of Jewish immigrants by country of origin not adjusted	6,053	656.5	471.4	96.1	15.7	73.3
21. Percentage distribution of Jewish admissions		100.0	71.8	14.6	2.4	11.2
22. Ratios of departures to admissions (%)	32.2	7.1	6.0	11.8	4.5	9.1

(*continued*)

Table 3.1 (*continued*)

The totals are based on annual series derived from several sources. The description deals separately with the estimates of total Jewish immigration (gross) and its distribution by country of origin, with particular emphasis on Russia.

Data on total immigration and on total immigration of Jews (Hebrews), the latter available only from fiscal 1899 onward, were taken directly, without adjustment, from two convenient sources (both using the annual reports of the Commissioner General of Immigration): Reports of the Immigration Commission, III, Statistical Review of Immigration, 1820–1910-Distribution of Immigrants, 1850–1900, 61 Cong., 3 Sess., Senate Doc. No. 756 (Washington, D.C., 1911), which is abbreviated below as *RIC*-III; and Walter F. Willcox, ed. *International Migrations*, vol. I (Statistics, compiled and annotated by Imre Ferenczi for the International Labour Office and the National Bureau of Economic Research New York, 1929). We also used the Annual Report of the Commissioner General of Immigration for 1912–14 (Washington, the relevant years). Data on departures available only since 1908 are from the same sources.

While total Jewish immigration (all immigrants to 1909, and immigrants admitted beginning with 1908) was taken as given, the apportionment by country of origin was adjusted to allow for the movement of Jews from Russia, Austria-Hungary, and Romania via other countries (including Canada)—an adjustment suggested by the swelling of immigrants reported from these transit countries whenever the movement from Russia became large. For years in which immigration reported from the other countries exceeded 2 percent of total Jewish immigration, the excess over a percent was allocated proportionately among the three major sources (Russia, Austria-Hungary, and Romania). The magnitude of the adjustment can be seen by comparing lines 20 with lines 5 and 16, for 1908–14 (when the proportions moving through other countries were particularly large).

For the years before fiscal 1899, reliance had to be placed on estimates of Jewish immigrants entering through three ports (New York, Philadelphia, and Baltimore) for 1894–98 and through New York alone (by far the dominant) for 1886–93. These data, collected by Jewish agencies, are found in Samuel Joseph, *Jewish Immigration to the United States from 1881 to 1910* (New York, 1914), which also shows the apportionment by country of origin, among Russia, Austria-Hungary, Romania, and all other.

For 1894–98, total Jewish immigration was estimated by raising the sum of entries for the three ports by so percent, a figure suggested by the comparison of similar entries in the subsequent years with the official totals (the former were given in successive issues of the American Jewish Yearbook, for 1900 and later years). For 1886–93, we raised the entries for the New York port by a factor that moved from 1.32 in fiscal 1893 to 1.25 in fiscal 1886 (to allow for the other two ports, on the assumption that ports other than New York played a lesser role in the earlier years). Once the annual totals for 1886–88 were estimated, the distribution among the four classes by origin (the three specific countries and "all other") were again adjusted for years in which "all other" accounted for more than 2 percent.

Given the estimates for 1886–98, total and for the four areas of origin, we calculated the proportions of Jewish to all immigrants from Russia, Austria-Hungary, and Romania. For Romania, the proportions had to be set at 100 percent since the actual figures estimated for Jewish immigrants were somewhat larger than the official figures for all immigrants from Romania. For Russia and Austria-Hungary, the denominator had to be adjusted to include immigrants from Poland, shown separately in the official data. For this purpose, we used the ratios from *RIC*-III, Table 9, 416, which indicate that of the Polish foreign born in 1900, 43 percent were from the Russian part of Poland, and 16 percent from the Austro-Hungarian part. Our calculation showed that the Jewish immigrants for 1886–98 accounted for 70 percent of total immigration from Russia plus 43 percent of total immigration from Poland, and 16 percent of the total immigration from Austria-Hungary, plus 16 percent of the total immigration from Poland. The application of these ratios to total immigration from Russia and Austria-Hungary (plus the indicated portions of total immigration from Poland), and of the 100 percent ratio to total immigration from Romania, yielded the estimates of Jewish immigration from the three areas of origin for 1881–85. The 2 percent allowance for "all other" rounded out the totals.

For 1871–80, gross immigration from the Russian Empire was 39.3 thousand; from Poland, thirteen thousand. The net change between 1870 and 1880 in foreign born was 31.1 thousand for those born in Russia, and 34.1 thousand for those born in Poland.[8] Apparently, an appreciable proportion of Poles born in Russia (or other countries) did not report themselves as Poles when they immigrated, but did appear as such in the Census of Population.

If we were to apply the ratios used for 1881–85 in Table 3.1, the total of Russian-Jewish immigration for 1871–80 would have been [39.3 + (13.0 × 0.43)] × 0.7, or about thirty-one thousand. The annual average would have been less than a fifth of that estimated for 1881–89 (see line 7, column 3). But a total of thirty-one thousand would still be a marked overestimate: the state distribution of the Russian foreign born in 1870 and 1880 indicates that of the total rise of 31.1 thousand, an addition of about twenty thousand is shown in four agricultural states—Kansas, Minnesota, Nebraska, and the Dakota Territory—where Jewish immigrants were not likely to settle.[9] Over the same decade the increase of Russian foreign born in the North Atlantic division was only 5.4 thousand, or less than a fifth of the total. By contrast, in the interval from 1880 to 1890, the North Atlantic division accounted for about 60 percent of the 147,000 increase in the foreign born from Russia. One should, therefore, scale down the gross number of Russian-Jewish immigrants for the decade 1871–80 to between fifteen thousand and twenty thousand at most.[10]

Both total Jewish and Russian-Jewish immigration began at moderate rates in the 1880s and accelerated to a peak in 1905 and 1906—when the effects of dislocation and the revolution exacerbated the endemic pressures of Russian government and society on the country's Jews—and continued at high levels up to the outbreak of World War I. As a result, of the total gross immigration of some 1.6 million Jewish immigrants from Russia over the thirty-four-year period, about two-thirds are concentrated in the last twelve years, 1903–14. This pattern of immigration—an insignificant trickle over decades, then more substantial but moderate levels, then high levels, both absolute and relative to the originating population—can be observed for several other groups in the United States immigration statistics. For example, gross immigration from Norway and Sweden (not shown separately in earlier decades) for 1820–64 was less than two thousand per year; and then rose after 1865, first to about twenty thousand per year, then to a peak of over seventy thousand per year in the 1881–85 quinquennium,

Table 3.2 Total immigration to the United States from Tsarist Russia, Jewish, and other, 1871–1914 (fiscal years, absolute figures in thousands)

				Per year	
	Total (1)	Jewish (2)	Other (3)	Jewish (4)	Other (5)
1. 1871–80	44.9	15.0	29.9	1.5	3.0
2. 1881–89	195.2	139.5	55.7	15.5	6.2
3. 1890–98	435.9	279.1	156.8	31.0	17.4
4. 1899–1902	344.4	136.8	207.6	39.2	51.9
5. 1903–7	940.7	482.0	458.7	96.4	91.7
6. 1908–10	464.0	186.2	277.8	62.1	92.6
7. 1911–14	867.8	329.0	538.8	82.3	134.7

Column 1: For lines 4–6 derived directly from *RIC*-III. For lines 1–3 derived by taking total immigration from Russia plus 43 percent of immigration from Poland (see notes to Table 3.1). For line 7 taken from the *Annual Report of the Commissioner General of Immigration* for 1911–14.

Column 2: For line 1 see the estimate in the text. For the years from 1881 onward see Table 3.1. In the table here, we give the total for Russian-Jewish immigration adjusted to include immigrants via Western European countries or Canada. The official totals are, for the periods beginning with line 4: 1899–1902—136.8; 1903–7—457.7; 1908–10—171.0; 1911–14—301.4. Use of these unadjusted totals would not affect the major movements in the residual in column 3.

Column 3: Column 1 minus column 2.

and subsequently, to World War I, varied between twenty thousand and fifty thousand. Even more striking is immigration from Greece, which was well below 100 per year until the second half of the 1880s and then climbed rapidly to a peak of almost ten thousand per year in the 1901–5 quinquennium. Similar patterns were followed by other emigrant populations, both small and large—from Belgium, Denmark, the Netherlands, and Switzerland.[11]

Particularly important for our explanatory discussion of the factors inducing Jewish immigration from Tsarist Russia is the evidence that non-Jewish immigration from that country also exhibited, with some lag, the explosive rise from a trickle to a large flow. Table 3.2 shows clearly that the number of non-Jewish immigrants was also small in the 1870s, then rose rapidly, and in the decade and a half preceding World War I accelerated as rapidly as that of the Jewish immigrants.

As is indicated below (Table 3.5C), most of this non-Jewish immigration was from ethnic stocks other than Russian as such (i.e., other than Russians, Ukrainians, and White Russians). The official data for 1899–1914 show that the largest groups among non-Jewish immigrants from Russia were the Poles, the Lithuanians, the Finns, and the Germans, who together accounted for 8.1 percent of the non-Jewish total. The "Russian" component was only 13.3 percent. The non-Jewish total used here is the larger residual, obtained by subtracting the unadjusted total of Jewish immigration from Russia.

Immigration of Jews from Russia was well over three-quarters of the total Jewish immigration to the United States for the full period (Table 3.1, line 17, column 3). We stress this point because in later discussion we shall be compelled to use, for 1899–1914 or for 1908–14, data for all Jewish immigration as representing effectively the Jewish immigration from Tsarist Russia. Such treatment is in large partly justified because in these two periods, the proportion of Russian Jews within the total Jewish immigration was as high as 70 and 80 percent. If, as will be noted below, the economic and social structures of Russian Jews and those from Austria-Hungary (largely Galicia) are fairly similar, the use of United States data on all Jewish immigrants to derive characteristics of Russian-Jewish immigrants is not likely to result in large errors.

Though the proportions of Jewish and Russian-Jewish immigration to total immigration rose, once the higher proportions were reached in 1890–98, the movements of Jewish, Russian Jewish, and total immigration were fairly similar. Thus all three show a moderate rise in immigration per year from 1890–98 to 1899–1902, a more than doubling between 1899–1902 and 1903–7, and a moderate decline from 1903–7 to 1908–14. This similarity in the short-term changes of Jewish (and implicitly Russian Jewish) immigration and of total immigration is revealed even more sharply by the annual data underlying the period averages in Table 3.1. Short-term changes in total immigration are found responsive to business cycles—the short-term fluctuations in the economic conditions of the United States—at least in periods free from wars. Consequently, despite long-term trends in the immigration from various groups of countries that respond to the push, the short-term changes in immigration generally respond to the pull of economic conditions in the United States—so long, again, as legal constraints or wars do not restrict the movement.[12]

In the six decades since the outbreak of World War I, both total and Jewish immigration into the United States were reduced sharply from the high levels shown in Table 3.1 for 1903–14. The explanation is obvious: the effects of the war pre-1919, legal restrictions taking effect after 1924, further reductions during the depression decade and World War II, and continued restrictions thereafter. A brief summary of the data is presented in Table 3.3, and our main interest is in the estimates of Jewish immigration of Russian origin.

Two lacunae in the basic data necessitate somewhat arbitrary procedures, and the conclusions we can derive are subject to greater relative error than the data summarized in Table 3.1. Since we wanted to retain some continuity between the Jews of Tsarist Russia and Russian Jews after World War I, the first problem was created by changes in the boundaries of the Russian state after World War I. A necessarily crude allocation had to be made of Jewish immigrants from post–World War I Poland between those who could be credited to Congress Poland (the Polish part of the old Tsarist Empire) and others. The second difficulty was created by the discontinuance, after fiscal 1943, of the "Hebrews" category in the official United States statistics of immigration. We had to use unofficial estimates of total Jewish immigration, which did not permit the separation of the Russian-Jewish component.

Despite these difficulties, the major endings of Table 3.3, relevant to our theme, are clear and unlikely to be significantly affected by qualifications. Gross Jewish immigration declined sharply after 1914 and continued to do so throughout the period. Compared with an annual average of over two thousand in 1903–14 (see Table 3.1, lines 10–11, column 2), the average was twenty-seven thousand in 1915–29, 13.4 thousand in 1930–43, and 10.6 thousand in 1944–68.

Second, the proportion of Russian Jews among the total of Jewish immigrants also declined. It was less than a quarter in 1915–29, compared with over eight-tenths in the decade before 1914 and declined to less than a tenth in 1930–43. While no data are available for 1944–68, one may assume that the proportion of Jews of Russian origin was probably not more than a tenth.

Third, as in the earlier period, the proportion of departures to admissions was far lower for Jewish than for total immigration—and the contrast sharpened as the departure proportions for Jewish immigrants dropped to 2 percent or lower, compared with 7 percent just before World War I. But despite this high ratio of net to gross migration, the additions, over the recent five and a half decades, to the cumulative inflow of Russian-Jewish immigrants were relatively small. If for 1881–1914 we allow for an average 6 percent departure ratio (implying fewer departures in earlier decades because of greater costs and difficulties of transport), the net cumulative Russian-Jewish

Table 3.3 Total and Jewish immigration into the United States, 1915–68 (fiscal years, absolute values in thousands)

	Total immigration			Jewish immigration			
	Admissions (1)	Departures (2)	Col. (2) as percent of Col. (1) (3)	Total admissions (4)	Total departures (5)	Col. (5) as percent of Col. (4) (6)	Admissions from Russia (7)
1. 1915–19	1,173	618	52.7	65.7	3.1	5.0	26.0
2. 1920–24	2,775	893	32.2	286.5	2.3	0.8	107.7
3. 1925–29	1,521	390	25.6	56.2	1.3	2.3	19.5
4. 1930–34	427	336	78.7	26.5	1.8	6.8	6.8
5. 1935–39	272	153	56.3	85.8	1.3	1.6	4.0
6. 1940–43	175	51.1	29.2	79.6	0.6	0.8	1.5
7. 1944–49	672	99.2	14.8	107.5	NA	NA	NA
8. 1950–54	1,099	131	11.9	48.4	NA	NA	NA
9. 1955–59	1,400	123*	8.8*	36.0	NA	NA	NA
10. 1960–64	1,418	NA	NA	43.0	NA	NA	NA
11. 1965–68	1,436	NA	NA	29.7	NA	NA	NA
Longer periods, totals							
12. 1915–29	5,469	1,901	34.8	408.4	6.7	1.7	153.2
13. 1930–43	874	540	61.8	191.9	3.7	1.9	12.3
14. 1944–68	6,025	NA	NA	264.6	NA	NA	NA

Longer periods, per year							
15. 1915–29	365	127	34.8	27.2	0.45	1.7	10.2
16. 1930–43	62.4	38.6	61.8	13.7	0.26	1.9	0.9
17. 1944–68	241	NA	NA	10.6	NA	NA	NA

*Based on 1955–57 only.

Na, not available.

Lines 1–2: The underlying data are from *International Migrations*, vol. I, Table XIII, 460–70, and Table XV, 473. The major problem was to estimate Jewish immigration from the former Tsarist Empire, which by 1920 was reduced to post–World War I Russia. For 1920–24 the question related to Poland, which for 1924–29 accounted for 127,000 Jewish immigrants (compared with only thousand from Russia). For this and subsequent quinquennia we assumed that one half of the Jewish immigrants from post–World War I Poland could be credited to the former part of the Tsarist Empire (i.e., so-called Congress Poland). This fraction was based on Jacob Lestchinsky's estimates which showed, for 1915, a total of Jews in former Congress Poland of 1.475 million, compared with a total for all of Poland of 2.8 million (the former figure is from "Die Umsiedlung und Umschichtung des jüdischen Volks im Laufe des letzten Jahrhunderts," *Weltwirtschaftliches Archiv* 30, pt. 2 (1929), Table I, 132–33; the latter from "Die Zahl der Juden auf der Erde," *Zeitschrift für Demographie und Statistik der Juden*, first half year of 1925, *Heft* 1, 1–8). In subsequent quinquennia, the relatively small number of Jewish immigrants from Latvia and Lithuania (available only from 1924 on) were also included.

Lines 3–11, columns 1–3: The underlying data are from United States Bureau of the Census, *Historical Statistics of the United States* (Washington, D.C., 1960); the supplement to it, *Continuation to 1962* (Washington, D.C., 1965); and the *Statistical Abstract* for later years.

Lines 3–6, columns 4–7: These are official U.S. data, as reported in successive issues (from 1925 through 1943) of the *American Jewish Yearbook* (published annually in Philadelphia by the Jewish Publication Society). Immigration of Jews from Russia (to correspond to the former Tsarist Empire) is the sum of Jewish immigrants from Russia, Latvia and Lithuania, plus half of the Jewish immigrants from Poland.

Lines 7–11, column 4: The official statistics discontinued the identification of "Hebrews" among immigrants after fiscal 1943. Estimates for later years have been prepared and published in the *American Jewish Yearbook* (see particularly the issue for 1961 (vol. LXII) and selected later issues) by Ilya Djour, and later by Jack J. Diamond. The figures are for gross admissions and are based on data from Jewish agencies and some U.S. government agencies. Only a rough regional allocation is available for later years. The latest estimate is for 1968.

immigration was close to 1.5 million, whereas the net total since 1915 was less than 200,000. By concentrating on the period 1881–1914, we are dealing with the few decades during which mass migration took place and had a major impact on the structure of the Jewish population of the United States.

It is, of course, possible that in the post–World War I period, a large proportion of the Jewish immigrants from countries other than Eastern Europe may have been Jews who had migrated to these other countries from Russia in earlier years. This may have been particularly true in the late 1930s and those years that immediately followed World War II when Jewish immigration was swollen by refugees from Fascism. The refugees from Germany may have included a number of Jews who had moved from Russia shortly after World War I or earlier. But we have no ready basis for estimating the numbers; nor is it clear whether, in the event of a long sojourn in a transit country, the immigrants should still be associated with the country of birth. At any rate, we must rest with the conclusion suggested by Table 3.3: the net additions from migration of Russian Jewry after 1914 were quite moderate, less than a seventh of the net total accumulated in the brief three and a half decades before World War I.

We round out the statistical account of Jewish immigration from Tsarist Russia by considering movement to countries other than the United States (Table 3.4). Here we have to rely on estimates made by scholars in the field, estimates particularly affected by the difficulty of distinguishing, among immigrants with European destinations, between temporary and permanent movements.

Migration to the United States was by far the dominant component of total emigration of Jews from Tsarist Russia, as it was for several emigrant countries in Western, Central, and Eastern Europe. The share of the United States as the country of destination ranged from 75 to 80 percent; that of Europe was about 10 percent or more; and that of other overseas areas including Asia and Africa (i.e., particularly Palestine and the South African Republic) was between 10 and 15 percent. Since Europe and Canada were probably transit areas in many cases, the true share of the United States as the eventual destination may be somewhat higher. Unfortunately, it is impossible from the rough estimates to distinguish trends in the relation between emigration to the United States and to other countries by which to discover whether the proportions of emigration to Europe were higher in the earlier decades and dropped as emigration to the United States and other overseas destinations accelerated.

Table 3.4 Jewish emigration from Russia to United States and other destinations, several estimates

Period and estimator	Absolutes (thousands)	Percentage shares of destinations		
		Europe	United States	Other overseas, including Asia and Africa
1. 1899–1914, Hersch	1,421	9.8	75.2	15.0
2. 1880–1914, Kaplun-Kogan	1,969	12.4	80.9	6.7
3. 1880–1929, Ruppin	2,285	10.5	76.5	13.0

Line 1: L. Hersch, "Jewish Migrations during the Last Hundred Years," in *The Jewish People-Past and Present*, vol. I (New York: Central Yiddish Culture Organization (CYCO), 1946), 410.

Line 2: Wladimir W. Kaplun-Kogan, *Die Jüdischen Wanderbewegungen in der neuesten Zeit (1880–1914)* (Bonn: München, Dunker & Humblot, 1919), Table III, 19.

Line 3: Arthur Ruppin, *Soziologie der Juden*, vol. I (Berlin, 1930), Table XV, 157.

With estimates of total gross migration of Jews from Tsarist Russia, with estimates of total Jewish population for 1880 and 1900, and with some approximations to the rate of natural increase of Jews in Russia, gross migration can be related to total Jewish population. Table 3.5 provides the rough estimates and comparable proportions for Norway and Sweden, the two European countries other than Ireland with the highest migration rates. Ireland is a unique case: the catastrophic effects of the famine of the 1840s with its long-term consequences and the pull of the neighboring labor markets resulted in substantial emigration—so great an outflow, in fact, that total population declined by more than half between the mid-1840s and World War I.[13]

The evidence indicates that the rate of migration of Russian Jews, while not at the extraordinary levels of Ireland, was for the whole period 1881–1914 appreciably higher than even that of Norway. Furthermore, it brought the growth of the total Jewish population of Tsarist Russia to a standstill over the decade and a half before World War I. Only the relatively high rate of natural increase among the Jews of Tsarist Russia, to be discussed further below, prevented a substantial decline after 1904. But given the differential impact of emigration on the sex and age groups within the population, even with constant population totals some emigration-prone groups, particularly men in their prime working ages, would decline substantially. It is this differential impact of emigration, particularly of voluntary emigration in response to economic difficulties at home and greater opportunities elsewhere, that, if large enough and cumulative over a long time,

Table 3.5 Jewish emigration from Tsarist Russia as proportion of total Jewish population, 1881–1914

A. Proportions of Jewish emigration

	Jewish population (annual average, in thousands) (1)	Gross emigration, per year (thousands) (2)	Annual emigration, per 1,000 population (3)
1. 1881–85	4,140	12.3	3.0
2. 1886–90	4,421	28.9	6.5
3. 1891–95	4,720	49.8	10.6
4. 1896–1900	5,040	29.0	5.8
5. 1901–5	5,274	81.1	15.4
6. 1906–10	5,197	118.4	22.8
7. 1911–14	5,218	109.7	21.0

B. Comparison with proportions for Norway and Sweden gross emigration per 1,000 of population

	Russian Jews (1)	Norway (2)	Sweden (3)
8. 1851–60	Na	3.0	0.8
9. 1861–70	Na	7.8	3.6
10. 1871–80	Na	7.0	3.9
11. 1881–90	4.8	11.1	8.4
12. 1891–1900	8.1	5.5	5.0
13. 1901–10	19.1	9.5	4.9
14. 1911–14	21.0	4.5	2.8
15. 1881–1914	12.0	8.5	5.7

C. Proportions of emigration to the United States to total population, different ethnic stocks, Tsarist Russia, 1899–1914

	Estimated population mid-period (millions) (1)	Immigration to united states (thousands) (2)	Immigration per year (thousands) (3)	Annual immigration per 1,000 base population (4)
16. Jews	5.2	1,134.0 (1,066.9)	70.9 (66.7)	13.6 (12.8)
17. Poles	9.10	741.4	46.35	5.1
18. Lithuanians	3.54	243.2	15.2	4.3
19. Finns	2.54	185.0	11.6	4.6
20. Germans	1.92	150.4	9.4	4.8
21. Russians	90.2	205.8	12.9	0.14

Lines 1–4: Average population was calculated (for 1883, 1888, 1893, and 1898—midyears of the quinquennia) by straight-line logarithmic interpolation between the totals for 1880 and 1900 shown in Lestchinsky's paper in the *Weltwirtschaftliches Archiv*, cited in the notes to Table 3.3. Emigration (gross, with no allowance for returns) was derived by raising the annual immigration of Russian Jews to the United States, estimated for Table 3.1, to cover other destinations, on the assumption that United States immigration was eight-tenths of the total.

Lines 5–7: Average population was derived from an annual series. The latter was calculated by starting with Lestchinsky's figures of 5,175,000 for 1900, applying a rate of natural increase of 1.8 percent per year, and subtracting net annual emigration, to derive the next year's population total. The 1.8 percent (or eighteen per one thousand) rate of natural increase was based on the Bienstock-Novoselski figures, cited in Jacob Lestchinsky, "Probleme der Bevölkerungs-Bewegung bei den Juden," *Metron* 6, no. 1 (March 1, 1926), particularly Table XXV, 127. Emigration was derived as for lines 1–4, except that the ratio of gross emigration to the United States to total gross emigration was set at 0.75. To derive population we needed net emigration, which was calculated by assuming that return migration was 7 percent of gross emigration (suggested by the ratio of departures to admissions for all Jewish immigrants to the United States, for 1908–14, in Table 3.1).

Lines 8–15: Column 1 was calculated from data underlying lines 1–7. Columns 2 and 3 are from Adolph Jensen, "Migration Statistics of Denmark, Norway and Sweden," *International Migrations*, vol. II, ed. Walter F. Willcox (New York: National Bureau of Economic Research, 1931), 283–312. The series on overseas migration from Norway was raised to cover total migration by applying the ratio of total to overseas migration for Sweden (see particularly Tables 102 and 103, pp. 289–90).

(continued)

Table 3.5 (*continued*)

Line 16: Column 1 is from data underlying A. Entries in column 2 are total Jewish immigration from Russia to the United States, either as estimated for Table 3.1 above or without the adjustment for transit countries (in parentheses).

Lines 17–21, column 1: The totals for 1897 (for the Finns for 1900) are extrapolated to 1907, the midyear of the period, by assuming rates of increase of eighteen per thousand for the Russians, fourteen per thousand for the Poles and Lithuanians, and eleven per thousand for the Finns and Germans. The initial totals for either 1897 or 1900 are from *Reports of the Immigration Commission, Volume IV, Emigration Conditions in Europe*, 61 Cong., 3 Sess., Senate Document no. 748 (Washington, D.C., 1911), Table 16, 339. The rates of increase are based on the Lestchinsky article in *Metron* cited for A, Table XXVII, p. 130. The latter source shows rates of natural increase in the fifty provinces of European Russia for 1896–97 and 1900–4 by religion—about eighteen (per thousand) for the Greek Orthodox, about fourteen for the Roman Catholic, and about 11 for the Lutherans.

Lines 17–21, column 2: For 1899–1910 from *RIC*-III, Table 14, pp. 53–83; for 1911–14 from the Annual Report of the Commissioner General of Immigration for the relevant years.

distorts the sex and age structure of the remaining population and affects adversely both its demographic and economic prospects.

In Table 3.5C, we compare the proportions of emigration to the United States (not to all countries as in Table 3.5A and B) to base population, for Jews and other groups in Tsarist Russia. The limitation to United States destination is imposed by the lack of comprehensive estimates and the availability of the data in the United States official statistics. We find that the emigration proportion of Russian Jews is much higher than that of other ethnic minorities in Russia. Yet the levels for the latter, which range between four and five per thousand, are substantial by international standards of the tune, especially as they are limited to movements to the United States alone. Only the Russian majority shows rather low relative emigration levels, but the pace of its immigration was accelerating toward the end of the period. It is quite possible that the flow of this group too would have grown substantially if it had not been stopped by World War I and subsequent developments. Furthermore, unlike the Jews and other ethnic minorities, large numbers of Russian peasants were migrating to Siberia, particularly after the 1880s.[14]

Historical Background

Having reviewed the dating, magnitude, and time pattern of Russian-Jewish immigration to the United States, we shift to a central group of three related topics. The first covers those features of the historical background of Russian Jews that helped to produce the economic and social characteristics that the emigrant group showed when substantial emigration began in the late nineteenth century. The second is suggested by the timing of the start of substantial emigration and by the "slow beginning—later explosion" pattern, which was also typical of many other European migration streams to the United States. The third deals with the selectivity of migration, its greater attraction for some groups rather than others among Russian Jewry.

In beginning with the historical background, it must be stated that we are not attempting to present a relatively full and balanced review either of the historical antecedents of Russian Jewry or of the Russian state of which it was a part. Each of these would be an enormous task. The historical roots of the Jewish population in Russia can be traced back through centuries of the Diaspora. And the Russian state, even in terms of contacts of Jews with it and its reaction to Jews, also had, by the nineteenth century, a long and complex history. We realize, of course, that these long roots did have effects that, if traced, could help us understand much of the shorter historical stretch preceding the emigration period and the economic and social characteristics of the Jewish community at that time.

The progenitors of nineteenth-century Russian Jewry, the Polish-Lithuanian Jews in the territories annexed by Russia in the successive partitions of Poland (1772, 1793, 1795) and added to after the Napoleonic wars and the Congress of Vienna, constituted the terminal group in the eastward migration of European Jewry that had gone on for centuries and constituted merely a phase in the long Diaspora of Jews in Europe. Their social, institutional, and ideological structures reflected much of this past experience. Likewise, the Russian state, which in the course of its westward expansion acquired its large Jewish population at the end of the eighteenth century, had encounters with Jews that also went back centuries, and that, given the fundamentalist Christian nature of the Tsarist state and its reactions, left a heritage of distrust and hostility that proved to be an important factor in the nineteenth century. But a summary of these deep roots in the longer historical past is not feasible here. Nor can we attempt a full review of the sequential development of the structure of Russian Jewry during the nineteenth century and of the various shifts in the Jewish policy of the Russian state in the context of the relevant developments in the rest of Europe and among European Jewry. We present only selected aspects of the historical background and make brief references to those of its features that seem to have affected most directly the economic and social characteristics of Russian Jewry at the end of the nineteenth century. The selection is derived from some prior notions of causal relations between an aspect of the past and its results as observed in later periods, and may be misleading. Alternative aspects of the past or some counterforces to assumed causal influences may well have been neglected. It is one man's implicit formulation of explanatory hypotheses and choice of relevant evidence. But it does link some features of the historical background with characteristics of Russian Jewry in the late nineteenth century that are revealed by demographic and economic data, and it leaves the way open for alternative explanations on the basis of more historical evidence and knowledge than can be commanded here.[15]

The position of the immigrant Jewish community throughout its life in a Christian premodern state like Poland-Lithuania depended upon the protective charter of the dominant authority in the host country.

This charter extended protection and several privileges designed to permit the Jewish community to perform the functions for which its presence was desired. At the same time, however, it specified and thus limited such conditions of life as place of residence, family formation, pursuit of religion, choice of occupation, and relation to the Christian majority. The Jewish community became like one of the estates, with its own specific and limited rights and privileges but dependent upon the country's central authority for support and protection—or, when central authority became weak, as it did in Poland well before the partition, upon support and protection by the landed estates, which were served by Jewish managers, intermediaries, and traders. The protection was needed particularly against major groups within the country's population that for religious, economic, or social reasons assumed a hostile attitude to the strange newcomers. Since a similar situation, modified only by the greater strength of the Tsarist government, prevailed for Russian Jewry through much of the nineteenth century (especially during the first half), the general consequences of such integration of a newcomer religious minority within an unfriendly majority should be explicitly considered.

These consequences follow directly and logically from the basic conditions of the process. If we assume an actively or potentially hostile majority and no recognition, in premodern times, of the natural rights to life and pursuit of happiness by men as individuals regardless of religion, race, and so on, the acceptance and tolerance of a newly arriving, religiously different minority could be justified only by its specific contributions. These contributions—to finance, trade, or some special occupations—could be recognized as useful to the realm only by the central authority that presumably had the realm's welfare and power in mind, not by any narrower interest group—until the presence and operation of the Jewish minority was seen to aid the latter's interests (as was the case with the increasingly powerful landed nobility in Poland). And it was the central authority that usually had the power to extend the needed protection.

The specific contributions of the Jewish minority were the quid pro quo for its protection. The hostility of the established church, of some of the estates (like the local trade and crafts groups), and of the majority population had to be minimized by restricting the rights of the minority with regard to residence and free pursuit of occupations. The minority was thus isolated from the majority population and the latter was thereby "protected" from it. Given the actual or potential hostility of the majority and the reliance of the Jewish minority on the uncertain support of the central authority, the specific and restrictive character of the conditions of life that could be pursued inevitably follows.

First, the few economic functions for which the Jews were wanted and tolerated were clearly not those that were already performed by the Christian majority—agriculture, the simpler forms of trade, transportation, and crafts. The functions of the Jewish minority, particularly in the beginning, were financial and trade services in the interstices between the established estates and economic classes, and particularly in the service of the landed gentry and its apex, the crown and the regional nobility. Only as the Jewish minority grew and tended to saturate its trade and related functions did a substantial proportion of its labor force shift to consumer goods crafts. And the choice of the craft was limited by the competition of Christian craft guilds and the prevailing rule against employment of Christian workers by Jewish masters. The specialization in economic functions that implied an intermediary position for much of the Jewish minority—intermediary between the landed gentry and its peasants, between the crown and the other estates, and between the landed gentry and the cities—meant, in the long run, a precarious position. When there was strain among the majority estates which the Jewish minority served as an intermediary, the Jews became the first focus of attack. The emergence of native strength in functions performed by the Jewish minority—whether in trade or a craft—put pressure on the protecting authority to restrict Jewish activity further. Thus any weakening in central authority and any strain in the country's economic structure where the Jewish minority provided linkages threatened catastrophe and massacres in the prevailing climate of religious hostility. It is important to note that the Polish-Lithuanian Jewry that later formed the mass of Russian Jewry had, by the time its absorption by the Tsarist Empire began, already suffered grievous losses as a result of the decline in the power of the Polish-Lithuanian state.

Second, given the strong desire to retain religious identity, the effort of the religious leadership of the Jewish community to fortify it against continuous pressure, and the attempt by authorities of the host Christian state to limit contacts between Jews and others, the Jewish community tended to lead an autonomous and distinctive cultural and social life. It was distinctive not only in religion but in language, dress, and the pattern of individual and family behavior. The restrictions on residence, occupation, and, later, on Western-type education only strengthened this tendency toward autonomy and distinctiveness. Even at the end of the nineteenth century, after decades of exposure to secularization and to nontraditional, Westernizing education, Yiddish-Hebrew was the dominant language of the literate Russian Jews, and their everyday life still strongly reflected the autonomous tradition of a separate Jewish community. Also, in the nineteenth century, as the pressure for emancipation in Russia and Poland developed, it was countered with the argument that the Jewish minority had to abandon its separatism and adopt the behavior patterns of the majority before it could be granted full civil rights. This requirement meant abandonment of the protective features of separateness in return for what seemed to most of the Jewish community an uncertain benefit.

Third, the protective charter was issued by the dominant authority of the host state to the Jewish community as a whole. Consequently, the existence of joint responsibility led to the creation of autonomous government within the Jewish community. This autonomous government could supervise and decide on the allocation within the community of taxes to discharge the common obligations; it could oversee the application of the specific limitations whose transgression might injure the whole community; it could enforce its decisions by the power of excommunication, confiscation, and expulsion; and it could settle most intra-community disputes without subjecting them to the dangerous alternative of resolution in the general courts of the Christian realm. This autonomous government naturally merged with the religious government which provided leadership to the community in its exercise of religious precepts under difficult and changing conditions. With the emergence of the movement for civil rights and political emancipation, and the associated decay in religious traditionalism, these autonomous governing bodies that dominated the life of the Jewish community lost their strength, and they were abolished whenever the rights and responsibilities of the individual members of the community were recognized by the state. But the heritage of common organization and action remained, and so long as the state continued to discriminate against and limit the residence and the occupational, educational, and mobility rights of the Jews, the need for communal organization and the feeling of common responsibility remained.

Fourth, despite the existence of self-governing autonomous institutions and the strong community of religious life, economic and social differences were wide within the Jewish minority in any country where it had attained some magnitude. The economic differentials were created by the differing success of various members in establishing profitable relations with the authorities or other economically powerful groups within the host country. The social differentials were created not only by the economic differences but by the degrees of success various members had in attaining distinction in religious lore and hence in the power that such religious attainments bestowed on them. Later, when secular education began to spread, further economic and social differentials were created by different capacities to acquire such education.

Thus, despite a community of feeling within a discriminated against and oppressed minority, there was the wide range between the Jewish financier at the royal court and the miserably poor innkeeper on some provincial landlord's estate, between the head rabbi of a large Jewish city community and a poor tailor in a village, or, in later times in Tsarist Russia, between an international banker or major industrialist living in St. Petersburg and a poor peddler in villages like Sholom Aleichem's prototypical *shtetl, Kasrilevke.*

These wide economic and social differences were inherent in the basic conditions of life in the Jewish communities. The opportunities for substantial economic advance were limited by the restrictions imposed on the occupations and economic pursuits of the Jews. But once the more capable could avail themselves of the few opportunities, whether in financial services to the powerful or later in the organization of factories and the construction of railroads, the returns were high. The opportunities for social advance through religious learning were also limited, but once attained they could bestow great social power on those few who reached the pinnacles, and this was true also of secular learning. At the other end, the large masses of Jews were kept at low economic and social levels by the pressure of their numbers on restricted economic opportunities and by the limited number of socially advanced positions that could be reached through learning, religious or secular.

Finally, the Jewish groups in any Christian country, even long after in-migration, preserved ties with Jewish communities in other countries—ties that originally also may have been appreciated as useful by the protecting authorities. The preservation of such ties and community of feeling was based not only on a common religion and similar past but also, to a considerable extent, on similar problems of life as minorities discriminated against within an actively or potentially hostile Christian majority. Such ties were only strengthened when the movement toward full civil rights began—as in the earlier centuries when expulsion from some of the Western European countries resulted in a migration to Jewish communities already established in the East. The policies of the several European countries toward their Jewish communities differed, according to their level of social and economic development. But these policies affected all European Jewish minorities, which through the centuries were interrelated if only because some were direct offshoots of others in earlier migrations. Thus, when the shift from the precarious position of a barely tolerated and greatly restricted minority to full civil rights began in Revolutionary France, it affected not only the Jewish minorities in other European countries, but also the authorities which had to respond to the threat or promise that such a change elsewhere portended. One distinctive feature of the nineteenth-century history of Russian Jewry was the reaction to its worsening problems by other European Jews, particularly the British and French; another was the influence on Russian Jewry and on some Russian authorities and circles of society, not only of the civil rights movements, but also of the philosophy of separation of state and church that originated and spread in the Western European countries, both of which found their clearest practical embodiment in some of the European offshoots overseas.

Much of the above discussion of the basic social conditions and structure of a Jewish minority in a preindustrial Christian state like Poland-Lithuania also applies to Tsarist Russia in the long century after the partitions of Poland. Russia was largely a preindustrial Christian state, with a record of intolerance of Jews for centuries before the nineteenth and with an economic structure that left little room for the more advanced economic activities in which the Jewish minority had a comparative advantage. This was particularly true since the government was unwilling to grant the newly acquired population sufficient freedom of residence, choice of occupations, and free economic intercourse with the Christian majority to permit the minority to profit from access to a much larger population and potentially wider market than was available earlier.

The restrictions upon Jewish rights of residence, occupation, and education that characterized the 1800s in Tsarist Russia need hardly be reviewed here. It should be noted, however, that the Jewish minority enjoyed some advantages in its transition from the declining Polish-Lithuanian state to the stronger and more expansive Russian state.

First and foremost, until the 1880s when a wave of pogroms began, their lives and property were free from the ravages of war and internal turmoil during the peaceful period after the last Napoleonic war. Also, despite residence and other restrictions, they had increasing access to a wider internal market. In its efforts to reduce the distinctive and separatist characteristics of Jewish life and organization, the Russian government, in its Russification program, was instrumental in furthering a shift toward the Western type of education and modernization. Furthermore, in its unifying role, the Tsarist government came to view the Jewish minority as a group of subjects on a par with others rather than as an autonomously governable group, and after some delay, it reduced the power of the autonomous organization. However, it did not effectively enforce the rights of its Jewish subjects within the local guilds, city governments, and the like. Still, loss of the power of the Jewish autonomous government, which was bound to religious and economic traditionalism, in itself facilitated the social and economic development of Russian Jewry.

Yet there were grave disadvantages. Conservative and despotic, Tsarist power was wedded to its power base in the landowners and the church and was resistant to any movement toward legal and economic rights for the mass of its own subjects, let alone the Jewish minority. And guided by fears generated by the French Revolution and its aftermath, the Tsarist powers "protected" Russia against significant advance toward modernization until the 1860s when belated and incomplete reforms were introduced. With respect to its Jewish minority, the very power of bigoted and ignorant despotism led to the kind of forceful policy exemplified by Nicholas I's effort to recruit young Jews into the army and thus wean them from their ancestral religion and culture. And there was the brutality of sudden restrictive changes in rights of residence which displaced thousands of Jews from their homes and long-established economic bases. Furthermore, the Tsarist government, despite its attempts to join the Jews to the established estates, weakened or nullified any results it achieved in this direction by responding to the counterpressures of hostile majority populations, particularly of the Polish and Lithuanian groups within the Pale. The burdens of being at the uncertain mercy of an ignorant despotism—burdens only partially lightened by corruption and the government's occasional clarity of perception—were felt with increasing acuteness as the proportion of Westernized groups within Russian Jewry rose, as the acquisition of fuller civil rights led to a keener sense of relative deprivation, and as Western European Jewry generally made marked social and economic advances.

Aspects of Trends and Structure

Growth in Number

Before considering the factors relating to the dating and time pattern of the emigration flows of Russian Jewry after they began in the 1880s, we attempt to link our general observations on the historical background with whatever quantitative data are available on the trends and structure of Russian Jewry before the late nineteenth century. We begin with the most obvious base, the growth in number (Table 3.6).

We use for this purpose the estimates made by Jacob Lestchinsky, the scholar who has contributed most to the quantitative foundations of Jewish demography and economics. The period of most interest at this point is that between 1825 and 1880. The two decades from 1880 to 1900 were already affected by emigration, and as a result, the growth per year was lower than previously (compare columns 6 and 7, lines 1–4).

Interestingly, the growth rate was substantial, well over 1.5 percent per year between 1825 and 1880; and, particularly intriguing, the growth rate for the Jewish population was higher than for total population over that period (lines 5 and 6). The record is sparse before 1825. Still, we have a rough estimate of some 200,000 Jews in White Russia at the time of cession in 1772 and an official estimate of 617,000 in Poland in 1788 (i.e., after cession of White Russia, Galicia, and Polish Silesia). But in view of the tendency to underreport, Thaddeus Chatzki, a well-known Polish historian who made a special study of the Jewish problem, raised this figure to 900,000.[16] If we assume a total for 1788 of 1.1 million Jews in what became part of Russia by 1825, the annual growth rate over the thirty-seven-year period (to a total of 1.6 million, in line 4, column 1) is about 1 percent per year. The Urlanis source, used in line 5 for European Russia, shows a growth rate from 1775 to 1825 of 1.1 percent per year for total population. These results are not implausible. The growth rate of the Jewish population over this disturbed period probably was distinctly below the rates after 1825, and also lower than that of the total, because the Jews were more directly and adversely affected by the Napoleonic wars than the population of the Empire as a whole.[17]

How plausible are the findings in Table 3.6A, particularly the higher growth rate for the Jewish than for the total population between

Table 3.6 Data bearing upon growth in number of Jews in Tsarist Russia, 1825–1900

A. Jewish and total population at selected dates

	Absolute totals (millions)				Growth rates, percent per year		
	1825 (1)	**1850** (2)	**1880** (3)	**1900** (4)	**Col. 1– Col. 2** (5)	**Col. 2– Col. 3** (6)	**Col. 3– Col. 4** (7)
Jewish population, Lestchinsky's estimates							
1. Lithuania and White Russia	0.550	0.800	1.225	1.450	1.51	1.43	0.85
2. Congress Poland	0.400	0.575	1.005	1.325	1.46	1.88	1.40
3. All other	0.650	0.975	1.750	2.400	1.64	1.97	1.59
4. Total	1.600	2.350	3.980	5.175	1.55	1.77	1.32
Total population, 1914 Empire boundaries							
5. European Russia (Urlanis)	49.8	61.6	85.6	111.2	0.85	1.10	1.32
6. Tsarist Empire (CSC)	52.7	68.6	92.6* 105.7+	133.0	1.06	1.12	1.36

B. Crude vital rates (per 1,000), Jews and total population, selected countries

	Birth rates		Death rates		Rates of natural increase	
	Jews (1)	Total (2)	Jews (3)	Total (4)	Jews (5)	Total (6)
European Russia						
7. 1896–97	35.9	50.2	17.6	32.4	18.3	17.7
8. 1900–4	34.4	48.6	16.7	30.9	17.7	17.7
Galicia						
9. 1882	46.2	48.0	29.4	36.4	16.8	11.6
10. 1895–1900	40.4	44.3	20.8	28.1	19.6	16.2
11. 1901–2	38.1	44.0	19.2	26.9	18.9	17.1
12. 1904, 1907, 1910	34.6	40.9	16.8	25.3	17.8	15.6
Hungary						
13. 1891–95	35.6	41.7	19.1	33.1	16.5	8.6
14. 1896–1900	34.6	39.6	16.9	27.6	17.7	12.0
15. 1901–5	31.4	38.0	16.7	26.2	14.7	11.8
16. 1906–10	28.6	36.4	15.2	24.9	13.4	11.5
17. 1911–13	26.8	35.3	14.6	24.0	12.2	11.3
Romania						
18. 1871–75	46.5	34.2	33.6	31.3	12.9	2.9
19. 1881–86	46.8	41.3	26.0	26.3	20.8	15.0

(continued)

Table 3.6 *(continued)*

B. Crude vital rates (per 1,000), Jews and total population, selected countries						
20. 1891–95	43.2	41.0	23.5	31.0	19.7	10.0
21. 1896–1900	40.1	40.1	21.4	27.4	18.7	12.7
22. 1901–5	32.6	39.5	21.2	25.7	11.4	13.8
23. 1906–10	29.6	40.4	17.4	26.5	12.2	13.9
24. 1911–15	26.6	42.7	16.1	24.8	10.5	17.9
Bulgaria						
25. 1881–85	32.9	33.7	14.4	16.4	18.5	17.3
26. 1891–95	37.6	37.5	23.1	27.9	14.5	9.6
27. 1904–7	34.2	43.2	13.7	21.9	20.5	21.3
28. 1909–12	30.6	40.8	13.3	23.0	17.3	17.8
Prussia						
29. 1822–40	35.5	40.0	21.6	29.6	13.9	10.4
30. 1876–80	31.7	38.9	17.6	23.6	14.1	15.3
31. 1886–90	23.9	37.3	16.1	24.3	7.8	13.0
32. 1896–1900	20.4	37.1	14.3	21.4	6.1	15.7
33. 1906–10	17.0	32.5	13.7	17.3	3.3	15.2
34. 1911–13	15.3	28.9	13.8	15.9	1.6	13.1

*1877, +1883.

Lines 1–4: Based on the estimates in the article in *Weltwirtschaftliches Archiv*, cited in the notes to Table 3.3.

Line 5: From B. Ts. Urlanis, *Rost Naselenia v Yevrope* (Growth of Population in Europe) (Ogiz: Moscow, 1941), summary table, pp. 414–15.

Line 6: The estimate by the Central Statistical Committee, cited in E. Z. Volkov, *Dinamika Narodonaselenia SSSR za Vosiemdesiat Let* (Dynamics of the Population of the USSR for Eighty Years) (Gosizdat: Moscow and Leningrad, 1930), Table 1, p. 8. The figure covers the former Tsarist Empire, excluding Finland, Khiva, and Bokhara. Because of effects of acquisition of territory we had to terminate the second period in 1877 and begin the third period in 1883. The annual growth rates are, of course, adjusted for differences in number of years included.

Lines 7–34: Taken from the Lestchinsky paper in *Metron*, cited for Table 3.5, pp. 80–164. Lestchinsky sometimes refers to total population as non-Jews, but an internal check suggests that the entries refer to total rather than the non-Jewish population. The specific sources are as follows: European Russia-Table XXVII, p. 130; Galicia-table on p. 109; Hungary-Table XVII, p. 109; Romania (referred to as Old, i.e., pre-World War I)-Table XXI, p. 115; Bulgaria-Table XXII, p. 118; Prussia-Table VIII, p. 83.

In some countries, only live births are covered, in others stillbirths are included, but Jewish and total population in each country are treated alike.

The data for Russia are adjusted in the source for underreporting of female births and of total deaths.

1825 and 1880? The Jewish population was far more urban than was the total population, and under preindustrial conditions of health and sanitation, mortality was distinctly higher among the urban than among the rural population. Also, some Jews might have been lost by conversion to Christianity (the reverse flow can be disregarded). On the other hand, there might also have been some net immigration from Galicia or Romania, but there is no evidence of a substantial movement.

The loss by conversion appears to have been minor. Ruppin,[18] citing the de la Roi estimates of total conversions of Jews in the nineteenth century (for the world) of somewhat over 200,000, raises the total to 250,000 to allow for offspring of mixed marriages. For Russia, whose Jewish population in the mid-century was close to 2.5 million, the corresponding total would be about 100,000, thus constituting a cumulative total of some 4 percent for a population that grew over the century by 250 percent.

Since it is reasonable to assume that between 1825 and 1880 the Jews of Tsarist Russia were virtually a closed population, that is, affected only by births and deaths, the crude vital rates are the only variables to be considered. The rates shown in lines 7 and 8 are for European Russia and cover a short span rather late in the period. But we can learn from the crude vital rates for Jews and total population in other countries, particularly Eastern European, which confirm what the growth rates for the Jewish and total population show in Tsarist Russia (see lines 9–28).

Two conclusions stand out. First, the growth rate for the Jewish closed population of Russia of about 1.8 percent per year—a crude rate of natural increase of 18 per 1,000—was not exceptional. It was also found in Galicia, Hungary, Romania, and Bulgaria. There is little reason to doubt that the Jewish population of Tsarist Russia could grow at the rates indicated in Table 3.6A.

Second, almost uniformly the higher rate of natural increase of the Jewish population as against the total population in each of the Eastern European countries was due to the much lower death rate. (Only in Romania in the late nineteenth century was the Jewish birth rate higher than that for total population. See lines 18–20, columns 1–2.) It more than compensated for the somewhat lower Jewish birth rate. This was also the case for European Russia at the end of the century, and presumably through the decades back to the 1820s. So long as the general level of death rates was high, there was a substantial absolute difference in favor of a lower Jewish death rate; so long as the shortfall in the Jewish birth rate was not too large, the rate of natural increase of the Jews could be higher. In the course of social and economic modernization, as both birth and death rates declined, the absolute differential in death rates in favor of Jews necessarily decreased, while the differential in birth rates in disfavor of Jews, if anything, widened. Prussia, the most economically developed country given in Table 3.6, shows this typical trend of Jewish and total vital rates from an excess in the rate of natural increase in the former, at the beginning, to a marked shortfall in the later decades (lines 29–34).

The evidence indicates that the hostile commentators, in ascribing the fecundity of Jews to early marriages, were right in that the Jewish birth rate was fairly high, but they were wrong in that the greater growth of the Jewish population was far more the result of a lower death rate—a phenomenon that was largely ignored. It should be noted that the lower mortality rates among the Jews were also widely observed for infants (below one year of age) in almost all countries of the world (including even the United States before World War I), indicating that much of the difference was independent of the differentials in age structure between Jewish and total population.

For our discussion both the relatively high birth rates of the Jewish population of Tsarist Russia and the much lower death rates are important. They were the source of an increase in number that generated the pressures contributing later to emigration. They are also indexes of a traditional structure of the Jewish population, with distinctive characteristics that contained factors that tended to keep birth rates high and, even more, to keep death rates substantially below those of total population. The high birth rate reflected both a tendency toward early marriage, which was also fostered by the desire to avoid military service, and by the religiously and traditionally fostered desire for children. The low death rate was due to distinctive cultural factors operating despite the relatively low income position of the mass of the Jewish population. Numerous writers have commented that such characteristics of family life as absence of drunkenness, high standards of hygiene, devotion to children, and close family ties were more typical of the Jewish than of total population before widespread modernization of the economic and demographic aspects of life.[19] In Tsarist Russia, with a predominantly peasant population (most of which, through much of the century, had the status of serfs), at low economic levels and living under conditions conducive to high death rates, these distinctive characteristics of the Jewish minority indicate a difference in social conditions and patterns of behavior. But while these were a source of strength, they exacerbated the problem of continued restrictions of residence and occupation upon rapidly growing numbers.

Concentration in the Pale

For many of the distinctive characteristics of the structure of Russian Jewry in the late nineteenth century, we have to rely on the Population Census of 1897, the only comprehensive census taken in Tsarist Russia. Data on population in earlier basic sources (like the various "revisias") are characterized by serious shortages, and the further one goes back in time, the greater the difficulty associated with the obvious reluctance of the population to register—particularly the Jewish population, with the heavy head taxes, other onerous obligations, and the communal responsibility for their discharge.

The 1897 Census refers to the Empire, except Finland, at the beginning of the year. By that year, Jewish emigration had been fairly substantial for about seventeen years, but, as Table 3.5A indicates, emigration before 1901 was a limited fraction of total population, allowing for a substantial growth of Russian Jewry from 1880 to 1897. The really massive immigration occurred in the years after the census.

The restriction of the right of residence to a relatively narrow area within European Russia amid the vast Russian Empire was perhaps the most important legal limitation imposed on the Jewish minority by the Tsarist government. And it was continuously maintained, with a few exceptions relating to narrowly defined groups of merchants of high rank (first guild, involving large capital), professionals with higher education, and master craftsmen pursuing their crafts (further restricted by craft guild rules and regulations in the cities beyond the Pale). The Pale was essentially confined to fifteen Western gubernias of the fifty gubernias of European Russia and the ten gubernias of Congress Poland, thus forming a kind of Western outer rim of the Russian Empire. Even within the Pale, Jews were barred from the countryside (unless they were already established in rural colonies) and restricted to incorporated cities and to "miestechkos," the latter, prevalent in the northwest, being villages serving the countryside (Table 3.7).

Jewish population is defined in Table 3.7 by religion (hence the R in parentheses in the tide), whereas in the other tables, it is defined by mother tongue (Yiddish, with L in the parentheses). The distinction is interesting. Of the 5.216 million Jews classified by religion, 162,000, or about 3 percent, claimed a language other than Yiddish as their mother tongue, suggesting a small group of Westernized Jews in their second generation. Of the 5.063 million Jews classified by mother tongue, almost nine thousand were of a faith other than Jewish (presumably converts). It should be remembered that when Jews are classified by mother tongue, a small but distinctive Jewish group, upper class by occupation and literacy, is omitted.

Table 3.7A reveals that 94 percent of the Jews were confined to an area in which less than a third of the non-Jews was living. Even though the Pale was expanded in the nineteenth century to include some southern gubernias, the large Jewish population was living in a limited, and most densely settled, part of the Russian Empire. And it is likely that the 4 percent of Jews living in European Russia outside the Pale represented an economic elite.

Even more significant is the concentration of the Jewish population within the Pale in the cities and small villages. Whereas the proportion of Jews in the total Empire was a mere 4 percent, the calculations in Table 3.7B show that in the Pale it amounted to 11.5 percent. Moreover, Jews constituted over 40 percent of the urban population of the Pale, and in an older Pale region, like the northwestern (Lithuania and White Russia), they were 8 percent of the total, in contrast with only 26 percent in the more recently opened and less crowded southern (New) Russian region. We shall see that these differentials in density of Jewish settlement relative to total urban population affected the sectoral structure of Jewish occupations and, implicitly, the economic position of the Jewish population and its propensity toward emigration.

One aspect of the residence restriction deserves explicit notice. The requirements for exemption were fairly complicated, but they could be eased by bribery or other pressures on corrupt local authorities, or made worse by the arbitrariness of the same corrupt authorities. As a result, those members of the Jewish community who, like the handicraftsmen, were legally entitled to reside outside the Pale were neither economically nor socially strong enough to overcome local arbitrariness or control it by bribery, and therefore did not fully use the privilege. Under such conditions the limited movement of Jews to residence outside the Pale is even more understandable, and so is the suggestion made above that permanent residence outside the Pale must have signified a sufficiently strong economic and social position to qualify many such residents as an economic elite of the Jewish population.

Table 3.7 Concentration of the Jewish (R) population in the Pale, Russian Empire, 1897 (1898)

A. Total and Jewish population in the empire, 1897 (absolute figures in millions)

Regions (number of gubernias in parentheses)	Total population (1)	Jewish (2)	Jewish as percent of total (3)	Percentage non-Jewish (4)	Distribution Jewish (5)
1. Northwestern—Lithuania and White Russia (6)	10.06	1.422	14.1	7.2	27.3
2. Southwestern (5)	14.64	1.426	9.7	11.0	27.3
3. Southern (New) Russia (4)	8.23	0.730	9.0	6.2	14.0
4. 15 gubernias of European Russia (lines 1–3)	32.94	3.578	10.9	24.4	68.6
5. Poland (Congress)	9.40	1.321	14.1	6.7	25.3
6. The Pale (lines 4–5)	42.34	4.899	11.6	31.1	93.9
7. Remaining 35 gubernias of European Russia	60.51	0.211	0.3	50.1	4.0
8. Caucasus	9.29	0.057	0.6	7.7	1.1
9. Siberia	5.76	0.035	0.6	4.7	0.7
10. Middle Asia	7.75	0.014	0.2	6.4	0.3
11. Total	125.64	5.216	4.2	100.0	100.0

B. Total and Jewish population in the Pale, Urban and Rural, 1897 and 1898

	Total (1897) (1)	Incorporated cities (1897) (2)	Col. 2 as percent of Col. 1 (3)	Cities and "Miestechkos" (1898) (4)	Col. 4 as percent of Col. 1 (5)
Total population					
12. Northwestern Russia	10.06	1.184	11.8	2.093	20.4
13. Southwestern Russia	14.64	1.399	9.6	2.566	17.5
14. Southern Russia	8.23	1.613	19.3	1.945	23.6
15. Poland	9.40	2.159	23.0	2.703	28.8
16. The Pale	42.34	6.354	15.0	9.307	22.0
Jewish Population					
17. Northwestern Russia	1.422	0.623	43.8	1.213	85.3
18. Southwestern Russia	1.426	0.503	35.3	0.978	68.6
19. Southern Russia	0.730	0.454	62.2	0.512	70.0
20. Poland	1.321	0.813	61.6	1.106	83.7
21. The Pale	4.899	2.393	48.8	3.809	77.8

(continued)

Table 3.7 (Continued)

B. Total and Jewish population in the Pale, Urban and Rural, 1897 and 1898

Jewish as percent of total population	The Pale	Incorporated cities	Remainder rural	Cities	Remainder rural
22. Northwestern Russia	14.1	52.6	9.0	57.9	2.6
23. Southwestern Russia	9.7	35.9	7.0	38.1	3.7
24. Southern	9.0	28.2	4.2	26.3	3.5
25. Poland	14.1	37.7	7.0	40.9	3.2
26. The Pale	11.6	37.7	7.0	40.9	3.3

Derived from Isaac M. Rubinow, "Economic Conditions of the Jews in Russia," in *Bulletin of the Bureau of Labor*, no. 72 (Washington, D.C.: Department of Commerce and Labor, 1907), 491 and 493–94.

While most of the data are from the Census of 1897, those on the total and Jewish population of incorporated cities plus the "miestechkos" (in column 4 of B) are for 1898 and are from a special study by the Jewish Colonization Society. "Miestechko" can be described as a settlement other than an incorporated city that serves as a commercial and to a lesser degree industrial center of the surrounding country, and in which, unlike the countryside, the Jews had the right of residence.

We derived the "remainder rural" in B by subtracting either the incorporated city population (1897) or that of cities and "miestechkos" (1898) from total population for 1987. It was impossible to make even a crude adjustment for the error introduced by relating an 1898 urban total to an 1897 population aggregate, because of internal migration, and for the Jews also because of emigration. The implicit error, however, cannot be greater than one or two percentage points.

Occupational Structure

Broad categories of the gainfully occupied workers among Jews and non-Jews, in the Pale and in the Empire in 1897, are sufficient to reveal the most conspicuous and distinctive characteristics of the economic structure of Russian Jewry (Table 3.8). Much of the greater detail available does not lend itself to effective analysis.

The major, and familiar, distinction—the small share of the Jewish population gainfully occupied in agricultural pursuits (including forestry, hunting, and fisheries)—is conspicuous: and, in view of the legal limitations on active participation in these occupations and on ownership of and residence on the land, this finding is hardly surprising. In fact, it overshadows all other comparisons between the economic structures of Russian Jews and non-Jews. The share of agricultural pursuits in the non-Jewish labor force amounted to six-tenths of the total, which is comparable to the part of the total labor force so employed in any preindustrial country; if the total population is distributed by the major economic source, those dependent on agriculture would constitute an even higher proportion, probably over seven-tenths.

Interesting comparisons can, therefore, be made between the economic structure of Jews and non-Jews only by excluding agricultural and related pursuits, thus approximating a comparison of Jews with urban non-Jews (columns 4–6, lines 1–14). Here we find that while the proportion in manufacturing and mechanical trades is about the same for the Jewish as for the non-Jewish labor force, the proportion in commerce, predominantly trade, is distinctly higher for the former—about three-tenths; for the latter, it is only 7 percent. The main offset is in the share of the miscellaneous category of personal services (a mixture of labor and domestic services for hire, hotel and innkeepers, and military service), which is about four-tenths of the nonagricultural labor force for the non-Jewish population and only about half that, 20 percent, for the Jewish. To put it simply, the trade share is distinctly higher, and that of unskilled labor-domestic service is distinctly lower for the Jewish nonagricultural labor force. This is perhaps what should have been expected, since Jewish unskilled labor faced particular difficulties in finding employment, and Jewish women traditionally were reluctant to enter domestic service even within Jewish households, let alone in non-Jewish ones.

Thus the shares of Jews in the total labor force in the several major sectors differed markedly (lines 15–16). For the Empire as a whole, while the share of Jews in the total labor force was 4.5 percent, it was only a

Table 3.8 Structure of gainfully occupied, Jewish (L) and non-Jewish population, Tsarist Russia, 1897

A. Distribution within the Pale and the Empire

	Total occupied			Total, excluding agricultural pursuits		
	Pale (1)	Other (2)	Empire (3)	Pale (4)	Other (5)	Empire (6)
Jews						
1. Absolute (thousands)	1.332	99	1,431	1,292	97	1,390
Percent share of production sectors						
2. Agricultural pursuits	2.9	2.1	2.9	0	0	0
3. Mining and manufacturing	37.9	38.1	37.9	39.1	38.9	39.1
4. Transport	3.3	1.7	3.2	3.3	1.7	3.2
5. Commerce	32.0	25.8	31.6	32.9	26.4	32.5
6. Personal services	18.8	27.6	19.4	19.4	28.2	20.0
7. Professional services	5.1	4.7	5.0	5.3	4.8	5.2
Non-Jews						
8. Absolute (millions)	9.54	20.56	30.1	3.51	8.38	11.9
Percent share of production sectors						
9. Agricultural pursuits	63.2	59.2	60.5	0	0	0
10. Mining and manufacturing	11.2	17.3	15.4	30.4	42.4	39.0
11. Transport	1.8	2.4	2.2	4.9	5.9	5.5
12. Commerce	1.4	4.4	2.7	3.8	8.1	6.9
13. Personal services	19.8	14.5	16.2	53.8	35.5	41.0
14. Professional services	2.6	3.0	3.3	7.1	8.1	7.6

Portions of Jews in total, by production sector

	Total (1)	Total excluding agriculture (2)	Agriculture (3)	Mining and manufacturing (4)	Transport (5)	Commerce (6)	Personal services (7)	Professional services (8)
15. Pale	12.2	40.4	0.6	32.2	21.0	76.3	11.7	20.9
16. Empire	4.5	10.5	0.2	10.5	6.5	37.8	5.4	7.3

B. Structure of gainful occupations, Jews (L), four major regions of the Pale, 1897

	Jews as percent of total urban population (1)	Total gainfully occupied (thousands) (2)	Percent shares of sectors in total					
			Agricultural pursuits (3)	Mining and manufacturing (4)	Transport (5)	Commerce (6)	Personal services (7)	Professional services (8)
17. Northwestern	58	402.7	4.1	43.2	4.1	25.6	17.5	5.5
18. Southwestern	38	376.4	1.7	35.3	3.1	37.8	16.5	5.6
19. Southern (new)	26	214.4	4.5	34.7	2.9	35.5	17.5	4.9
20. Poland	41	338.0	1.8	36.6	2.9	31.1	23.6	4.0

Calculated from Isaac M. Rubinow, "Economic Conditions of the Jews in Russia," *Bulletin of the Bureau of Labor*, no. 72 (Washington, D.C.: Department of Commerce and Labor, 1907), 500–2.

(L) in the table caption means that Jews were defined by a linguistic criterion, that is, mother tongue. By this definition the total is 5.06 million, compared with 5.22 million defined by religion (R) in Table 3.7.

Agricultural pursuits include forestry, fishing, and hunting. Mining and manufacturing include all the mechanical arts, particularly handicrafts and construction. Transport includes communication. Personal services include, in addition to a large category described as personal and domestic service, military personnel, hotel and restaurant keepers, and dealers in spirituous liquors. "Occupations unknown," prostitutes, people dependent on property income alone or charity, and prisoners, and so on, are excluded.

Column 1 of lines 17–20 is from Table 3.7, lines 22–25, column 4.

fraction of a percent in agriculture, yet well over a third in commerce. For the Pale, the share of Jews in the total labor force of the trade sector was well over three-quarters, indicating a saturation of this sector in the Pale that may partly explain the high share of the Jewish labor force in manufacturing, particularly in small-scale handicrafts.

Several additional observations suggested by Table 3.8 can be briefly listed. First, the major role played by Jewish labor in the economy of the Pale resulted in an economic structure of the non-Jewish population that was significantly different from that of the non-Jewish population outside the Pale, where Jews formed a minor fraction (compare columns 1 and 2, or 4 and 5, lines 2–14). The non-Jewish labor force in the Pale shows a higher proportion in agricultural pursuits, lower proportions in industry and commerce, and a higher proportion in personal service, than the non-Jewish population outside the Pale. In other words, the proportions of the non-Jewish labor force in the Pale are high in the sectors in which the proportions of the Jewish labor force are low, and low where the latter are high. In this sense, the concentration of Jews in the urban part of the Pale made the economic structures of the Jewish and non-Jewish populations complementary. The implication is that the competition of the Jewish labor force displaced some of the non-Jewish labor from pursuits that they would otherwise have occupied. Saturation and pressures for employment must surely have been aggravated thereby.

Second, the broad categories in Table 3.8 conceal much detail, some of which is significant. Thus, the industrial category within the Jewish labor force is heavily dominated by one branch—the clothing industry, which accounts for close to a half of the total, a degree of concentration not found in the industrial sector within the non-Jewish labor force. In transport, the dominant group within the Jewish labor force is "carting and draying," the individual, small-town carriers, not the railroads and water transport, much of which was in government hands with employment barred to Jews. In professional services, the largest group among the Jews was "teachers and educators," most of whom were involved in the small "cheders" (private religious schools for Jewish boys), not the government servants or legal personnel that dominated professional services among the non-Jews. The distinctive characteristics of Jewish occupational structure, associated with bars to government employment, with the propensity to small-scale operations resulting from difficulties in securing adequate wage or salary employment in large enterprises, and with the concentration within industry on production of consumer goods, in labor—rather than in capital—intensive types of operation, would be further revealed by additional detail.[20]

Third, Table 3.8B strongly suggests that a greater density of Jewish concentration led to a lower proportion of the labor force in commerce and a higher proportion in manufacturing and mechanical arts (and transport). The implication is that the trade sector, though preferable, had reached the saturation point and forced a shift into industry, that is, largely handicrafts. Rubinow associated these shares of industry and trade with the proportion of Jews to total population.[21] But a more relevant association is with the percentage of Jewish urban population in total urban population, urban including both the incorporated cities and the rural villages ("miestechkos") where Jews had the right to reside (see column 1, lines 17–20). The association between the share of Jews in total urban population in the four regions of the Pale and the share of commerce in the Jewish labor force is negative, while its association with the shares of manufacturing and transport is positive.

Fourth, the suggestion that increasing density of Jewish relative to urban population made for a movement from trade to manufacturing or handicrafts is corroborated by evidence that the proportions among the Jews engaged in trade were much higher, and those engaged in the crafts, much lower in the earlier decades than in 1897. Thus for 1818, data for sixteen gubernias, largely coincident with the Pale but excluding Poland, show a share of population in trade (merchants and "mieszane," the latter identified as small traders) of about 86 percent and in handicrafts of about 12 percent (the rest being in agriculture).[22] Even if the allocation of all "mieszane" to trade (rather than of some to transport or services) exaggerates its share, that of handicrafts is clearly much below the 1897 proportion.

Economic Differentials

In any large population group with a diversity of occupations, and even in one whose members are all engaged in similar pursuits, there are significant economic differentials. For the 1880 population of 4 million Russian Jews (see Table 3.6), the economic differentials were probably quite wide. Undoubtedly there were marked contrasts between the majority of people at low income levels and a small top group whose economic standing was high despite legal discrimination and occasional bureaucratic arbitrariness. But we have no adequate data to demonstrate, or approximate, the width of the economic differentials that may have prevailed. There are, however, bits of evidence that can be cited to add realism to the comprehensive figures discussed so far for large economic or regional categories.

The existence of a large proportion of the population at the low side of the income and economic level distribution is suggested by the data on assistance that had to be extended for extraordinary consumption needs, for example, on the occasion of such a holiday as Passover, and on the presence, within each large occupational category, of masses of those employed who, given the character of their occupations and the small amounts of capital involved, could earn only a bare living. The data on assistance over Passover relate to some 133,000 families in 1,200 localities in 1898 and indicate that such help was extended to 19 percent of all families. Similar, though lower, proportions are shown for the years back to 1894. The descriptive data on some of the small-scale groups in trade and tile character of many of the occupations involved in the large handicraft sector show clearly tile presence of marginal components that eked out a small income. Rubinow notes the prevalence of the sweatshop type of handicraft operation, involving the work of many members of the family, in combination with the domestic industry system in which work was done on order and for sale to the bigger middlemen. He also mentions the "pauper merchants" and women peddlers with little capital operating on a shoestring.[23]

There is some evidence on the elite groups beyond the list of notable bankers, textile, sugar, and tea trade magnates and of the Jewish capitalists who helped to build the Russian railway.[24] A curious bit of information is from the 1897 Census on the structure of Jews (L) by estates ("soslovie"): of the total of 5.06 million, the group including nobles, honorary citizens, and merchants (top guild rank) amounted to some eighty-two thousand or 1.6 percent.[25] Also, the study by the Jewish Colonization Society shows that close to three thousand of the factories in the three regions of the Pale (excluding Poland) were owned by Jews; while they were appreciably smaller than the non-Jewish factories, they were substantial enough to suggest a relatively high economic position for the owners. Apparently, the proportion of Jewish factories in Poland was also high, particularly in the textile industry. Rubinow, in discussing trade, refers to large Jewish commercial establishments with a sizable body of employees, sufficient to generate salesmen's strikes and collective agreements.[26] Finally, as already mentioned in connection with Table 3.7, the 4 percent of Jews who lived in European Russia outside the Pale must have represented largely an economic elite, who could maintain the right of residence not only because of the legal status they occupied by virtue of higher education, or because they were merchants of the first rank, but also because of their economic power that protected them from the arbitrariness of local, and sometimes even of central, authorities.

The data are deplorably scanty, but the scattered evidence does suggest that alongside large groups, amounting to perhaps a fifth to a quarter of the population, at miserably low economic levels, there may have been a group (from 5 to 10 percent) with rather high incomes relative to the average for all Jews and particularly significant relative to incomes of the majority urban population. The existence of these wide economic differentials within Russian Jewry was a major factor underlying the selection process in the emigration that began in the 1880s. It also contributed to maintaining and perhaps strengthening the hostility of the majority population in reaction to both the seemingly low productivity and poor status of the Jewish masses at one extreme and the economic successes of the Jewish capitalist and professional elites at the other.

Literacy Proportions

We conclude our discussion of the characteristics of Russian Jewry by reviewing the proportions of the literate, with data again drawn from the Census of 1897 (Table 3.9). Literacy is defined as the ability to read in any language (including Yiddish), with the usual qualifications that attach to such definitions.

The much higher literacy proportions among the Jews than among the non-Jews could have been expected. The former were predominantly an urban group, and thus within the reach of schools, and the latter were predominantly a rural group, with schools hardly accessible. More interesting, from our standpoint, is the difference in literacy proportions between Jewish males and females and the differences between the literacy of Jews in any language and in Russian.

With respect to literacy in any language, the proportion of literates among the Jewish males was strikingly higher than among the Jewish females—about double. This finding is similar to that for the non-Jewish population, dominated by the Greek Orthodox majority, for whom the ratio of male to female literacy proportions is over two. The obvious implication is that both the Jewish and the Russian traditional institutions of the time, unlike modernized societies, put much greater emphasis on the education of men than of women.

Table 3.9 Literacy by sex and age, Jewish (L) and non-Jewish population, Tsarist Russia, 1897

	Percent literate, any language		Percent of Jews literate in Russian	Percent of Jews literate only in non-Russian—(2)–(3)
	Non-Jews (1)	Jews (2)	(3)	(4)
Males, by age				
1. 10–19	44.8	59.8	42.2	17.6
2. 20–29	43.8	71.0	52.5	18.5
3. 30–39	38.4	69.9	48.4	21.5
4. 40–49	32.0	67.5	40.5	27.0
5. 50–59	25.1	61.6	31.1	30.5
6. 60 and over	19.2	54.3	22.3	32.0
7. 10 and over	37.6	64.6	42.9	21.7
8. 20 and over	34.7	66.9	43.3	23.6
Females, by age				
9. 10–19	20.7	43.7	31.7	12.0
10. 20–29	18.4	45.6	29.7	15.9
11. 30–39	15.0	34.1	17.8	16.3
12. 40–49	12.1	25.7	9.8	15.9
13. 50–59	10.7	20.1	6.1	14.0
14. 60 and over	9.6	14.9	3.6	11.3
15. 10 and over	16.1	36.6	22.5	14.1
16. 20 and over	14.3	32.8	17.6	15.2
Males and females				
17. 10 and over	26.8	50.1	32.3	17.8
18. 20 and over	24.4	49.6	30.2	19.4

Excess of literacy proportions for males over those for females, non-Jewish and Jewish population, by age

	Any language		Jews	
Age	Non-Jews (1)	Jews (2)	Russian language (3)	Non-Russian language only (4)
19. 10–19	24.1	16.1	10.5	5.6
20. 20–29	25.4	23.4	22.8	2.6

(continued)

Table 3.9 (*continued*)

	Percent literate, any language		Percent of Jews literate in Russian	Percent of Jews literate only in non-Russian—(2)–(3)
21. 30–39	23.4	35.8	30.6	5.2
22. 40–49	19.9	41.8	30.7	11.1
23. 50–59	14.4	41.5	25.0	16.5
24. 60–69	9.6	39.4	18.7	20.7
25. 10 and over	21.5	28.0	20.4	7.6
26. 20 and over	20.4	34.1	25.7	8.4

Calculated from Rubinow (cited in the notes to Table 3.7), tables on pp. 577 and 579.

This emphasis on the education of men is associated particularly with literacy in languages other than Russian, as can be seen from noting the male–female differences by age for literacy in any language, Russian and non-Russian. These differences in favor of males are particularly marked for persons beyond the ages of twenty-nine or thirty-nine. They suggest that it is in comparison with older men, whose literacy was limited in Russian but was high in Yiddish or Hebrew, that the literacy of women was so low, even in the non-Russian language. This finding confirms two distinctive characteristics of Jewish literacy: it was secured through a widespread system of *cheders*, particularly for the older generation before the spread of literacy in Russian; and, given the religious framework of this learning, it was extended largely to men and not to women. But even when literacy in Russian began to spread, by 1897 at significant levels only among the younger ages, the proportion among males was still substantially higher, if only because of their greater need for literacy in pursuing their economic activities. The findings thus corroborate the usual view of both the traditional position of women within the household and the separate cultural life of the Jewish community, particularly with respect to the older generations.

This widespread literacy in the traditional languages, evident at least as early as the second quarter of the nineteenth century, was important when the enlightenment movement began. For by the late nineteenth century, there existed a flourishing literature in Hebrew through which modern knowledge and ideas could spread among the Jewish intelligentsia, and it appeared to be more effective than the literature in the newly acquired Russian language. There were also the beginnings of a literature and press in Yiddish, which became stronger as the spread of socialist ideas concentrated attention on the needs of the masses and on their vernacular. The prevalence of learning in the Jewish community, however hampered by religious limitation and by orthodox resistance to secular learning, colored the attitudes and aspirations of the younger generations, and it had significant consequences for the orientation toward learning of Jewish emigrants in the countries of their destination, particularly in the United States.

Factors Relevant to Time Pattern and Dating

We shift now to the factors that may explain the time pattern of emigration observed for the Russian Jews—a trickle for decades, a slow beginning in the 1880s, and then a rapid rise to high levels sustained until other circumstances, either war or legal restrictions, shut off the flow. First we consider the likely determinants of this time pattern, observed also in immigration flows to the United States from other countries. Then we deal with the more specific question as to why this long-term pattern in the emigration of the Russian Jews holds for the particular dates observed in Table 3.1.

Several conditions can be suggested that would account for the slow beginning–explosive growth time pattern of emigration to a country like the United States from an older country (assuming no significant legal barriers at either end).

First, there must be, at the emigration end, a population subjected to strains and pressures that have accumulated to a point where substantial proportions of that population will be induced to migrate. We deliberately emphasize here pressures at the emigration end, the push rather than the pull (with the latter assumed as given but present over a long period before massive emigration begins). The multiple costs of emigration—the separation from familiar and native surroundings and ties, the substantial expense of moving overseas, and the major adjustments in the country of destination—are great. For most people, other than the relatively few adventurous souls, these costs far outweigh the perception of possible long-term differential advantages overseas. Even though it had been apparent for decades that the long-term prospects were far better in the United States than at home, significant migration from many of these countries did not begin until quite late—in the 1850s from Germany and in the 1870s and 1880s from Italy and Eastern Europe. It is the worsening of economic and social conditions at home, not their low absolute level, that provides the push needed to initiate migration on a significant scale.

Second, if migration is to be large and sustained over a long period, the potential population affected must be large, and the push or pressure must be capable of exerting cumulative influences on a substantial population group. Obviously only those factors that can produce a worsening of the situation affecting a sufficiently large population are significant. Thus a deterioration in the position of a small traditional craft, displacing a few hundred workers and their families, would not be sufficient to generate a massive emigration flow sustained over several decades. By contrast, the competitive effect of the newly introduced factory system in important industry and transport areas could destroy opportunities for thousands of small-scale producers and craftsmen. Likewise, a natural calamity affecting agriculture in a narrow segment of the country with a small population is unlikely to generate mass emigration, but an increasing pressure of population on land under traditional agricultural practices, or displacement of agricultural labor by "industrialization" of agriculture, means a large reservoir for emigration considering the size of the agricultural labor force in preindustrial countries. Since factors of large effect also imply a diversity in pressure and strain, the movement might begin with those most pressed but still capable of emigration and then extend to increasing circles as pressure extends and the cost of emigration declines.

Third, the cost of migration, particularly overseas, must decline to the point of mass availability, in two respects: a fall in the financial expense of transport and a reduction in the cost of information and learning about the country of destination. The efficiency of transportation, communication, and spread of knowledge has probably increased at much higher rates than that of most other economic activities—with a resulting reduction of relative costs. Furthermore, the beginnings of industrialization and modernization of a country expose its population and remote areas to both the competitive and instructive effects of the outside world, thus sharply reducing the cost of migration and learning. Once the mass migration gets under way, other cost-reduction factors are created. The early migration streams establish channels that facilitate the movement of later migrants, such as means of transport, emigrant-aid organizations, institutional patterns of movement, and the like. Also, the additions to the body of immigrants in the receiving country provide further information to their relatives, neighbors, and friends still in the sending country and, after a while, resources and facilities of great help and protection to would-be new emigrants. We shall see below how frequently the immigrants to the United States had their passage paid for by relatives in the country, who also provided initial hospitality to the newcomers. In short, the costs of travel, information, and adjustment are all reduced sharply as the early immigration streams become settled in the country of destination. This reduction of costs undoubtedly was an added incentive for additional groups to emigrate—even with less intensive pressures than those that impelled earlier emigration despite the greater cost of movement.

Fourth, among the general conditions that underlie mass emigration movements, the acceleration aspects of the process explain the mushrooming effects once substantial emigration begins. It is not only that the reduction in cost of migration increases the volume of potential migrants. Early emigrants settled overseas attract other members of their families, or circles with close ties, left at home. If this attraction is assumed to spread over, say, three to four quinquennia, one could set up a model in which, all other conditions being equal, this attraction capacity of the initial migrants would create an acceleration over the assumed span in the volume of total emigration. All of these sources of what may be designated autocatalytic or self-stimulating characteristics of the emigration process, reflected in the time pattern we are dealing with, could be more elaborately formulated, but this brief description should suffice for present purposes.

Finally, under the basic conditions assumed—no legal restrictions at either end and no major conflicts or other exogenous obstacles—the migration flow would reach a peak and begin to decline, although not to the insignificantly low levels that prevailed in the much earlier decades when the country of origin was in a preindustrial state and the costs of migration, there and elsewhere, were much greater. For if the country of emigration does become industrialized and its agriculture modernized, within a few decades it should be able to absorb internally any further displacements and dislocations that may occur. Emigration to the United States from Germany, the Scandinavian countries, and other northwestern European countries (including Great Britain) was clearly at much lower levels after the 1880s (or, for some, after an earlier peak decade) and continued to drift down to World War I, without any legal restrictions at either end and without wars or other obstacles to block the flow. It was merely that the dislocative, transitional period was completed in all these countries, while it was just starting after the 1880s in Italy and Eastern Europe. In reaching a crest and then diminishing, the emigration flow is similar to an autocatalytic process in chemical reactions in which the reaction is first stimulated by its very unfolding and then is brought to a halt by exhaustion of the supply of elements in the combination.

One may well ask whether this rather general model of the tune pattern of emigration from an old European country to the United States (or to any other of the open countries overseas) has much relevance to the emigration of the Russian Jews, for they were subject to continuous legal restrictions and they suffered from adverse political pressures. These two conditions alone could explain their emigration, once the high costs of movements were lowered and it became evident, as it did in the 1880s, that restrictions would be intensified and there would be little hope for amelioration in the situation of the Jewish masses in the Tsarist Empire. Even the acceleration of Jewish emigration after 1902–3 could be explained by the intensification of persecution—by the mounting wave of pogroms initiated by the Kishinev pogrom of 1903—rather than by the effects of the earlier emigration on the circle of would-be migrants through family and personal ties with those already settled in the United States and through further reduction of costs of migration.

The question cannot be answered unequivocally. Obviously, legal restrictions and the intensifying persecution contributed to the growth of Jewish emigration from Russia. Nevertheless, the model outlined above still has substantial relevance to our case. This is suggested by concurrent, or only slightly delayed, substantial expansion of emigration of non-Jews from the Tsarist Empire—Poles, Lithuanians, Finns, Germans, and, in the few years preceding World War I, even Russians. Disturbed as these groups may have been by economic and political strains, legal limitations on their activities and persecutions were surely only a minor element compared with the weight of these factors in the case of the Jewish community. Table 3.5 shows that for several of these groups, the gross emigration ratio to base population was as much as a third of the ratio for the Jews. Another item of evidence is the record of emigration of Jews from Austria to Hungary in the years 1881–1914, given in Table 3.1. Unlike Tsarist Russia and Romania, where legal restrictions were severe, the Austro-Hungarian monarchy granted civil rights to Jews in the 1860s, and by whatever yardstick one measures, the policy of the government and the legal situation were mild compared with those in Russia and Romania. To be sure, in the transition period toward greater industrial development, hostility to the Jewish population was mounting, particularly in Galicia. But given the identification of the Jewish population as a distinctive social group, its concentration in certain pursuits, particularly trade, and its movement up the scale once freedom and civil rights were granted, economic competitors were bound to exploit longstanding prejudices of the Christian majority. We can cite no case in which hostility to Jews by the groups whose economic or social standing was constrained or endangered did not exist. In any event, in Austria-Hungary, legal restriction and official persecution were much less virulent. Yet, with a Jewish population in 1880 in the areas that comprised the old dual monarchy (Galicia, Hungary, Bukowina, Bohemia, Moravia, and Lower Austria) of some 1.6 million[27] compared with almost 4 million in Tsarist Russia, the total immigration into the United States for 1881–1914 was about a quarter of that for Russian Jews (see Table 3.1, line 6, columns 3 and 4). The basic emigration ratio for Austro-Hungarian Jews was thus over six-tenths of that for Russian Jews (i.e., 0.25/0.4), a relatively high emigration ratio for the former community. Interestingly, a similar comparison for Romania yields as high an emigration ratio for Romania as for the Russian Jews. The Jewish population in Romania in 1880 was 200,000, and total immigration into the United States for 1881–1914 was eighty thousand; both population and United States immigration were one-twentieth of those for Russian Jews.

These oversimplified statistical comparisons only suggest that while legal restrictions and persecutions contributed greatly to the increase in emigration of Jews from Tsarist Russia, a considerable component could be accounted for in terms of the model outlined above. But two general arguments are perhaps more telling. The first is the repetition of the same time pattern of emigration where the emigrants were members of a large, ethnically homogeneous population (as was the case in the Scandinavian countries or in Italy) and where, though there were economic differentials and strains within the native population, no religious persecution or significant legal restrictions were involved. All these countries had, however, gone through a period of transition from premodern agriculture and technology to the more modern, industrialized type of economy—with all the dislocations and strains that such transition involved. Just such a transition we know began in the Tsarist Empire in the 1880s and 1890s, and it can thus be argued that even without persecutions and restrictions the Jewish minority could hardly have escaped dislocation and economic strain and that the inducement to migrate overseas would have existed. An argument against emigration would hold only if it could be proved that the economic composition of the Jewish working force and the institutional structure of Russian Jewry were both adaptable to the transition process without substantial dislocation—an unlikely hypothesis. Of course, one may conjecture that if the transition toward industrialization in Tsarist Russia were to have been accompanied by effective abolition of all restrictions on residence, economic activity, and education of its Jewish subjects, much of the resulting migration might have been eastward, within the Empire, rather than overseas. But even this speculative conjecture would not have excluded substantial emigration abroad, particularly to the United States.

The second, closely related argument has to do with the possible connection between intensification of restrictions and barriers and the acceleration of the dislocative and pressure effects of the transition process. Not only did this process involve shifts in economic weight from one sector to another and thus in the position of the groups attached to them, but it also required modernization of political and social institutions. Without such changes, the potentials of the modern economy could not be utilized effectively. Was the increasing severity of the restrictions on the Jews in Tsarist Russia that began with the reign of Alexander III in 1881 and continued in that of Nicholas II—particularly the spread of pogroms in the decade preceding World War I—a response by the conservative and autocratic central power to the obviously threatening aspects of social and economic changes? Was it a response to the pressure for reform and modernization that would give greater voice to the land cultivators, workers, and industrial classes? Was it an effort to relieve the general discontent through discharging hostility upon the Jews—a means of gaining credit with those groups in the population that showed continued and intensified animosity toward Jews as increasingly effective competitors? These questions indicate that the increased severity of legal restrictions and persecutions that clearly set off the long trend toward mass emigration among Russian Jewry in the 1880s can itself be interpreted as a response to the threats that the transition process posed to the traditional centralized powers of the country and to the classes on whose strength they rested.

In trying now to explain why significant emigration of Jews from Russia to the United States and elsewhere began in the 1880s and rose to a high level by the first decade of the twentieth century, we face the usual difficulties of causal analysis of a specific historical movement. How far back should one go in accounting for the roots and hence timing of the movement? How does one establish the timing of both the factors that stimulated the movement and the ones that restrained it (whose weakening at a given date served to release it)? And how does one gauge the continually changing weights of the various positive stimuli and negative obstacles to the movement—a changing balance over a specific stretch of time that explains the specific dating of the movement once it begins? To illustrate: should one ask why the Jews in the declining Polish-Lithuanian Kingdom failed to emigrate in the early eighteenth century? After all, some sectarian groups had emigrated to the American shores at that early date. Should we ask to what extent the weakening of communal authority among Russian Jewry after the 1840s was an important factor in freeing individual responses to emigration prospects? To what extent were the intensified anti-Jewish measures and actions beginning in Russia in the 1880s reflections of, or facilitated by, the resurgence of anti-Semitism in Western Europe (particularly Germany, but also France) that also emerged in those years? And, as already noted above, how do we secure the proper weights of the interrelated variables? How do we gauge the relative weights, in the history of Russian Jewry, of the several inducements and obstacles to emigration, not only economic but others involving adherence or non-adherence to traditional religious ties, or ties to the revolutionary and other streams in Russian life?

The attempt to explain fully the timing of the emigration of Russian Jews overseas and its intermediate stages within Europe would involve a wide canvas and yield at best only tentative hypotheses. Under the circumstances, we must again be selective, as in dealing with the broad historical background. And perhaps it is not essential, in the present connection, to attempt a fully tested and relatively complete analysis. We will consider only a few broad propositions, reflections on the sweep of well-known history but directed toward our specific question and offering tentative, but we hope plausible, suggestions.

First, we may justifiably limit our attention to the nineteenth century, indeed to the decades after the 1820s. Mass migrations overseas or within Europe, economically motivated and peaceful or voluntary in character, are a product of the nineteenth century—of the changed political structure in the countries of emigration, of the establishment of independent sovereign states overseas that welcomed the prospect of immigration, and of the appreciable lowering of the cost of movement. Substantial immigration from overseas to the United States did not begin until the 1830s, and it came even later to the offshoots overseas that were still colonial in status. The migrations of sectarian groups in the earlier centuries were quite small and relied on their capacity to establish self-sufficiency through the pursuit of agriculture. The Jewish community in Eastern Europe was too large, too ill-adapted to the pursuit of agriculture, too attached to the network of European Jewry, and too foreign to the still unsecularized overseas colonies of the eighteenth century to be a likely source of mass migration overseas or even within Europe.

Second, if we limit our discussion to the period from the 1830s to World War I and ask why overseas emigration of Jews from Russia was insignificant before the 1880s, several explanations at the sending and receiving ends can be suggested. Thus, the number of Russian Jews (as indicated in Table 3.6) rose from 1.6 million in 1825 to about 4 million in 1880. The pressure of numbers in a limited range of occupations and area was felt only toward the end of the century. The limited spread of Western education and literacy and the self-contained corporate life of Russian Jewry in the first half of the century isolated the Jewish population from outside contacts and inhibited emigration despite the repressions of Nicholas I, whose reign began in 1825 and ended in at the receiving end, the substantial immigration of European Jewry, largely German, into the United States occurred by the middle of the third quarter of the century; before that time the United States was not seen as a haven for Jews, particularly of the traditional and religious type that predominated in Eastern Europe. The liberalization and reform era of Alexander II (who reigned from 1855 to 1881) spread Westernization and Russification, and the condition of Russian Jewry improved for a while. The right of residence outside the Pale was extended to selected economic and professional groups; there were more civil rights for the population, including Jews, and there was hope for more to come. Meanwhile, through part of this period, the United States was engaged in the War between the States; immigration was largely suspended in the early 1860s, to be resumed vigorously only in the 1870s.

With the 1880s came a reversal toward greater conservatism, a more virulent repressive policy toward Russian Jewry, and the outbreak of pogroms, encouraged and perhaps organized by the Tsarist government. All of this was quite overt and found favor among the Christian majority, including some revolutionary groups that mistook the anti-Jewish violence of the mobs for the expression of revolutionary fervor. These beginnings of a new policy initiated in the reign of Alexander III were accompanied by outspoken authoritative statements that pointed to emigration as one obvious solution open to Russian Jewry–policy declarations that were recognized by contemporaries to be, and unquestionably were, direct stimuli to emigration. The short-term impact of these policies can be observed quantitatively; their cumulation into long-term trends became apparent as repressions and social strains and strife continued throughout Alexander III's reign and into that of Nicholas II, which began in 1894.

Finally, one should note the position and role of Western European Jewry, which rendered active service in assisting and directing the mass emigration of Russian Jewry overseas.[28] Three lines of connection should be briefly mentioned. First, the economically and socially more developed Western European Jewry exercised pressure on the Tsarist government to relax its persecution and at least tolerate mass emigration of its Jewish subjects. Second, the Jewish organizations of Western Europe provided most of the economic resources and organizational skills needed to facilitate migration overseas without excessive human costs, and thus contributed to a reduction in real costs when the movement began. Finally, with the emergence of anti-Semitic moods and policies in Western Europe in the 1880s, the potential flow of Russian Jews into the Western European countries was reduced. Such an inflow, if it continued, would have elicited restrictive legislation, as it did in the United Kingdom in the first decade of this century. In that sense, the timing of conditions among Western European Jewry was a factor in determining the timing of the emigration of Russian Jewry overseas. One may also note that the attainment of civil rights and better economic standing by Western European Jewry would have contributed to the dissatisfaction and resulting emigration of Russian Jewry even without the reactionary policies of Alexander III and Nicholas II—as did the known freedom and economic success of the small Jewish groups in the United States within the surge of economic achievement there in the 1870s and 1880s.

Selectivity of the Emigration Flow

Despite their comparatively high levels, the proportions of emigration to base population of Russian Jewry in the three and a half decades from 1881 to 1914 permitted a wide range of selectivity. Records for most flows, including that of Russian Jewry, show that the propensity to emigrate was greater among men than among women, among people in prime working ages than among children and the aged, and among the lower income groups, more adversely affected by the dislocation in the transition to industrialism and modernization; in addition, for the Jews, there was a greater tendency to emigrate among those more oppressed by the intensified legal restrictions and active persecution.

Documentation of these selective aspects of the emigration of Russian Jews to the United States is difficult. Since much of that emigration was illegal, if tolerated, and since Russian authorities had little interest in the process, there are no acceptable data on the emigration at the source. We can only derive some rough notions for a single point of time, using the Census of 1897 for comparative analysis of the Jewish population in the various regions. Juxtaposition of this comparison with the information we have on Russian-Jewish immigrants into the United States yields revealing results. Unfortunately Jewish immigrants are distinguished in the immigration records of the United States only beginning with fiscal 1899, and the demographic and economic information is given for all Jewish immigrants, with no distinction by country of last residence. We are, therefore, compelled to use the characteristics of all Jewish immigrants into the United States for 1899–1914 as proxy for the characteristics of Russian-Jewish immigrants. However, as Table 3.1 shows, the proportion of Russian Jews among all Jewish immigrants was about three-quarters for 1899–1914, and over seven-tenths even in the decades back to 1881. Therefore, we can assume that the procedure followed introduces only a limited error. For some aspects of the structure, such as occupation, we have a check in the data on the characteristics of Austrian Jewry, the second-ranking, though much smaller group of Jewish immigrants into the United States; in some cases, there are partial data for years before 1899. At any rate, it seems preferable to make rough comparisons rather than to forgo completely the tentative insights that they provide.

Sex and Age Structure

Two main conclusions are suggested by the evidence on the sex and age structure of Jewish immigration, taken to represent that of Russian Jewry (Table 3.10). First, the Jewish immigrants reflect the same selectivity from the base population as many other long-distance immigration flows: a greater proportion of men than of women and a greater concentration in working ages. Second, this selectivity among Russian-Jewish immigrants was far less marked than among non-Jewish immigration in that the proportion of women and children was

Table 3.10 Sex and age structure, Jewish and total immigration before 1899, Jews in Russia (1897), Jewish and non-Jewish immigration, 1899–1914

A. Jewish and total immigration, 1886–98

	1886–89 (1)	1890–94 (2)	1895–98 (3)	1886–98 (4)
Sex structure				
1. Jewish immigrants, Port of New York (thousands)	101.3	193.1	85.9	380.3
2. Females as percent of adults (16 and over) in line 1	38.3	41.9	45.3	41.6
3. Females as percent of total in line 1	41.5	44.7	47.2	44.4
4. Females as percent of immigrants from Russia (excluding Poland)	35.6	39.3	41.2	38.9
5. Females as percent of total immigration	38.5	38.0	40.4	38.7
6. Females as percent of non-Jewish immigration	38.3	37.2	39.9	38.3
Age structure				
7. Children (under 16), as percent of Jewish immigration, Port of New York	27.9	34.0	40.4	33.8
8. Children (under 15) as percent of immigration from Russia (excluding Poland)	24.2	21.2	22.8	22.2
9. Children (under 15) as percent of total immigration	19.3	15.1	15.0	16.5[+]

B. Jews in Russia (1897), Jewish and non-Jewish immigration, 1889–1914 (Percent proportions in relevant total)

	Male (1)	Female (2)	Under 14 (3)	14–44 (4)	45 and over (5)
Russia, population, 1897					
10. Jews (L)	48.8	51.2	38.4 (43.1)	46.6	15.0
11. Non-Jews	49.8	50.2	36.4 (38.5)	47.8	17.8
Gross immigration, Jewish					
12. 1899–1902	57.3	42.7	24.4	69.7	5.9
13. 1903–7	57.2	42.8	24.8	70.2	5.0
14. 1908–14	54.4	45.6	24.0	69.5	6.5
15. 1899–1914	56.0	44.0	24.4	69.8	5.8
Gross immigration, non-Jewish					
16. 1899–1902	69.8	30.2	10.9	83.5	5.6
17. 1903–7	72.3	27.7	10.0	85.3	4.7
18. 1908–14	67.9	32.1	11.6	83.1	5.3
19. 1899–1914	69.8	30.2	10.9	84.0	5.1
Departures and net immigration, 1908–14					
Departures as percent of gross immigration					
20. Jews	9.9	3.8	1.8	8.3	13.6
21. Non-Jews	39.7	18.3	12.8	31.6	63.8
Net immigration					

(continued)

Table 3.10 (*continued*)

22. Jews	52.7	47.3	25.4	68.5	6.1
23. Non-Jews	61.0	39.0	14.7	82.7	2.6

C. Immigration, gross and net, 1920–924 (Percent proportions in relevant total)

	Male (1)	**Female** (2)	**Under 16** (3)	**16–44** (4)	**45 and over** (5)
Gross immigration					
24. Jews	45.6	54.4	29.7	57.7	12.6
25. Non-Jews	58.2	41.8	17.3	73.9	8.8
Departures as percent of gross immigration					
26. Non-Jews (or total)	40.5 (1.3)	18.6 (0.4)	6.9	30.4	87.4
Net immigration					
27. Jews	45.4	54.6	(29.7)	(57.7)	(12.6)
28. Non-Jews	50.3	49.7	23.5	74.9	1.6

Lines 1, 2, and 7: From Samuel Joseph (cited in the notes to Table 3.1), Tables XXXIV and XXXVI, pp. 176–77.

Line 3: Estimated on the assumption that for children (under sixteen) the numbers of males and females are the same. The proportions under sixteen years of age are from line 7.

Lines 4, 5, 8, and 9: From United States Bureau of Statistics, *Immigration into the United States Showing Number, Nationality, Sex, Age, Occupation, Destination, etc. from 1820 to 1903* (Washington, D.C., 1903), 4347–62.

Line 6: Calculated by applying the percentages in line 3 to the total estimated Jewish immigration into the United States (from annual estimates underlying Table 3.1).

Lines 10–11: Calculated from Rubinow (cited in the notes to Table 3.7), p. 577. Because Rubinow's age distributions were in ten-year intervals, we had to estimate the groups shown (which are those of the United States immigration statistics, and of the Joseph monograph cited in the notes to lines 1, 2, and 7). The estimation was by linear interpolation between the successive age classes (1–9 and 10–19, and 30–39 and 40–49). The entry in parentheses in column 3, line 10, is the percentage proportion of population under the age of sixteen; that in parentheses in column 3, line 11, is the percentage proportion of population under the age of fifteen.

Lines 12–23: Calculated from the annual data on United States immigration assembled for 1899–1910 in *RIC*-III and shown in the successive annual reports of the Commissioner General of Immigration for fiscal years 1911–14. No departure data are available before fiscal 1908.

Lines 24–28: Calculated from the series in Willcox, ed., *International Migrations*, vol. I, Tables X, XI, 432–49; and Tables XVI, XVII, and XIX, 474, 476–78. The entries in parentheses in line 26 are the proportions of departures to gross immigration, male and female, for Jewish immigration. The source does not provide data on departures by race and age, but in view of the minute proportion of departures to gross immigration for the Jewish component (less than 1 percent for the period), we assumed an identical age distribution for both gross and net immigration of Jews (hence the parentheses in line 27, columns 3–5). See also Table 3.3.

much higher among Jewish immigrants. Thus the latter approximated more closely the structure of families and "normal" population than the non-Jewish immigration.

The selectivity aspects are revealed by the comparison of the sex and age structure of Jewish immigration into the United States with that of all Jews in Russia in 1897. For the years before 1899, data on immigrants arriving at the Port of New York (accounting for close to three-quarters of all Jewish immigration) show the proportion of women to be 44 percent (see line 3, column 4), and for 1899–1914, it was about the same (see line 1, column 2). This proportion is distinctly smaller than the 51 percent share of women in the total Jewish population in Russia in 1897. Even if we adjust the latter for the effect of emigration, it is not likely to fall below the 50 percent share shown for Russia's non-Jewish population (lines 10 and 11, column 2). Likewise, the proportions of the very young (under fourteen) and the older groups (forty-five and over), 24.4 and 5.8 percent, respectively, for 1899–1914, are well below the 38 and 15 percent shares shown for all Jews in Russia in 1897 (compare line 1, columns 3 and 5). This underrepresentation in immigration of the young is confirmed by the data on the proportions of immigrants under sixteen among all Jewish immigrants passing through the Port of New York; the figure for 1886–98 of 33.8 percent (line 7, column 4) can be compared with the 43 percent for the same age group among Russian Jewry in 1897 (entry in parentheses, line 10, column 3). It follows that men and people in working ages were overrepresented in the immigration of Russian Jews, as they are in all relatively free immigration flows: men were well over a half of the total through all the periods (lines 12–14, column 1), and for age groups fourteen to forty-four, for 1889–1914, the proportion was 70 percent (line 15, column 4), compared with 47 percent among Jews in Russia in 1897. Thus the propensity of this age group toward emigration was 1.5 times the average, while that for people aged forty-five and over was less than 0.4 times (line 15, column 5, divided by line 10, column 5).

Yet while the selectivity of emigration among Russian Jewry followed the common pattern, it was far narrower than among the non-Jewish immigrants into the United States—certainly in the years 1899–1914, for which we have data, and probably also for the earlier years. For 1899–1914, the proportion of females to all Jewish immigrants was 44 percent (line 15, column 2), but among non-Jewish immigrants, it was only 30 percent (line 19, column 2). Thus the male–female ratio for Jewish immigrants was 1.3 while that for non-Jewish immigrants was 2.3. Again for 1899–1914, children (under fourteen) were 24.4 percent of all Jewish immigrants (line 15, column 3), but only 10.9 percent of the non-Jewish immigrants (line 19, column 3). And since the shares of people forty-five and over were about the same in the two streams, those fourteen to forty-five years of age were 70 percent of the Jewish immigrants but as high as 84 percent of the non-Jewish. This lesser concentration among Jewish immigrants of men and people of working ages would be even more conspicuous if the age brackets were more detailed and distinguished the younger working ages from about eighteen to the early thirties. Despite the difficulties of comparison, it is clear that for 1886–98, females were a somewhat higher proportion and children a distinctly higher proportion of Jewish immigrants than of all immigrants (and hence of the non-Jewish: compare column 4, lines 3 and 6, and lines 7 and 9).

The contrast between what might be called the "family" or "permanent" sex and age structure of Jewish immigration and the more "individual" and "temporary" character of the sex and age structure of non-Jewish immigration is strengthened by the departure rates shown in lines 20–21. The proportions of departures to gross immigration are far higher for men than for women—both Jewish and non-Jewish—but the proportions for the Jewish immigrants are only a quarter or a fifth of those for the non-Jewish. The ratios of departures to gross immigration are lowest for the younger age groups and highest for those forty-five and over—but here again in every age bracket, the ratios are very much lower for Jewish immigration than for non-Jewish. The distribution of net immigration by sex and age (lines 22–23) also shows the much higher proportions of women and children among the Jewish than among the non-Jewish immigration flows.

Although the period 1920–24 falls beyond our scope, it is the only post-1914 quinquennium with substantial Jewish immigration to the United States. We cover it here (and in Table 3.11, which deals with a broad occupational structure) only to indicate the substantial differences from and some similarities with the pre-World War I movement that is the focus of our discussion. Table 3.3 shows that in 1920–24, Russian-Jewish immigrants were about four-tenths of total Jewish immigration, much lower than in 1881–1914. Lines 24–28 of Table 3.10 show that both Jewish and non-Jewish immigration flows contained higher proportions of women than before World War I and appreciably higher proportions of older people, that is, forty-five and over. Indeed, in the case of Jewish immigration, women outnumbered men. But in this shift toward what might be called refugee or relief immigration, reflecting the desire to reunite families broken by World War I, Jewish immigration still retained its higher proportions of women and children in comparison with non-Jewish immigration. However, unlike the situation in the period before World War I, the aged also began to form higher proportions than among non-Jewish immigrants. The important point here is the marked change in the character of immigration, particularly Jewish, toward a refugee type—an element also present in immigration of Russian Jews during the period of our coverage but not nearly as dominant as it became after World War I.

Two aspects of the difference in sex and age structure between Russian Jewish (and total Jewish) and non-Jewish immigration into the United States are significant. First, the ratio of dependents to people of working ages was much higher among Jewish than among non-Jewish immigrants. Table 3.11 below shows the ratio of gainfully occupied to total number for gross Jewish and non-Jewish immigration in 1899–1914 (lines 2 and 3, column 2). The ratio of dependents to gainfully occupied was 0.8 for Jewish immigrants, 0.3 for non-Jewish. In other words, each Jewish working immigrant had to support 1.8 persons and each non-Jewish working immigrant only 1.3. Thus the attainment of economic adequacy was a greater problem for the more burdened Jewish immigrant than for the non-Jewish. But, second, the larger proportion of children and women implied a greater preservation of family structure among the Jewish immigrants. This may have meant an easier adjustment of Jewish immigrants to the difficulties of their early years in the United States. Also, a proportion of children as high as a quarter (which, for our argument, should be increased to include younger people a few years above fourteen) meant a sizable group whose education and assimilation in the United States was relatively easier than that of older people beyond the ages for formal education. It is reasonable to suggest that once the initial difficulties compounded by a high ratio of dependents to workers were overcome, the "family" structure of Jewish immigration was an important factor in the rapid and successful assimilation of Jewish immigrants in the United States.

Occupational Structure

We have already commented on the high proportion of dependents or, what is the same, the low proportion of gainfully occupied to the total of Jewish immigrants, compared with non-Jewish, referring to Table 3.11. This table also assembles data on the occupational structure of the gainfully occupied, among all Jews in Tsarist Russia in 1897, among Jews of Austria in 1900 (to fill out the background), and among both Jewish (largely Russian Jewish) and non-Jewish immigrants in 1899–1914. Data on the occupational structure of Jewish immigration are not available before 1899; the available data on the occupational structure of immigrants from Russian part of Poland are not a good proxy for Russian Jewry, and the occupational statistics for immigration for these earlier years are not comparable to the more detailed, and apparently more complete, data beginning in fiscal 1899.

The selectivity of immigration among Russian Jews with respect to sex and age meant also selectivity with respect to gainful occupation. With the base population in 1897 having far higher proportions of children, women, and aged—all groups with lower than average labor force participation ratios—it is not surprising that the ratio of gainfully occupied to the total is only 28 percent, whereas among Jewish immigrants to the United States, it is 57 percent (lines 1 and 2, column 2). But if we allow for differences in sex and age structure between the emigrants and the base population and between the Jewish immigration and non-Jewish, the differences in the proportion of gainfully occupied to total population either disappear or are markedly reduced (see lines 1–3, column 4). This adjustment still leaves the proportions of gainfully occupied among Jewish immigrants higher than among Jews in 1897 Russia, but a more detailed reweighting with narrower age breaks would probably have removed that difference also. We can therefore say that the selectivity with respect to sex and age, already discussed in connection with Table 3.10, explains almost completely the selectivity with respect to gainful occupation.

In dealing with the sectoral structure of the gainfully occupied, we have to use broad divisions to assure adequate comparability between the data for the gainfully occupied in Russia (or Austria) and those for the immigrants into the United States. Complete comparability is impossible, and only major differences can be treated as significant. There is also the question whether the occupational information provided by immigrants on arrival in the United States corresponds to their occupational attachment in the home country, although the analysis in Table 3.12 below (on structure within the manufacturing and mechanical category) shows a reassuring agreement.

Table 3.11 Structure of gainfully occupied, Jews in Russia, 1897 (L), Jewish and non-Jewish immigrants to the United States, 1899–1914

A. Ratio of gainfully occupied to total population

	Total population (millions)	Percent gainfully occupied		
		Base not adjusted	Adjusted for sex structure	Adjusted also for age
	(1)	(2)	(3)	(4)
1. Jews, Russia, 1897 (L)	5.06	28	43	80
2. Gross immigration, Jewish, 1899–1914	1.49	57	80	110
3. Non-Jewish immigration, 1899–1914	12.20	76	95	110

B. Structure of gainfully occupied, gross immigration, 1899–1914

	Percent shares in total of gainfully occupied						Percent of gainfully occupied in total population
	Agricultural pursuits	Manufacturing, mechanical arts	Commerce	Laborers and servants	Professional	Residual	
	(1)	(2)	(3)	(4)	(5)	(6)	(7)
4. Jews in Russia, 1897 (L)	2.8	37.7	31.4	18.6	5.0	4.5	28.4
Jews in Austria, 1900							
a. Including dependents	11.9	29.8	36.5	9.6	6.8	5.4	
b. Excluding dependents	11.6	28.6	33.4	11.9	7.8	6.7	37.7

Gross immigration, Jews, 1899–1914							
5. 1899–1902	1.6	62.7	7.2	23.3	1.0	4.2	49.8
6. 1903–7	1.3	64.2	5.0	23.4	1.3	4.8	57.3
7. 1908–14	3.5	64.0	5.4	18.2	1.5	7.4	58.3
8. 1899–1914	2.3	64.0	5.5	21.0	1.3	5.9	56.7
Gross immigration, Non-Jews, 1899–1914							
9. 1899–1902	16.4	13.2	1.4	66.0	0.7	2.3	73.9
10. 1903–7	26.6	15.7	2.0	51.9	1.6	2.2	78.2
11. 1908–14	36.1	13.4	1.6	43.6	1.7	3.6	74.5
12. 1899–1914	29.9	14.3	1.7	49.7	1.5	2.9	75.8

C. Structure of gainfully occupied, gross immigration, 1908–1914 and 1920–24

	Percent shares in total of gainfully occupied					
	Agriculture (1)	**Industry and mining** (2)	**Trade and transportation** (3)	**General labor and domestic services** (4)	**Professional and government** (5)	**Percent of gainfully occupied in total population** (6)
1908–14						
13. Jewish immigration	3.9	65.9	10.3	18.4	1.5	57.4
14. Non-Jewish immigration	36.8	13.2	4.0	44.3	1.7	73.3
1920–24						
15. Jewish immigration	3.0	36.4	17.5	37.6	5.5	43.4
16. Non-Jewish immigration	13.2	23.2	10.9	47.8	4.9	59.5

(continued)

Table 3.11 (*continued*)

Lines 1–3: The basic data are from the sources cited in Table 3.10 relating to Jews in Russia in 1897 and United States immigration, respectively.

For Russia, gainfully occupied exclude people dependent on property incomes or charity, prostitutes, and prisoners.

The entries in column 2 are the percentage proportion of gainfully occupied to total population, the latter unadjusted for possible differences among the several population bases in sex and age structure.

In the adjustment for sex structure, we assume that the female propensity to engage in gainful occupations was one-third of the male (based on the data for Russian Jews in 1897), and we therefore divide the percentages in column 2 by a fraction which the adjusted base forms to unadjusted (the latter taken as one). In the adjustment for age structure we assume that there are no gainfully occupied for ages under 14 and that the proportion for ages and over is only half of that for the 15–44 group; we take the age structure of males and females to be the same. Then, for column 4 we divide the entries in column 2 by the product of the two ratios: one reflecting the sex adjustment, the other the age adjustment.

Line 4: Agricultural pursuits (column 1) include not only agriculture, animal husbandry, and so on, but also forestry, fishing, and hunting. Manufacturing and mechanical arts include all industrial occupations, a minor group of clerks, and so on, employed in manufacturing, and construction and mining. Commerce includes credit and trade. The laborers and servants group here includes, in addition to the group so designated, members of the armed forces, and the draymen and carters—on the ground that these are two large groups of potentially unskilled workers (who would be so classified in the United States immigration statistics).

Lines 5a–b: The data are for Austria, excluding Hungary, but immigration statistics for 1910–14 show that Jewish emigration to the United States from Austria was eight-tenths of the total from Austria-Hungary (see Willcox, ed. *International Migrations*, vol. I, Table XIII, 464). The data are from Dr. J. Thon, "Die berufliche Gliederung der Juden in Österreich," *Zeitschrift für Demographie und Statistik der Juden* 1, no. 8 (August 1905): 1–6. The detailed classification is given for total population alone (see Table III in source, p. 2): agriculture includes forestry and fisheries; manufacturing and mechanical arts also include mining and construction; trade includes credit and finance, and miscellaneous trade; laborers and servants include workers in land and water transport, and military service; professions include government employees and other free occupations; miscellaneous is limited to occupation unknown. The total excludes people living on rent and subsisting on charity. Estimates in line 5b are derived by applying to the large groups the ratios of occupied to total shown in Table V. p. 4; with the estimate for professional services being a residual (from the ratio of gainfully occupied to total at 37.7 percent as given in the source).

Lines 6–13: Agricultural pursuits are represented here by farmers and farm laborers. Manufacturing and mechanical arts are represented by all skilled workers, except for two groups—barbers and hairdressers, and clerks and accountants. Commerce is represented by bankers, agents, and merchants and dealers. Laborers and servants are the sum of these two large groups, shown separately. Professional pursuits are defined separately in the immigration data. The residual is the difference between the total gainfully occupied and the categories distinguished separately in columns 1–5. In general, here as elsewhere, the percentage shares are derived from absolute totals of the annual data.

Lines 14–17: Derived from *International Migrations*, vol. I, Table VIII, 400, and Table XII, 450ff. The classification by sector differs from that used for lines 6–13 in three respects:

(a) the skilled workers group is taken here to represent industry and mining and includes the barber and clerk groups omitted for lines 6–13; (b) transport workers are included with trade (which also includes bankers and agents); (c) a miscellaneous group is combined with those not reporting any occupation, rather than listed separately, but as comparison for 1908–14 shows (compare entries in lines 14 and 15, column 6, with those in lines 8 and 12, column 7), this component accounts for barely 1 percent of the total population of immigrants, Jewish or non-Jewish.

Granted the limitations of the data, the differences between the structure of gainfully occupied Jewish immigrants and that of Jews in Russia in 1897 (and in Austria in 1900) are wide and indicate significant selectivity. The sector that is markedly overrepresented among the Jewish immigrants is that of skilled workers—manufacturing and mechanical arts—which accounted for 64 percent of Jewish immigrants in 1899–1914, but for less than 40 percent of gainfully occupied Jews in Russia in 1897, and less than 30 percent in Austria in 1900 (lines 4, 5, and 9, column 2). The laborers and servants group also showed a slight excess—21 percent compared with 18.5 percent for Russian Jews and about 10 percent for Austrian Jews. But this difference may reflect our inclusion of draymen and carters in that sector in the immigration data. On the other hand, the commerce and professional groups are underrepresented. The former is only 5.5 percent and the latter only 1.3 percent of Jewish immigrants for 1899–1914, but the share of commerce is over 30 percent of both the Russian Jews in 1897 and Austrian Jews in 1900, and that of the professional group is 5 and 7 percent, respectively (lines 4, 5, and 9, columns 3 and 5).

The differences in sectoral structure of the gainfully occupied between gross Jewish immigration to the United States and the base population, either in Russia in 1897 or in combination with that for Austrian Jews in 1900, are far too wide to be due to statistical incomparabilities. Why, then, were the proportions of skilled workers, mostly artisans in manufacturing, construction, and related mechanical arts (the structure to be discussed in Table 3.12 below), so much higher for the immigrants than for the base population? Why were the proportions of those in unskilled labor and domestic service somewhat higher, but the shares of commerce and professional services so much lower? Lacking more detailed data at the source (and also in the immigration statistics), we can only offer conjectures, but they may be of some help in evaluating the factors involved in the selectivity thus observed.

The unskilled labor and domestic service group represents "transitional" occupations, in the sense that in a growing economy and relatively mobile society men and women enter these occupations either as an interim step or in preparation for more skilled and responsible jobs. Thus a farm laborer or an unskilled urban worker would, generally, hope to become a farmer or a skilled worker; a young woman might enter domestic service before marriage. One would expect this group to be younger than the others and its family burdens to be lighter or nonexistent. It would thus represent a mobile group with emigration ratios higher than those of the other sectors. Indeed, one might even have expected a greater excess in the proportion of all Jewish immigrants than in the base population. In fact, the unskilled labor–domestic service group is the most dominant among non-Jewish immigrants to the United States over the same period.

Nor is there much doubt that the lower proportions of professional services among the immigrants than among the base population are due partly to the difficulty in transferring these skills from one country to another. Even the teachers, employed chiefly in the cheders in Russia, were probably not equipped for similar employment in the United States, where Jewish education played a lesser role. And perhaps substantial groups of professionals in Russia may have enjoyed economic returns above average and had, therefore, less desire to lose an established position through emigration.

The one puzzling aspect of the sectoral structure of the Jewish immigrants is the very low share of commerce contrasted with its high share in the base population. To be sure, the average returns in trade in Russia may have been higher than in the handicrafts or factory employment, but there must also have been a substantial group within trade whose incomes were low indeed. And if handicrafts were particularly overcrowded in the northwestern part of the Pale because of the saturation of the trade sector, this implies a situation in the latter in which, all other conditions being equal, the outflow of tradespeople should have been substantial. Yet, even if we shift some peddlers from the unskilled workers or miscellaneous category to the trade sector in the immigration statistics, the under-representation is still striking. The average share in the total of immigrants might then be 10 percent, compared with a share of over 30 percent in the base population.

Transferability of skill is probably the major factor accounting for this difference in sectoral structure between the immigrant and base population. The manufacturing and mechanical arts group is dominated by handicraftsmen or artisans. Their skills as tailors, seamstresses, shoemakers, carpenters, and so on can be assumed to have had some prospect of application in the country of destination, even in the initial stages. The commercial dealer and trader immigrants had no such transferable skills, and the vast majority of those engaged in commerce had so little liquid capital that it could not play a significant role in any transfer abroad. According to Rubinow, of the 426,000

Jews engaged in commerce (excluding hotels, restaurants, and saloons) in the Pale, well over 200,000 were dealers in cattle, grains, fur pelts, and agricultural products.[29] Their skill, primarily a knowledge of the Russian agricultural markets, had little obvious relevance to conditions in the United States. Furthermore, in many cases, success in trade rested on the ability to build up a local clientele; this facility, unlike such skills as tailoring and cabinetmaking, was an item of human capital not readily transferable to another country. Finally, the commerce group among the Jewish gainfully occupied in Russia had easier access to the wider markets of the Empire than the small-scale handicraftsmen and artisans concentrated in the western part of the Pale.

Granted that both commerce and professional services attained higher economic standing in Russia (and probably Austria) than the overcrowded handicrafts, the selectivity among immigrants may have been due in large part to the differences in transferability of skills. Obviously, both sets of factors were involved. The separate analysis of both would require detailed data on incomes and age distribution by occupations in the country of origin, which are not available.

The differences in sectoral structure of gainfully occupied between Jewish and non-Jewish immigrants into the United States are also conspicuous. Needless to say, the share of agriculture is lower among Jewish than among non-Jewish immigrants: for 1889–1914, it was about 2 percent for the former and close to 30 percent for the latter (see Table 3.11A, lines 9 and 13, column 1). However, there are also differences in the nonagricultural occupations. The dominant sector among the Jewish immigrants was the manufacturing and mechanical arts sector, with a share of almost two-thirds; among the non-Jewish immigrants, it was the laborers and servants category, essentially unskilled labor, which accounted for seven-tenths of the nonagricultural labor force (49.7 percent divided by 70.1 percent, i.e., line 13, column 4 divided by 100 minus column 1). To put it simply, Jewish gainfully occupied immigrants were largely skilled, urban workers; the non-Jewish were largely farmers and farm laborers (30 percent) and unskilled workers and servants (50 percent.)

The comparison of 1908–14 with 1920–24 (lines 14–17) indicates a major change in the occupational structure of Jewish immigration to the United States. Before World War I (and presumably in earlier periods), this structure was largely a reflection of a flow from Russian Jewry due to the dislocative pressures of transition to industrialism and the legal restrictions and intensified political persecution. The structure in 1920–24 reflects the stoppage of the dominant source of such migration by the Communist revolution. And the change in the sectoral structure of gainfully occupied Jewish immigrants was far greater than the changes—also marked—in the structure of the non-Jewish immigrants. Thus the share of gainfully occupied in skilled work (manufacturing, etc.) in total Jewish immigration dropped from 66 to 36 percent (lines 14 and 16, column 2) while that of unskilled labor rose from 18 to 38 percent, that of trade and transport from 10 to almost 18 percent and that of professional groups from about 1.5 to 5.5 percent. And with non-Jewish immigration moving toward the relief type, from European countries affected by World War I, the disparity in sectoral structure between Jewish and non-Jewish immigration dropped sharply between 1908–14 and 1920–24: the sum of differences in sectoral percentage shares (signs disregarded) between the two immigration groups in the earlier period was 118.0 points, in the later period only 40.8 points.

In view of the dominance of the skilled workers (manufacturing and mechanical arts) sector among the gainfully occupied Jewish (Russian Jewish) immigrants before World War I, we may compare the structure of this particular sector among the Jewish immigrants with that of the gainfully occupied Jews in Russia (Table 3.12). To do this we grouped selected occupations shown in the immigration statistics for 1899–1914 (for all Jewish immigrants), used the essentially industrial divisions of the 1897 Russian Census, and also took data from the field study of the Jewish Colonization Society covering Jewish artisans in the Pale in 1898. The data on artisans are of value because they accounted for most of the Jewish industrial labor (factory employees were roughly only a tenth of the total) and because the clothing industry was defined more precisely than in the Census. Although only the largest subdivisions could be distinguished and the findings are necessarily crude, they are sufficiently revealing to be of interest.

For the sake of comparability between columns 1 and 2, the clothing industry, which apparently includes shoemaking in the 1897 Census,[30] is combined with the animal products industry (including other leather crafts). Whatever the definitions, the clothing industry and related branches are dominant in the structure of industry among the Jewish population of Russia, and even more dominant in the sectoral distribution of skilled workers among Jewish immigrants for 1899–1914 (line 2 or line 4). This finding is confirmed by line

4a which shows that the shares of just two related occupations—tailors and seamstresses—comprise 44 percent of all skilled Jewish immigrant workers. Since the share of the latter among all Jewish immigrant workers is 64 percent, the two occupations alone accounted for close to three-tenths of all gainfully occupied. That this Jewish inflow was a major factor in developing the clothing industry of New York and the United States is hardly a surprise.

For the other subsectors, Table 3.12 suggests rough agreement between the structure for all Jews or for Jewish artisans in 1897 and 1898 and that shown for Jewish immigrants to the United States. The shares for wood industries and construction were between 15 and 16 percent. For food industries and metals, the shares in the immigration totals were smaller than those shown for the Jews in Russia. But the general impression is that the structure of the large skilled workers (manufacturing–mechanical arts) sector in the data on the base population in Russia is sufficiently similar to that in the immigration data in the United States to be taken as comparable. We can assume, therefore, that there was not too much distortion in the occupational information provided by the Jewish immigrants on their arrival in the United States.

In terms of initial adjustment to conditions in the United States, the distinctive occupational structure of Jewish (and Russian Jewish) immigrants had several advantages. It permitted, as it did in Russia, small-scale and often home-located activities, an advantage in view of the linguistic and religious difficulties that would impede the employment of newly arrived Jewish immigrants in larger scale plants. The pursuit of some of the dominant crafts (clothing, millinery, and the like) permitted employment of women and children. Furthermore, with the low ratio of total gainfully occupied to the dependents at time of entry into the United States, immigrants not previously employed could be drawn into the labor force. Low paying and strenuous as these initially available occupations were, with particularly extreme conditions in the sweatshops and often at home, they did provide opportunities for sustenance without breaking up the family and allowed sufficient support for the younger generation to attain the education required for upward occupational mobility. An occupational structure that relied heavily on agriculture or on blue-collar employment in large-scale industry would not have provided such opportunities.

Also, because of the urban concentration of Jewish immigrants and the underrepresentation of commerce within their occupational structure, it was not too difficult for them to shift into small-scale trade. And professional pursuits were open to the younger generation once they had climbed the educational ladder. Despite the absence of agriculture as a possible outlet, and despite the difficulties of entry by Jewish immigrants into large-scale industry and commerce or the professions, the occupational structure of Jewish immigrants permitted a fair amount of elasticity. It enhanced the flow of additional groups into the labor force; it permitted the pursuit of familiar skilled crafts, and it allowed the shift into small-scale commerce which, in Russia, was impeded by the overcrowding of that sector within the Pale.

Miscellaneous Characteristics

Table 3.13 summarizes several items in the United States immigration statistics which, while adding neither to the demographic nor to the basic economic data, do shed further light on Jewish immigration, as distinct from non-Jewish.

The choice of New York State (more precisely probably the New York City metropolitan area) as the place of future residence, so much greater among the Jewish than the non-Jewish immigrants, is not surprising (lines 1–2). But the high level of concentration is striking, although it drops from 1899–1902 to 1908–14. This finding reflects the tendency to gravitate to the place where the established Jewish community was large and to settle in an area—New York—where the immigrants' skills might have value.

The other findings in Table 3.13 point to the greater importance of family ties in the Jewish immigration than in the non-Jewish. And this too, if we assume that there was already a substantial Jewish community in New York by 1908 (or by 1899), explains the concentration on it as the state of expected residence in line 1. Relatives paid the passage of more than six-tenths of Jewish immigrants but of less than three-tenths of the non-Jewish immigrants (lines 3–4). Also, 94 percent of the Jewish immigrants planned to join relatives, compared with 78 percent of non-Jewish immigrants.

We return to the question of literacy, and compare Jewish immigrants with all Jews in 1897 Russia, and Jewish with non-Jewish immigrants (Table 3.14). The former comparison shows that for both men and women, literacy was appreciably higher among the Jewish (and Russian Jewish) immigrants than among the base population in Russia in 1897. Thus, the literacy ratio for male immigrants was 83 percent in 1899–1902, compared with 68 percent for all male Jews

Table 3.12 Structure of gainfully occupied within the manufacturing-mechanical (skilled workers) group, Jews in Russia (1897, L), Jews in the Pale (1898), gross Jewish immigration to the United States, 1899–1914

	Jews in Russia, 1897	Jewish artisans in the Pale, 1898	Gross immigration, Jews to the United States			
	(1)	(2)	1899–1902 (3)	1903–7 (4)	1908–14 (5)	1899–1914 (6)
1. Absolute totals (thousandth)	536.6	483.5	66.8	226.5	244.8	538.1
			Percent within total			
2. Clothing (differing definitions, columns 1 and 2)	47.2	37.6	45.4	51.5	54.6	52.2
3. Animal products (column 1), leather goods (column 2)	4.0	17.6	11.0	8.5	7.7	8.5
4. Sum of lines 2 and 3	51.2	55.2	56.4	60.0	62.3	60.7
4a. Tailors and seamstresses	Na	Na	42.7	44.9	43.9	44.2
5. Wood industry and construction	15.2	16.2	17.7	17.9	12.9	15.2
6. Food industry	8.6	8.4	4.5	6.0	5.9	6.2
7. Metal industry	8.1	7.1	4.5	5.7	3.8	4.6
8. Sum of above	83.1	86.9	83.1	89.6	85.0	86.7
9. All other	16.9	13.1	16.9	10.4	15.0	13.3

Column 1: From Rubinow (cited in the notes to Table 3.7), detailed breakdown, pp. 498–99. The data refer to Jews in all of Russia, according to the Census of 1897. The total in line 1 is for all mining, manufacturing, and construction activities, excluding the "all other" (line 40), not allocated by branches. The branches used here are manufacture of clothing; manufacture of animal products; manufacture of wood, plus building industry, plus carriage and wooden ship making; production of food, animal and vegetable; and manufacture of metal.

Column 2: Calculated *from Recueil de Matériaux* (cited in footnote 23), vol. II, Appendix, Table 45–51, no page numbers. These data relate to Jewish artisans in the Pale in 1898 and were collected by the Jewish Colonization Society. The branches used are clothing and wearing apparel, except laundresses and barbers/coiffeurs (the whole group is described as *objets de toilette*); leather goods—in toto; food products—as given, excluding one half of "bakers and restaurateurs"; wood manufactures plus building, excluding ceramics; crude metals and locksmiths, and so on (excluding finer metal workers and watchmakers). The total excludes the barbers and one half of the bakers and restaurant keepers subgroup.

Columns 3–6: Calculated from the United States sources cited for Tables 3.10 and 3.11. For some of the detailed occupations here, separate entries begin only in fiscal 1904; for those the "all other skilled" was used to estimate the missing entries for the earlier years—on the basis of the ratios to an expanded "all other" for 1904–7 and 1908–10, comparable to the "all other" for the years before 1904. These estimates relate to small occupational groups, and any errors in the procedure would have little effect on the results.

The following occupational groups were added to form the sectors in columns 3–6: for line 2—tailors, seamstresses, dressmakers, milliners; for line 3—furriers and fur workers, saddlers, and so on, shoemakers, tanners and curriers; line 5—cabinetmakers, carpenters and joiners, wheelwrights, woodworkers not otherwise classified, masons, painters and glaziers, plasterers, plumbers, stonecutters; line 6—bakers, butchers, millers; line 7—iron and steel workers, locksmiths, timers, metal workers other than in iron, steel, and tin.

aged fourteen and over in 1897 (line 1, column 3, and line 4, column 1). The comparison for women shows literacy proportions of 66.5 percent for immigrants and 36.8 percent for women aged fourteen and over in 1897 Russia. These differences may reflect a younger age composition of immigrants (fourteen and over) than of the base population. However, the literacy proportions for immigrants are higher than even those for the fourteen to forty-four age group in the base population in 1897 (see lines 1 and 2, column 1). Another source of the difference may be that the immigration data, even for 1899–1902, are for a period with a midpoint several years later than 1897, and literacy may have risen over these years. Yet the proportions for immigrants show no such trend over the three intervals from 1899 to 1914.

It may well be that the net difference in literacy between the base population of Jews in Russia and the Russian-Jewish immigrants to the United States was in favor of the latter. We may also suggest that on the basis of column 1, lines 4 and 5 and lines 1 and 2, the difference was more marked for men than for women. Such a showing could easily be attributed to the greater propensity of literate men to migrate, and even to the acquisition of literacy in preparation for migration. And if Russian-Jewish migration was dominated by Jews from the northwestern region (Lithuania and White Russia), a hypothesis to be discussed briefly below, the higher cultural levels of that part of Russian Jewry might also have contributed to the differences observed in Table 3.14 between the immigrants and total Jewish population in 1897 Russia.

However, as already noted, for both the immigrants and the base population, the literacy ratios are much higher for men than for women. The differential is clearly associated with the traditional character of the Jewish culture in Russia even as late as the 1890s. Both in Russia and among the Jewish immigrants, the literacy ratios for men were almost twice those for women. But in this respect there was a marked contrast with total (and hence non-Jewish) immigration, for which the literacy proportions for the two sexes were about the same, indeed slightly higher for the women than for the men (see lines 4 and 5, column 4).

Because of this difference between the Jewish and non-Jewish immigrants in the comparative literacy proportions for males and females, the male Jewish immigrants show a distinctly higher literacy proportion than all male immigrants—83 percent compared with 74 percent for 1908–14. By contrast, female Jewish immigrants show lower proportions of literacy than all female immigrants—66 percent

Table 3.13 Immigrants, Jewish and non-Jewish, by state of intended residence, source of passage payment, and type of person to be joined

	Percentage with New York as state of intended residence			
	1899–1902 (1)	1903–7 (2)	1908–14 (3)	1899–1914 (4)
1. Jews	70.6	63.7	58.8	62.4
2. Non-Jews	29.3	26.9	25.6	26.6
	Source of passage payment, 1908–14			
		Distribution by passage payment (%)		
	Total immigration (thousands) (1)	Paid by relative (2)	Paid by self (3)	Other (4)
3. Jews	656	61.8	37.8	0.4
4. Non-Jews	6,054	28.9	69.9	1.2
	Type of person to be joined, 1908–14			
		Distribution by person to be joined (%)		
	Total (thousands) (1)	Relative (2)	Friend (3)	None (4)
5. Jews	656	94.2	4.0	1.8
6. Non-Jews	6,054	78.1	15.4	6.5

Calculated from *RIC*-III, Tables 29, 39, and 40; and the annual reports of the Commissioner General of Immigration for fiscal 1911–14.

compared with 74 percent (see columns 3 and 4). The differences in male literacy presumably have a direct effect on the adjustment of male workers to economic opportunities. However, the records of literacy are in terms of ability to read in any language, and, as already indicated, literacy for Jewish immigrants must have been preponderantly in Yiddish or Hebrew. The measures are, therefore, reflections of learning and ability to participate in the Jewish cultural life—for much of which the ability to read was indispensable. The high levels of literacy indicated for Jewish immigrants, particularly men, are more in the nature of an index of participation in Jewish culture and of whatever general endowments such participation developed than they are of a language tool widely applicable within the context of economic adjustment in the new country.

Table 3.14 Literacy ratios, Jews in Russia, 1897 (L), Jewish and non-Jewish immigration, 1899–1914, by sex

	Ratios for Jews in Russia, 1897			
	14–44 (1)	45 and over (2)	14 and over (3)	
1. Male	70.2	59.8	67.6	
2. Female	57.6	18.8	36.8	
3. Total	63.7	39.3	57.8	
	Ratio for immigrants, 14 and over			
	Jewish immigrants			All immigrants
	1899–1902	1903–7	1908–14	1908–14
4. Male	83.0	81.6	82.7	73.7
5. Female	66.5	64.0	66.0	73.9
6. Total	76.4	74.5	75.3	73.7

Lines 1–3: Calculated from Rubinow (cited in the notes to Table 3.7), the literacy ratio being of those able to read in any language. The data, shown for age classes of 1–9, and by ten-year intervals, had to be interpolated to secure the ratios for the age groups (14–44, and 45 and over) used in the United States immigration statistics.

Lines 4–6: For Jewish immigration (and other), neither the literacy ratios nor the age groups are shown by sex before 1908. We assumed (a) that male and female immigrants under the age of fourteen were equal in number for a given year, period, or race—so that by subtraction we could obtain the numbers of men and women, each fourteen years of age and over; (b) that the ratios of male to female literacy among Jewish immigrants for 1908–14 (at 1.25) prevailed also in the earlier periods—which permitted us, knowing the numbers of males and females fourteen and over and the total literacy ratio, to derive this ratio separately for men and women fourteen and over.

Regions of Origin within Russia

In discussing the characteristics of Russian Jewry in section Aspects of Trends and Structure, we distinguished the several major regions within the Pale. These regions differed markedly with respect to density of Jewish population, proportionately to total, and the associated structure of occupations, with particular reference to the share of manufacturing and mechanical arts versus that of commerce (see Tables 3.7 and 3.8). To repeat, in the northwestern region, a combination of Lithuania and White Russia, which accounted for about 27 percent of all Russian Jewry in 1897, the ratio of Jews to total urban population was particularly high (58 percent). In that region, too, the share of crafts and manufacturing within the total Jewish labor force was high and that of commerce low (43 and 26 percent, respectively). In contrast, the southern (New) region (with 14 percent of total Jewish population) or the southwestern (with 27 percent) were marked by relatively low ratios of Jewish to total urban population (26 and 38 percent, respectively) and low shares of crafts and manufacturing (35 percent in each region) compared with relatively high shares of commerce (36 and 38 percent). One would thus expect that the selectivity of emigration of Russian Jewry would reflect a greater propensity to migrate from the more crowded northwestern region, with its dominance of crafts in the occupational structure, than from the much less crowded southern and southwestern regions. The propensity to migrate would also be greater than that in Congress Poland, where the situation was mitigated by lesser restrictions and more employment opportunities in the rapidly growing factory system of that region. If the northwestern region was the dominant source of Russian-Jewish immigration to the United States, the finding would be of particular interest because of the associated cultural differences. The region was characterized by more advanced learning and a more rationalist movement in religion, in contrast to the greater role of pietistic and Hasidic movements in the South and in Poland.

But firm data to test the hypothesis of differential propensity toward emigration among the regions of the Pale are lacking. Moreover, it is easy to find conflicting statements in the literature. To be sure, the data for 1897 show that the ratio of women to men was 1.08 for the northwestern region, 1.06 each for Poland and the southwestern regions, 1.02 for the southern region, and 0.87 for the Jewish population outside the Pale.[31] This difference in the female/male ratio is a strong indication that emigration proportions were higher in the northwestern region than elsewhere. A similar suggestion is provided by the ratio of Jewish men aged twenty to fifty-nine to all Jewish men, cited in the same source: this ratio was lowest in the northwestern region (40.1 percent), high in the southwestern and southern regions (43.2 and 43.3 percent, respectively), and intermediate in Congress Poland (40.6 percent). But these data are for 1897, before the major migration flows of the decade and a half preceding World War I. While they suggest that in the early emigration the share of the northwestern region might have been appreciably larger than its share in total Russian Jewry, some shifts might have occurred—for example, after the Kishinev pogrom (1903) in the southern region.

We cite two of the conflicting statements in the literature. I. M. Rubinow wrote in 1907:

> The Jews living in Lithuania, as well as those who live in White Russia, are known as Lithuanian Jews; the Jews of the ten Polish Provinces as Polish Jews, and those who have settled in the Southwestern region and in New Russia [i.e., Southern region] as southern Jews. From the American point of view the distinctions are not without some practical significance, because the Lithuanian Jews have until recently constituted the vast majority of the Russian Jewish immigrants to the United States. The general culture of the Polish Jews s considerably lower than that of Lithuanian Jews. The economic condition of the Jews in the South of Russia is so much better than that of those in the northwest that only since the recent disturbances has the immigration fever touched the Jews of that region.

It would not be difficult to quote from other pre-World War I writings emphasizing the large share of Lithuanian Jews in the Russian-Jewish immigration into the United States.[32]

In contrast, V. V. Obolensky-Ossinsky (a past president of the Central Statistical Board of the U.S.S.R.), writing on this question in the late 1920s in a chapter on emigration from Russia, stressed the pogroms of the pre-World War I decade, which were largely concentrated in the southwest and the south, and thus "reduced the predominance of Poland and the northwestern region in tranquil years." He concluded, relying on the rather uncertain regional distribution data of applications to the Hebrew Emigration Society and Jewish Colonization Society in 1901–11, that "in general, the distribution of emigrants from different parts of the Hebrew Pale corresponds roughly with the distribution of population."[33]

The conclusions are perhaps less contradictory than they seem, because the two writers stress different periods in the emigration flow. Furthermore, Obolensky-Ossinsky tends to contrast the total of Lithuanian and Polish Jews, combined, with the southwestern and southern Jews. (The Jewish Colonization Society applications for 1906–13 still show that the average share of the northwestern region was well above 30 percent, while that of the base population in 1897 was about 27 percent.)

The following conclusions seem justified. First, before 1903 the share of Lithuanian Jews in Russian-Jewish immigration to the United States must have been much larger than its share in the total Jewish population of Tsarist Russia. Whether, to use Rubinow's terms, they were the "vast majority" cannot be demonstrated with the available data. Second, with the outbreak of pogroms and disturbances in the last decade or so before World War I, this significant overrepresentation of Lithuanian Jews in total Russian-Jewish immigration was probably reduced. However, the proportion of Lithuanian Jewish immigrants in Russian-Jewish immigration to the United States may still have been larger than that in the Russian base population. Third, because of their weight in the early stages of Russian-Jewish immigration, their contribution to, and role in, the economic and cultural life of Russian-Jewish immigrants in the United States may have been all the greater.

We are touching here upon cultural and institutional differences among various groups of Russian Jews that may have been important in the historical background of the emigration flow, in the selectivity of emigration, and in the adjustments that the Russian-Jewish immigrants and their children made upon settling in the United States. But since this analysis is limited to demographic and economic processes for which quantitative measures are available, it is not feasible to elaborate here on this aspect. It must be stressed, however, that not only the demographic and economic trends and structure but also the structural differences and movements in the religious and cultural life of Russian Jewry played important roles in the selectivity of the Russian-Jewish migrations to the United States, and later in the adjustment within the country of destination.

Concluding Comments

The facts of Russian-Jewish immigration to the United States are fairly clear, despite the gaps in the data and the amount of estimation that is involved. An insignificant trickle for decades, Russian-Jewish immigration acquired momentum in the 1880s, and for fiscal 1881–1914 reached a total of about 1.5 million, three-quarters of all Jewish immigrants. Also, during the same period, about three-quarters of the roughly two million Jews who emigrated from the Tsarist Empire came to the United States. Total Jewish population in the United States in 1880 was estimated at 250,000. Obviously the inflow in the following three and a half decades of two million Jewish immigrants, three-quarters of them from Tsarist Russia and most of the rest from other countries in Eastern Europe, radically changed not only the magnitude but also the structure of United States Jewry.[34]

After 1914, Jewish immigration declined even more than total immigration, and during the five and a half decades to the late 1960s, only about 860,000 Jewish immigrants were admitted. However, probably not more than a quarter of these were immigrants from the former areas of the Tsarist Empire. Even so, Russian-Jewish immigrants from fiscal 1881 to date must have totaled some 1.75 million out of less than 3 million Jewish immigrants. Furthermore, the structure of Russian Jewry was not dissimilar to that of Jews in Austria-Hungary and Romania, the two other major sources of Jewish immigration to the United States. Inclusion of these may raise the total of Jewish immigrants from Eastern Europe to about 2.5 million for the decades since 1881. We concentrated on the Russian-Jewish immigration for 1881–1914 because that group and period were dominant not only in the mass migration of Jewry from Eastern Europe but also in the mass migration of Jews into the United States.

Emigration of Jews from Tsarist Russia amounted over 1881–1914 to two million; total Jewish population in Russia at its peak in the early 1900s was about 5.3 million. Some of the forces involved in the emigration were those that made for mass migrations from many European countries to the United States (and elsewhere in the New World) in the nineteenth century. The transition from preindustrial and premodern structure in these countries to industrialization and modern organization meant dislocation of people from the land, competitive pressures of new technology on handicrafts and small-scale industry and transportation, and the exposure of previously isolated communities and regions to the rest of the world. This shift began in Russia in the late nineteenth century, following the abolition of serfdom in the early 1860s, the construction of railways, and the attempts to promote industrialization. The movement, as always, had disruptive aspects; and one result was intensified emigration from Tsarist Russia not only of Jews but also of other ethnic groups (Poles, Finns, and Germans) and eventually even of the Russian majority (Great Russians, Ukrainians, and White Russians). This pattern of an explosive rise, after barely a trickle for decades, typifies emigration from many European countries (e.g., the three Scandinavian countries, Greece, and Italy).

Yet other factors clearly affected emigration of Russian Jewry, and they were quite distinctive and specific to it. These had to do with the precarious legal and social position of the small Jewish minority within a hostile, autocratic state that rested its authority on identification with the Orthodox Christian church. The far-reaching restrictions on residence, choice of economic activity, and education, the constant political pressure, the intensification, beginning in the 1880s, of repression and persecution—all of this, in magnitude and time pattern, was specific to the Jewish position within the Tsarist Empire. Much of this represented an attempt, in the strains and stresses of the transition, to use the persisting hostility of some groups to the Jewish minority to focus discontent on that minority rather than on the traditional authority. It is thus hardly surprising that the proportion of emigration to base population (either total emigration or that to the United States) was distinctly higher for Russian Jews than for any other European population, with the single exception of Ireland, whose population was affected by the catastrophic famine of the 1840s and by the open market for emigrant labor in neighboring Great Britain.

This combination of general (common to all or most populations) and specific (limited to Jews) factors affected several aspects of Russian-Jewish immigration to the United States—and would probably characterize all Jewish immigration in the period 1881–1914, when the flows were relatively free at both ends. Like all emigration flows, Jewish emigration was selective with respect to sex and age—including higher proportions of men than that of women and of people in working ages than that of the young and the old, both compared with base population. But Jewish emigration, as reflected in the immigration to the United States, differed in structure from non-Jewish immigration: it had a much higher proportion of women and of children under fourteen and a lower proportion of persons in working ages (fourteen to forty-four). Jewish immigration was distinctly more family-oriented than non-Jewish immigration.

Also, like that of all emigration flows, the occupational structure of Jewish immigration into the United States reflected selectivity in favor of the lower-income occupations, combined with transferability of skill. However, the restriction of Russian Jewry to urban occupations and the overcrowding of handicrafts meant a low share of farmers and a dominant share of skilled workers, largely artisans in the needle and similar consumer-goods trades. For the non-Jewish immigration over the same period, this selectivity meant a dominant share of unskilled workers and domestic service, and a large share of farmers.

In addition, while all relatively free migration flows were reduced, particularly in the decades just before World War I, by a return stream of departures, usually within a few years after arrival, the departures ratio was markedly lower for Jewish than for non-Jewish immigration to the United States. The data are available only beginning with fiscal 1908; for 1908–14, the ratio of departures to arrivals was only 7 percent for Jewish immigration but was over 32 percent for non-Jewish.

This double approach can be applied broadly. The movement of Russian (and Eastern European) Jews to the United States can be viewed as that of a distinct group among many affected by the spread of industrialization and modernization in Europe, whose departure reduced some of the strains and pressures of the situation. But the emigration of Russian and other Eastern European Jews can also be seen as a late phase in the centuries-old migration of Jews in the European and Near Eastern Diaspora. After all, these Russian Jews, a short time before, had been Polish-Lithuanian Jews, who, in turn, were immigrants or descendant immigrants from Western Europe who had themselves been part of a migration that had begun in the thirteenth and fourteenth centuries.

This point needs no further elaboration. Obviously immigration to the United States and to other immigrant-receiving countries outside Europe since the 1820s was a process that affected more than one country or ethnic group; it was part of the adjustment to dislocations caused by the spread of industrialization and modernization that also affected various countries and groups. Yet any one country or ethnic group has some distinctive characteristics in its base population and some selectivity in emigration upon which the push and pull of the migration process play, resulting in differences in timing and structure of emigration. And these distinctive, specific characteristics of the single country or ethnic group are the heritage of whatever history shaped the country or group. This heritage was particularly distinctive for the Russian-Jewish population, with its long coexistence with hostile majorities and long record of migration.

Our account dealt mainly with the measurable characteristics of the base population and selectivity of Russian-Jewish immigration to the United States. These records do not reflect directly the major features of the historical heritage of Russian Jewry that shaped the human capital transferred to the United States by immigration. It is this transfer of human capital that constitutes the essential content of migration, internal or international; while sex, age, occupational structure, and literacy tell us much about this human capital, they do not help us to distinguish the more fundamental characteristics of capacity for social organization and for adjustment to the challenges of a new environment. Nor do they describe the long-standing scale of priorities inherited from the past and likely to shape the goals of immigrants and their descendants for several generations after their arrival in the country of destination. One may assume that after centuries of coexistence with hostile majorities, after migrations from one country to another in Europe and the Middle East, and after self-selection over time by the loss of some of its members, the Jewish people in Europe, and especially its largest subgroup in Tsarist Russia, must have acquired a distinctive equipment of human capital. Such equipment is transferable to new surroundings and may be of great value in making the necessary adjustments. If one could establish the characteristics of this heritage of human capital other than the basic demographic and economic characteristics, one might be able to explain, in tracing their consequences in the history of the Jewish community in the United States, aspects of American social history that are otherwise obscure. But the tools needed for such a study of the historical heritage of Russian or East European Jewry are not those of economics and demography, and the account above, long as it is, must be left incomplete.

Notes

1. Reference to the group under discussion as Russian Jewry may be somewhat misleading. Before the first partition of Poland (1772), the Jews of Tsarist Russia were subjects of Poland (and Lithuania) and had been for centuries. A more precise designation would be Russian, formerly Polish-Lithuanian, Jewry. Though obviously awkward, this compound designation would help stress the earlier historical roots of Russian Jews, which affected their social and economic structure through much of the nineteenth century.

   It would also have been useful to include the Jews who immigrated from other parts of Eastern Europe. particularly Galícia—a large subgroup of Polish Jewry inherited in the partitions by the Austro-Hungarian Empire. But inclusion of this subgroup would have presented statistical problems and also difficulties in analyzing its economic and social structure next to the much larger body of Russian Jewry. The latter dominated the mass immigrations of Jews into the United States, overshadowing the other Eastern European Jews.
2. Throughout the chapter, fiscal years are used in citing United States immigration and emigration statistics.
3. See the comment on omission of passengers arriving by first and second class in the notes on the official migration statistics in U.S. Bureau of the Census, *Historical Statistics of the United States, Colonial Times to 1957* (Washington, D.C., 1960), 49. Cabin passengers, included in the series before 1869, were "not included as immigrants until 1904." On the possible exclusion of assimilated Jews, see Arthur Ruppin, *Soziologie der Juden*, vol. I (Berlin: *Jüdischer Verlag*, 1930), 136. Ruppin comments on the fact that the United States data on immigration distinguished Jews on the basis

of language and culture, not religion—so that identification was, in effect, practicable only for Jews from Eastern Europe and the Orient, not for Jews from Western and Central Europe. He suggests that the understatement may have been in the order of 5 percent, but does not indicate the basis for this estimate.

4. U.S. Bureau of the Census, *Historical Statistics of the United States, Colonial Times to 1957*, 49–50.
5. See U.S. Senate, *Reports of the Immigration Commission, Volume III, Statistical Review of Immigration, 1891–1910—Distribution of Immigrants—1850–1900*, 61 Cong., 3 Sess., Senate Doc. No. 756 (Washington, D.C., 1911), Table 14, (Total population and number and per cent of foreign-born, in continental United States, by class and place of residence: 1900), 421, hereafter cited as *RIC*-III).
6. In this connection one can ask: When does a Jewish immigrant from Russia, coming eventually to the United States after a long interval, cease to be a Russian Jew and become an English, German, or Canadian Jew? We assume that transitory delays of a few years still meant retention of the historical and social heritage of a Russian Jew, but when the transit interval is long, the question remains.
7. The data are from *RIC*-III, Table 9, 14–44.
8. *RIC*-III, Table 9, 416.
9. The data on foreign born by states are from the *Compendium of the 1870 Census* (Washington, D.C., 1872), Table XIV, 392–93; *Census 1880, volume I, Statistics of the Population of the United States* (Washington, D.C., 1883), Table XIII, 492–95; and *Census 1890, volume 1, Part I. Population* (Washington, D.C., 1897), Table XXXII, 606–9.
10. See also comment on the "non-Jewish" type of state distribution of the foreign born from Russia in 1870 and 1880, in U.S. Senate, *Reports of the Immigration Commission, Immigration Conditions in Europe*, vol. IV, 61 Cong., 3 Sess., Senate Doc. No. 748 (Washington, D.C., 1951), 271.
11. All the data cited are from *RIC*-III, supplemented for 1911–14 by Walter F. Willcox, ed., *International Migrations*, vol. I (New York: National Bureau of Economic Research, 1929).
12. On the similarity between short-term changes in Jewish and total immigration see the chart in Liebmann Hersch, "International Migration of the Jews," in *International Migrations*, vol. II, ed. Walter F. Willcox (New York: National Bureau of Economic Research, 1931), Diagram 12, 476. On the responsiveness of immigration to business cycles, see Harry Jerome, *Migration and Business Cycles* (New York: National Bureau of Economic Research, 1926), 243–44.
13. Sec D. A. E. Harkness, "Irish Emigration," in *International Migrations*, vol. II, Table 97, 274.
14. See *Reports of the Immigration Commission*, vol. IV, 251–53.
15. I have relied on the following monographs: Simon M. Dubnow, *History of the Jews in Russia and Poland*, vols. I–III (Philadelphia: Jewish Publication Society of America, 1916–1920); Simon M. Dubnow, *History of the Jews*, translated from the Russian, vol. V (New York, 1973), which corresponds to IX and X of the 4th definitive ed. (*Istoriya Yevreiskovo Naroda na Vostoke* [Riga. 1939]); Bernard D. Weinryb, *The Jews of Poland*

(Philadelphia, 1973); Yuli Gessen, *Istoriya Yevreiskovo Naroda v Rossii* (History of the Jewish People in Russia), vols. I and II (rev. ed. Leningrad, 1925–1927); Salo W. Baron, *The Russian Jew under Tsar and Soviets* (New York, 1964); and Isaac Levitats, *The Jewish Community in Russia 1772–1844* (New York, 1943).

16. The estimates are given in Dubnow, *History of the Jews* in *Russia and Poland*, vol. I, 263–64, 307. Dubnow considers this estimate conservative in the light of a liter report by the "Jewish Commission" of the Quadrennial Diet (see p. 264).

17. The estimate for Jewish population in 1788 used here appears larger than those suggested in Weinryb, *The Jews of Poland*, Appendix 3, 308–20 (although there are some difficulties in the comparison). But our estimate seems reasonable in the light of the acceptable birth and death rates and the 1897 Census population total. If the Census total for 1897 is taken as a firm estimate, with some bias toward understatement, and the birth and death rates (subject to minor effects of migration and conversion) are acceptable, a lower initial Jewish population total in 1788 would imply too high a growth rate either between 1788 and 1825 or between 1825 and 1880.

18. See Ruppin, *Soziologie der Juden*, vol. I, 295–97.

19. See Jacob Lestchinsky, "Problems der Bevölkerungs-Bewegung bei den Juden," *Metron* 6, no. 3 (June 1, 1927): 87–112.

20. For discussion of the economic structure of the Jewish communities in several countries, see Simon Kuznets, "Economic Structure and Life of the Jews," in *The Jews: Their History, Culture, and Religion*, vol. II, 3rd ed., ed. Louis Finkelstein (New York: Harpers, 1960), chap. xxxix, 1597–1666.

21. See Isaac M. Rubinow, "Economic Conditions of the Jews in Russia," *Bulletin of the Bureau of Labor*, no. 72 (Washington, D.C.: Department of Commerce and Labor, 1907), 502.

22. The figures are from Gessen, *Istoriya Yevreiskovo Naroda*, vol. I, 186. The same figures, with similar identification but much less detail, are cited by Lestchinsky in the second part of his article in *Weltwirtschaftliches Archiv*, 32, pt. 2 (1930): 573.

23. Rubinow, "Economic Conditions," 571–72, 525, 561. Much of this evidence is *from* the economic study of the Jewish community in 1898 by the Jewish Colonization Society and can be found in the two summary volumes of its studies. *Sbornik Materialov ob Economicheskom Polozhenii Evreev v Rossii* (Collection of Materials on the Economic Condition of the Jews in Russia) (St. Petersburg, 1904–1905). (These volumes also appeared in French: *Recueil de Matériaux sur la Situation Économique des Israélites de Russie [D'Après L'Enquete de la Jewish Colonization Association]* [Paris, 1904–1906].)

24. Brief and informative biographies of the most prominent—the Baron Guenzburg (finance), Polyakoff (railroad construction), Brodsky (sugar refineries), and Wissotzky (tea trade)—can be found in various volumes of *Encyclopaedia Judaica* (Jerusalem, 1972).

25. See Arthur Ruppin, "Die Russische Juden nach der Volkszahlung von 1897," *Zeitschrift für Demographie und Statistik der Juden* 2, no. 3 (March 1906), Table XII, 45.

26. Rubinow, "Economic Conditions," 537–41, 561–66.

27. See Jacob Lestchinsky, "Die Umsiedflung und Umschichtung des jüdischen Volkes im Laufe des letzten Jahrhunderts," *Weltwirtschaftliches Archiv* 30, pt. 2 (1929), Table I, 132–33.
28. A useful, detailed account is presented in Mark Wischnitzer, *To Dwell in Safety: The Story of Jewish Migration Since 1800* (Philadelphia: Jewish Publication Society of America, 1948), chaps. i–iv.
29. Rubinow, "Economic Conditions," 556.
30. See Liebmann Hersch, *Le Juif Errant d'Aujourd'hui* (Paris: Giard and Brière, 1913), 240–43.
31. The data, and those on proportions of men aged twenty to fifty-nine, from the summary article "Naselenie" ("Population"), in *Yevreiskaia Enziklopedia* (Jewish Encyclopedia, in Russian), vol. XI (Petersburg, 1906), 537, 541.
32. See Rubinow, "Economic Conditions," 491–92, 502. See also Charles S. Bernheimer, ed., *The Russian Jew in the United States* (Philadelphia: J. C. Winston Co., 1905). Particularly the article by Peter Wiernik ("The Jew in Russia" in the Russian Jew in the United States, ed. CS Bernheimer. Philadelphia: J.C. Winston Co, 1905: 18-21) in which he comments on the depressed conditions of Lithuanian Jews and stresses their high propensity to migrate, to the interior of Russia and abroad.
33. Willcox, *International Migrations*, vol. II, chap. xvii, 521–80. The quotations are from the discussion of the regional distribution of Jewish immigration on pp. 543–46.
34. The 1880 figure is from Kuznets, "Economic Structure," Table 10 and discussion on pp. 1634–35. The analysis suggests that, speaking as of 1950, "Over eight tenths of the Jewish population today derived from immigrants since 1880" (p. 1635). While the calculations underlying this statement need revision, the major conclusion will probably stand. If restricted to Russian-Jewish immigration alone, the contribution is probably no less than six-tenths.

Index

S

T

U

W